Matrices and Society

Ronald L. Meek was born in 1917 in New Zealand where he first studied law, graduating with a Masters degree in law in 1939. During the intervening war years his interests changed to economics, and he obtained an M.A., again from New Zealand, in 1946. From then until 1948 he was a postgraduate student in Cambridge and gained his Ph.D in 1949.

In 1948 he was appointed to a lectureship at Glasgow University and in 1963 he moved to Leicester as Tyler Professor of Economics, a post which he held until his death in 1978. He was not a narrow specialist, but firmly believed that economics could be studied in conjunction with subjects such as sociology, history and anthropology and his books illustrate the breadth of his vision. They include *The Economics of Physiocracy* (1962), *Figuring Out Society* (1971), *Studies in the Labour Theory of Value* (1973), *Social Science and the Ignoble Savage* (1976), *Smith, Marx and After* (1977), as well as a small guidebook – *Hill-walking in Arran* (1972). Ronald Meek was also an enthusiastic teacher, and he had planned to dedicate *Matrices and Society* to his students.

Ian Bradley is a lecturer in economics at the University of Leicester. He was educated in Liverpool, and read economics at Cambridge. Currently he is engaged in a United Nations programme to develop graduate and undergraduate courses in 'Western economics' in China.

Ian Bradley and Ronald L. Meek

Matrices and Society

Princeton University Press
Princeton, New Jersey

Published by Princeton University Press, 41 William Street,
Princeton, New Jersey 08540

Copyright © Ian Bradley and Ronald L. Meek, 1986

Made and printed in Great Britain by
Cox & Wyman Ltd, Reading
Filmset by Northumberland Press Ltd, Gateshead,
Tyne and Wear

LCC 86–42891
ISBN 0–691–08454–8
ISBN 0–691–02404–9 (pbk.)

6/12/92

Contents

Preface

It is no longer necessary to justify a book on the use of mathematics in the social sciences. There is general recognition that the application of mathematics in all the social sciences has brought a multitude of results that would never have been obtained if researchers had been confined to languages such as English. Despite their richness, such languages are unsuitable for expressing complicated quantitative and logical relationships. Indeed such relationships do not have to be very complicated before mathematics becomes the only language to describe them. Translating the following simple mathematical argument into English would not produce anything intelligible.

$$x^2 - 5xy + 6y^2 = 0$$
$$\therefore (x - 2y)(x - 3y) = 0$$
$$x = 2y \text{ or } 3y$$

The translation might start something like this. 'Suppose there are two quantities. They are such that if the first one is multiplied by itself and from this is subtracted five times the product of the two quantities, and then to this result is added six times the second quantity multiplied by itself then we will end up with nothing.' This is bad enough but just try making the logic of the next step clear in English!

While the benefits of using mathematics in the social sciences are now well recognized this has not always been so. Mathematics grew up with the physical sciences and to a considerable extent was moulded by them. This means that much of mathematics is not of great use to economists, sociologists and so on, and branches of mathematics that would be suitable for handling certain problems in the social and behavioural sciences have not been developed. However, certain well-developed branches of mathematics are of immense use. A typical social-science problem may well have many more variables than physicists may be used to handling. In an economy, for instance, there are many different commodities that can be produced using many different inputs in many different places to produce them. It turns out that matrix algebra which can cope as easily with expressing a problem with three hundred commodities as it can with two is of considerable power in analysing many social processes and phenomena. Let us look at a small part of the economy, a firm, to indicate how matrix algebra may be useful.

Suppose we are interested in looking at the profit of this firm. For simplicity we will assume it produces only two commodities. Let y_1 be the amount it produces of commodity one, y_2 the amount of commodity two. Let the price per unit it receives for the two commodities be p_1 and p_2. Let us also suppose that it has to use a different combination of inputs to produce each commodity. Thus a can of tomato soup requires a certain amount of tomatoes, sugar, etc. and a can; while a jar of pickled onions requires somewhat different ingredients. Looking at the various recipes we might find that there were a total of say three different kinds of input. To make a unit of the first commodity may require a_{11} of input one, a_{21} of input two and a_{31} of input three. Similarly unit production of the second commodity may require a_{12} of input one, a_{22} of input two, and a_{32} of input three. In general then to produce a unit of commodity i requires a_{ji} of input j.

To look at the firm's profit we need to know the prices it has to pay for its three inputs. Let these be w_1, w_2 and w_3. Its profit from making commodity one is the revenue it gets from its sales minus the cost of production.

$$\text{Revenue} = p_1 y_1$$

Cost per unit production $= w_1 a_{11} + w_2 a_{21} + w_3 a_{31}$.
So cost to produce $y_1 = (w_1 a_{11} + w_2 a_{21} + w_3 a_{31}) y_1$.
Profit from producing $y_1 = p_1 y_1 - (w_1 a_{11} + w_2 a_{21} + w_3 a_{31}) y_1$.

We could do this for every commodity and then add up the profit from producing each, to get the profit for the firm as a whole.

Total profit $= p_1 y_1 + p_2 y_2$
$$- (w_1 a_{11} + w_2 a_{21} + w_3 a_{31}) y_1$$
$$- (w_1 a_{12} + w_2 a_{22} + w_3 a_{32}) y_2.$$

Imagine how complicated this would look if the firm produced fifty-seven commodities and used ninety-two inputs.

As the reader will discover, one of the great advantages of matrix algebra is that it saves an awful lot of ink and paper. Somebody versed in the subject on seeing the calculation above would immediately write something like this:

$$\text{Let} \quad y = \begin{bmatrix} y_1 \\ y_2 \end{bmatrix}$$

$$\text{and let} \quad p = \begin{bmatrix} p_1 & p_2 \end{bmatrix} \quad \text{and} \quad w = \begin{bmatrix} w_1 & w_2 & w_3 \end{bmatrix}.$$

That is, they would let one symbol y stand for a column of all the ouputs, and symbols p and w stand for the prices of all outputs and all inputs respectively with these prices arranged along a row.

$$\text{Then they would let} \quad A = \begin{bmatrix} a_{11} & a_{12} \\ a_{21} & a_{22} \\ a_{31} & a_{32} \end{bmatrix}.$$

That is, they would let a single symbol A represent the whole recipe book arranged in some order in a rectangular table. In this case the recipe for output one is given by the first column and that for output two by the second column. They would then say:

$$\text{Total profit} = \text{revenue} - \text{costs}$$
$$= py - wAy.$$

The uninitiated reader will not understand this at this stage – they can come back and look at it again after reading the first three chapters of the book. What we have done is to express profit in a concise fashion by using definitions of matrices and how they are manipulated. But matrix algebra is much more than shorthand. Having expressed profit in this way we would find it easy to find out how profit would change if the prices of inputs and outputs changed, if the amount the firm produced changed or if recipes changed. There are many examples in this book where, by expressing problems in matrix form and knowing the mathematical properties of particular kinds of matrices, seemingly very complicated problems become very simple indeed.

I mentioned earlier that mathematics grew up with the physical sciences, but matrices are so useful to social scientists that the properties of certain types of matrix have been discussed and discovered because of the needs of the social sciences. The most obvious example is what is known as game theory and this is the subject of the last three chapters of this book. Game theory is applicable where agents, be they individuals, unions, governments or whatever, strive for their own advantage but are not in control of all the variables on which any outcome depends. Thus it is applicable to many conflict situations of a military, economic, political or strictly social kind. The classic expository work on the subject, *The Theory of Games and Economic Behaviour* by J. Von Neumann and O. Morgenstern, first published in 1944, indicates by its title that here is mathematics specifically developed for use by social scientists.

The intention of our book is to show the usefulness of not only game theory but also of many other matrix methods in the social sciences. It attempts this by giving students and other interested people a knowledge of basic matrix algebra and, by its examples, an idea of the many diverse problems in economics, anthropology, sociology, political science, geography and so on that matrix algebra has helped to illuminate. The book is not simply a matrix text, nor is it a comprehensive guide to the use of matrix methods in the social sciences. Examples of application have been chosen from diverse fields both to illustrate the widespread usefulness of the techniques and because I think the problems that are discussed should be interesting to all social scientists, and to men and women in the street interested in the workings of society. Although the various disciplines within the social sciences have become more quantitative, students arriving to study these disciplines at universities and polytechnics are generally not expected to have strong mathematical backgrounds. Nor is it necessary that they should have. However, they must be prepared to investigate and learn mathematics appropriate to their disciplines. This book is intended for such students and anyone else interested in the successful ways that mathematics can be used in often rather unexpected fields. Broadly speaking the structure of the book consists of discussing a particular matrix technique in a not too complicated mathematical way and then illustrating by example how this technique can be useful. The mathematics should not be beyond anybody who at some time or other has reached 'O' level standard or the equivalent – but as with all serious subjects the reader may have to think quite hard. There are exercises placed strategically throughout the book which readers are encouraged to complete in order to check their understanding. It is hoped that readers will wish to pursue their own particular interests further than this book takes them. Further reading is suggested as a guide to the beginning of such a pursuit.

Ronald Meek started this book with the idea very much in mind that the reader should realize that matrix algebra really does help one to understand very important and interesting problems. It is not the intention to convert all would-be social scientists into expert practitioners of the finer points of matrix algebra. That is unnecessary. Ronald Meek liked to think of himself as a mathematical simpleton, which he certainly was not – his clear, logical mind prevented such a possibility. However, he was educated at a time when it was not universally recognized that all economists should be numerate, and he came to understand and reap the advantages of using mathematics in social science and economics in particular a little later than he would have liked. He was always eager to embark upon learning new techniques that would help him understand society. Having undertaken a voyage of discovery himself through what he liked to call 'the magic of matrices', he wanted to share his experience and enthusiasm with others. His untimely death prevented him finishing the book. Chapters 1, 3, 4, 5 and most of 6 and 7 are based upon drafts that Ron Meek wrote. I hope that his inimitable style still remains after the alterations and additions that have been made. Any errors, omissions and misinterpretations in these chapters and in the rest of the book are unfortunately my sole responsibility.

IAN BRADLEY

1

Matrices and How to Manipulate Them

What Is a Matrix?

You are at home in the evening; there is nothing good on television; and you are at a loose end. There are three possibilities open to you: to go out to the pub, to go out to the theatre, or to stay at home and invite some friends round for a game of cards. In order to weigh up the comparative advantages and disadvantages of these three alternatives, you decide to put certain basic facts about each of them down on paper. And, being an orderly, methodical type you put them down in the form of a table, like this:

	Motoring (miles)	Admission charge (£s)	Liquor (pints)	Crisps (packets)
Go to pub:	3	1	4	3
Go to theatre:	2	3	1	1
Cards at home:	0	0	12	9

If you went to the pub, you would have to take your car out and drive three miles. It would cost you £1 to get in, since there is a special entertainment on there tonight, and you would also have to pay for the four pints of liquor and three packets of crisps which you calculate that you would consume on the premises. If you went to the theatre, it would cost you £3 to get in, but as compared with the pub you would save a little on motoring costs and quite a lot on liquor and crisps. If you stayed at home and asked some friends round for cards, you would have to provide a comparatively large quantity of liquor and crisps, but to compensate for this you would not have to take the car out and there would not of course be any admission charge.

Suppose now that just for fun you extracted the array of numbers from this table and put a pair of large square brackets around them, like this:

$$\begin{bmatrix} 3 & 1 & 4 & 3 \\ 2 & 3 & 1 & 1 \\ 0 & 0 & 12 & 9 \end{bmatrix}.$$

No doubt much to your surprise, you would then have succeeded in constructing a *matrix*, which is simply a rectangular array of numbers. The individual numbers in a matrix are called its *components* or *elements*. This particular matrix, since it has three rows and four columns, is said to be a 3 × 4 matrix. If you had considered only two alternative courses of action – omitting, say, the 'Go to theatre' possibility – the matrix you constructed would have looked like this:

$$\begin{bmatrix} 3 & 1 & 4 & 3 \\ 0 & 0 & 12 & 9 \end{bmatrix}.$$

This matrix has two rows and four columns, and is therefore said to be a 2 × 4 matrix. If on the other hand you had retained all three rows but omitted one of the columns, your matrix would have been a *square* one with three rows and three columns – that is, a 3 × 3 matrix.

Suppose now that you had seriously considered only one possible course of action – going to the pub, say. Your table would then have consisted of a 1 × 4 matrix – that is, a single row of four numbers:

$$\begin{bmatrix} 3 & 1 & 4 & 3 \end{bmatrix}.$$

An ordered collection of numbers written in a single row like this is a special (and very important) kind of matrix which is called a *row vector*.

Suppose finally that you had been interested only in the different quantities of liquor consumption associated with the three alternative courses of action. Your table would then have consisted of a 3 × 1 matrix – a single column of three numbers:

$$\begin{bmatrix} 4 \\ 1 \\ 12 \end{bmatrix}.$$

An ordered collection of numbers written in a single column like this is another special (and equally important) kind of matrix which is called a *column vector*.

Matrices in the Social Sciences

The next question, of course, is why matrices are important in the social sciences, and why so many textbooks spend so much time instructing you how to play around with them. What is it all about?

A short answer is that the social sciences are often concerned with unravelling complex *interrelationships* of various kinds, and that it is often extremely convenient and illuminating to put these interrelationships down on paper in matrix form.

In economics, for example, we may be interested in the implications of the fact that some of the things which an industry produces (that is, its '*output*') may be used as ingredients (that is, as '*inputs*') in the production of other things – or even in their own production. A large part of the electricity produced in this country, for example, is not consumed directly by you and me, but is used as an input in the production of things like corn, machines, clothes and so on – and of electricity itself. Imagine, then, a very simple economy where there are only three industries, which we

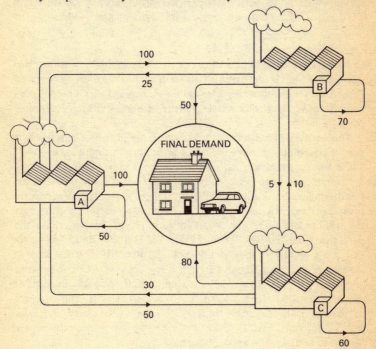

shall imaginatively call A, B and C. Industry A produces 300 units of its particular product – tons of steel, kilowatt hours of electricity, or whatever we suppose it to be – every year. It sells 50 of these 300 units to itself (as it were) for use as an input in its own production process; it sells 100 units to industry B and 50 to industry C for use as inputs in *their* production processes; and the remaining 100 units are sold to final consumers like you and me. Industry B produces 150 units, 70 of which go to itself, 25 to A, 5 to C, and the remaining 50 to final consumers. Industry C produces 180 units, 60 of which go to itself, 30 to A, 10 to B, and 80 to final consumers.

The way in which the total outputs of the three industries are disposed of can be very conveniently set out in the form of a simple matrix like this:

$$
\begin{array}{c}
\qquad\qquad\qquad\qquad \textit{To} \\[4pt]
\begin{array}{c c}
 & \begin{array}{cccc} \text{A} & \text{B} & \text{C} & \begin{array}{c}\text{Final}\\\text{Demand}\end{array} \end{array} \\
\textit{From}\quad
\begin{array}{c} \text{A} \\ \text{B} \\ \text{C} \end{array}
&
\left[
\begin{array}{cccc}
50 & 100 & 50 & 100 \\
25 & 70 & 5 & 50 \\
30 & 10 & 60 & 80
\end{array}
\right].
\end{array}
\end{array}
$$

One of the advantages of setting out the facts in this way is that two interrelated aspects of the overall situation are presented to us at one and the same time: the three rows tell us where each industry's output goes to, and the first three columns tell us where each industry's physical inputs come from.

Another type of matrix which often crops up in the social sciences is one which sets out the gains and losses accruing from some kind of '*game*' which two (or more) participants are supposed to be playing. Suppose, for example, that two persons, Tom and Jerry, find themselves in some sort of conflict situation in which they are obliged to choose (independently of one another) between several alternative courses of action, and in which the final outcome – the gain or loss for each 'player' – depends upon the particular combination of choices which they make. Tom and Jerry, let us say, are two rival candidates for political office. At a certain stage in the election campaign a crisis arises, in which Tom has to choose between two possible strategies and Jerry between three. If we could calculate the numbers of votes which would be gained (or lost) by Tom – and therefore we assume, lost (or gained) by Jerry – in the event of each of the six possible outcomes, our calculations would be usefully presented in matrix form. The matrix might appear like this:

$$
\begin{array}{c}
\textit{Jerry} \\
\begin{array}{ccc}
1 & 2 & 3
\end{array} \\
\textit{Tom}\;\;
\begin{array}{c}
1 \\
2
\end{array}
\left[
\begin{array}{ccc}
1000 & 0 & -1000 \\
-3000 & 2000 & 1000
\end{array}
\right]
\end{array}
$$

Tom's gain matrix

From this we can immediately see, for example, that if Tom adopts his first strategy and Jerry adopts his third strategy, the outcome will be that Tom will lose (and Jerry will therefore gain) 1000 votes. If Tom adopts his second strategy and Jerry adopts *his* second, then Tom will gain (and Jerry will therefore lose) 2000 votes. And so on. The advantage of this way of presenting the facts is once again that it puts them before our eyes simultaneously from two points of view – the rows, as it were, from the point of view of Tom, and the columns from the point of view of Jerry.

In sociology, again, we might be interested in what is called a *dominance situation*, in which the pattern of dominance between three individuals (Pip, Squeak and Wilfred, say) can be represented in a matrix, where

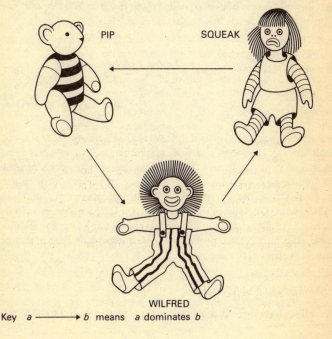

PIP   SQUEAK

WILFRED

Key *a* ⟶ *b* means *a* dominates *b*

the entry 1 indicates that the person whose row the entry is in dominates
the person whose column it is in; at the same time an entry 0 in a row
means that the person whose row it is in does not dominate the person
whose column the 0 entry is in.

$$
\begin{array}{c}
 & \text{Pip} & \text{Squeak} & \text{Wilfred} \\
\begin{array}{c} \text{Pip} \\ \text{Squeak} \\ \text{Wilfred} \end{array} &
\left[\begin{array}{ccc}
0 & 0 & 1 \\
1 & 0 & 0 \\
0 & 1 & 0
\end{array} \right]
\end{array}
$$

Thus the rows of this matrix show us that Pip dominates Wilfred,
Squeak dominates Pip, and Wilfred dominates Squeak; and if we look at
the columns we can immediately see whom Pip, Squeak and Wilfred
respectively are dominated *by*.

Or, to take a final example, we might be interested in some kind of
transition matrix, setting out the probabilities of a person's proceeding
from (for instance) one social class to another in some given time period –
a generation, say. Take the following matrix, which might represent the
probability of the sons of upper-, middle- and lower-class fathers moving
into the upper, middle and lower classes respectively:

$$
\begin{array}{cc}
 & & \textit{Sons} \\
 & & \text{Upper} & \text{Middle} & \text{Lower} \\
\textit{Fathers} & \begin{array}{c} \text{Upper} \\ \text{Middle} \\ \text{Lower} \end{array} &
\left[\begin{array}{ccc}
.4 & .5 & .1 \\
.1 & .7 & .2 \\
.1 & .5 & .4
\end{array} \right]
\end{array}
$$

Here the rows show us the probabilities of the son's class when that of the
father is known. The son of a middle-class father, for example, has a one
in ten chance of moving to the upper class, a seven in ten chance of staying
in the middle class, and a one in five chance of moving to the lower
class. In this case the interpretation of the columns is not quite so
straightforward. Obviously the first column, for instance, does not tell us
what the probabilities are of an upper-class son having an upper-, middle-
or lower-class father. Such probabilities must depend on the number of
fathers there are in each class.

The Manipulation of Matrices

So far, all we have done is to explain what a matrix is, and to establish that the matrix form may sometimes be a neat and convenient way in which to set out some of the interrelationships in which social scientists are interested. But if that was all there was to it, there would hardly be any need for a book like the present one. The point is that it is often useful not merely to set out the interrelationships in matrix form, but also to be able to *manipulate* the matrices themselves in various ways. What is meant by this?

In ordinary arithmetic, where we deal with individual numbers, we use certain simple techniques, which we all take in with our mother's milk, in order to add, subtract, multiply and divide them. Suppose, however, that you want to deal not with individual numbers but with arrays of numbers in matrix form. Suppose you think that it might be useful to treat each of these matrices as a unit, and to perform operations upon them analogous to those of addition, subtraction, multiplication and division in ordinary arithmetic. How would you go about it?

Essentially, what you would require is a set of conventions establishing what you are going to *mean* by addition, subtraction, multiplication and division, when you are dealing with matrices rather than with individual numbers. And the conventions you adopted would depend largely upon their convenience in relation to the particular problems which you were hoping to be able to solve with the aid of these operations.

So far as *addition* is concerned, the convention usually adopted is a fairly simple and commonsense one. To add two matrices of the same dimensions, or order as it is often called (that is, having the same number of rows and columns), you simply add the corresponding components. For example:

$$\begin{bmatrix} 2 & 0 \\ -1 & 4 \\ 3 & 7 \end{bmatrix} + \begin{bmatrix} 6 & -2 \\ 0 & 4 \\ -2 & 1 \end{bmatrix} = \begin{bmatrix} 8 & -2 \\ -1 & 8 \\ 1 & 8 \end{bmatrix}.$$

Here are two more examples, in the first of which we add two 1×3 row vectors, and in the second 2×2 square matrices:

$$\begin{bmatrix} 3 & -2 & 4 \end{bmatrix} + \begin{bmatrix} 0 & -3 & -2 \end{bmatrix} = \begin{bmatrix} 3 & -5 & 2 \end{bmatrix}$$

$$\begin{bmatrix} 1 & 2 \\ -1 & 3 \end{bmatrix} + \begin{bmatrix} 3 & 2 \\ -1 & 0 \end{bmatrix} = \begin{bmatrix} 4 & 4 \\ -2 & 3 \end{bmatrix}.$$

But, you may be asking, what about matrices which do not have the same number of rows and the same number of columns? How do you add *them*? The simple answer is that you don't, and can't. The operation 'addition', when applied to matrices, is defined in terms of the addition of the *corresponding* components, and is therefore applicable only to matrices of the same dimensions.

The operation *subtraction* is defined analogously to that of addition, and it is also therefore applicable only to matrices of the same shape. Examples:

$$\begin{bmatrix} 1 & 2 \\ -1 & 3 \end{bmatrix} - \begin{bmatrix} 3 & 2 \\ -1 & 0 \end{bmatrix} = \begin{bmatrix} -2 & 0 \\ 0 & 3 \end{bmatrix}$$

$$\begin{bmatrix} 6 \\ 4 \\ -2 \end{bmatrix} - \begin{bmatrix} 3 \\ 5 \\ -3 \end{bmatrix} = \begin{bmatrix} 3 \\ -1 \\ 1 \end{bmatrix}.$$

That is all easy enough, I suppose. But *multiplication* is defined in a different, less obvious way, and will take a little longer to explain.

First let us get what is called *scalar multiplication* out of the way. Sometimes we may want to multiply each component of a matrix by a single number, say 2, in which case we just do precisely that, setting out the operation as in the following example:

$$2 \begin{bmatrix} 1 & -3 \\ 2 & 4 \end{bmatrix} = \begin{bmatrix} 2 & -6 \\ 4 & 8 \end{bmatrix}.$$

More often, however, as we shall see later in this book, we will want to multiply the matrix not by a single number but by another matrix, or by itself. What meaning is it most useful for us to give to such an operation?

Let us approach this problem indirectly by having another look at the matrix which we constructed at the beginning of this chapter:

	Motoring (miles)	Admission Charge (£s)	Liquor (pints)	Crisps (packets)	
Go to pub:	3	1	4	3	
Go to theatre:	2	3	1	1	= A.
Cards at home:	0	0	12	9	

In order to identify this matrix, let us call it *A*. Suppose now that you want to take a further step in weighing up the advantages and disadvantages of the three alternatives by calculating the respective *total money costs* involved in each of them. Suppose also that for some reason best known to yourself you want to separate out the tax element in these money costs, so that you finish up with two separate figures relating to each of the three options – one showing the total money costs of the option, and the other showing the total amount of tax included in these costs.

The motoring cost per mile, reckoned in pence, is, let us say, 20p which includes a tax element of 10p; the admission charge per £1 is (not unnaturally) 100p, which includes a tax element of 25p; the price of liquor per pint is 80p, which includes a tax element of 20p; and the price of crisps per packet is 10p, the tax element here being zero. It will be convenient to put this information in the form of a second matrix – a 4 × 2 one this time – which we will identify as matrix B:

	Cost including tax	Tax element	
Motoring cost per mile	20p	10p	
Admission charge	100p	25p	$= B$.
Liquor per pint	80p	20p	
Crisps cost per packet	10p	0	

Given these two matrices A and B, it is of course simplicity itself to make the calculations you have in mind. To work out the total money costs involved in going to the pub, you multiply each of the components in the first row of A by the corresponding components in the first column of B, and then add up the four products, thus:

Cost (including tax)
of going to the pub $= (3 \times 20) + (1 \times 100) + (4 \times 80) + (3 \times 10)$
$= 510$p.

And to work out the tax element included in this total of 510p, you multiply each of the components in the first row of A by the corresponding components in the second column of B, and then add up the four products, thus:

Tax element in cost
of going to the pub $= (3 \times 10) + (1 \times 25) + (4 \times 20) + (3 \times 0)$
$= 135$p.

Similarly to work out the total money costs involved in going to the theatre, you multiply each of the components in the second row of A by the corresponding components in the first column of B, and then add up the four products, thus:

Cost (including tax) of
going to the theatre $= (2 \times 20) + (3 \times 100) + (1 \times 80) + (1 \times 10)$
$= 430\text{p}.$

And to work out the tax element included in this total of 430p, you multiply each of the components in the second row of A by the corresponding components in the second column of B, and then add up the four products, thus:

Tax element in cost of
going to the theatre $= (2 \times 10) + (3 \times 25) + (1 \times 20) + (1 \times 0)$
$= 115\text{p}.$

You should now have no difficulty in making the third and last pair of calculations yourself, or in seeing that the most convenient way of presenting the final results is in the form of a third matrix – a 3×2 one – which we shall identify as matrix C:

	Total cost including tax	Total tax element
Go to pub:	510p	135p
Go to theatre:	430p	115p
Cards at home:	1050p	240p

$= C$.

All right – let us now make a mighty intellectual leap and agree to say that we have arrived at matrix C by *multiplying* matrix A by matrix B so that:

$$\begin{bmatrix} 3 & 1 & 4 & 3 \\ 2 & 3 & 1 & 1 \\ 0 & 0 & 12 & 9 \end{bmatrix} \begin{bmatrix} 20 & 10 \\ 100 & 25 \\ 80 & 20 \\ 10 & 0 \end{bmatrix} = \begin{bmatrix} 510 & 135 \\ 430 & 115 \\ 1050 & 240 \end{bmatrix}.$$

In other words, let us *define* the multiplication of two matrices as consisting of the set of arithmetical operations we have just been describing.

Just to make absolutely sure that we understand what this amounts to, let us go over each of the six operations involved:

1. The number in the *first row* and *first column* of C is obtained by multiplying each component in the *first row* of A by the corresponding components in the *first column* of B, and adding the products.

2. The number in the *first row* and *second column* of C is obtained by multiplying each component in the *first row* of A by the corresponding component in the *second column* of B, and adding the products.

3. The number in the *second row* and *first column* of C is obtained by multiplying each component in the *second row* of A by the corresponding components in the *first column* of B, and adding the products.

4. The number in the *second row* and *second column* of C is obtained by multiplying each component in the *second row* of A by the corresponding components in the *second column* of B, and adding the products.

5. The number in the *third row* and *first column* of C is obtained by multiplying each component in the *third row* of A by the corresponding components in the *first column* of B, and adding the products.

6. The number in the *third row* and *second column* of C is obtained by multiplying each component in the *third row* of A by the corresponding components in the *second column* of B, and adding the products.

The *general* rule should be pretty clear from this. If two matrices A and B are to be multiplied together in order to arrive at a product matrix C, then any particular component of C – the component in the mth row and the nth column, let us say – is obtained by multiplying the components in the mth row of A by the corresponding components in the nth column of B, and adding the products. Clearly it is useful in the homely case we have been using as our illustration to define *multiplication* in this way, since it gives us a sensible answer to the problem we set ourselves. And since it also does this in a great many other cases, of somewhat greater practical importance, this is the way in which the multiplication of matrices is conventionally defined.

Before going any further, you might like to check that the same definition of multiplication has been employed in the following additional examples:

(1)
$$\begin{bmatrix} 2 & -1 \\ 0 & 4 \end{bmatrix} \begin{bmatrix} 6 & 0 \\ -2 & -2 \end{bmatrix} = \begin{bmatrix} 14 & 2 \\ -8 & -8 \end{bmatrix}.$$

(2)
$$\begin{bmatrix} 6 & 0 \\ -2 & -2 \end{bmatrix} \begin{bmatrix} 2 & -1 \\ 0 & 4 \end{bmatrix} = \begin{bmatrix} 12 & -6 \\ -4 & -6 \end{bmatrix}.$$

(3)
$$\begin{bmatrix} 3 & 4 & -1 \end{bmatrix} \begin{bmatrix} 2 & 4 \\ 3 & -1 \\ -2 & 0 \end{bmatrix} = \begin{bmatrix} 20 & 8 \end{bmatrix}.$$

(4)
$$\begin{bmatrix} 3 & 1 & 3 \\ 2 & 5 & 0 \end{bmatrix} \begin{bmatrix} 1 & 2 & 0 & 1 \\ 1 & 0 & 1 & 0 \\ 0 & 3 & 1 & 1 \end{bmatrix} = \begin{bmatrix} 4 & 15 & 4 & 6 \\ 7 & 4 & 5 & 2 \end{bmatrix}.$$

You will probably have noticed that in each of these cases the number of columns in the first matrix is equal to the number of rows in the second. This is not accidental, of course: indeed, if you think about it for a moment you will see that it follows necessarily from our definition of multiplication that a matrix A can be multiplied by another matrix B only if A has the same number of columns as B has rows. It also follows from our definition – and this too can be seen from the examples above – that the matrix which is the product of two other matrices A and B will have as many rows as A and as many columns as B.

So if you are presented with two matrices A and B and asked to multiply the first by the second, a good tip is to begin by putting the dimensions of A and B side by side – for example:

$$\begin{array}{cc} A & B \\ 3 \times 2 & 2 \times 5. \end{array}$$

If the second and third numbers (representing respectively the number of columns of A and the number of rows of B) are equal – as they are in this example – then you know for certain that the matrices *can* be multiplied. And if so, the first and fourth numbers – 3 and 5 in this case – will give you the dimensions of the product matrix. Examples:

A	B	Multipliable?	Dimensions of product matrix	
3×5	5×4	Yes	3×4	
5×4	3×5	No	–	
2×3	3×1	Yes	2×1	(a column vector)
1×5	5×4	Yes	1×4	(a row vector)
2×2	2×2	Yes	2×2	
2×3	2×3	No	–	
1×4	4×1	Yes	1×1	(a single number)

24

This is known as the DOMINO rule. Think of *A* and *B* as dominoes and their product *A B* as being the end values of the domino chain:

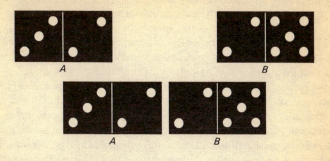

And now to play another domino you need a 3 or a 5.

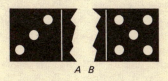

The final thing to note about the multiplication of matrices – and it is a very important thing indeed – is that the *order* in which they are to be multiplied matters. In ordinary arithmetic, of course, the order does not matter at all. If 6 can be multiplied by 7, then 7 can be multiplied by 6; and whichever way round you do the sum the resulting product will naturally be the same. But in both these respects the arithmetic of matrices is strikingly different.

First, if matrix *A* can be multiplied by matrix *B* (in that order), it does *not* follow that matrix *B* can be multiplied by matrix *A* (in *that* order). This can easily be seen from the first two examples in the list in the last paragraph but one: you can multiply a 3 × 5 matrix by a 5 × 4 matrix, but you *cannot* multiply a 5 × 4 matrix by a 3 × 5 matrix.

Second, even if you *can* multiply two matrices in either order (two 2 × 2s, for example, or a 5 × 3 and a 3 × 5), the product matrix will not necessarily – or indeed usually – be the same. This is obvious enough if A is 5×3 and B is 3×5: AB will then be 5×5 and BA will be 3×3, so that no question of the possible equality of AB and BA can arise. In the case of two square matrices of the same dimensions – two 2×2s, for example – it is not quite so obvious. If you look back at examples (1) and (2) on p. 23 above, however, where two 2×2s are multiplied first in one order and then in the reverse order, you will see that the two resulting product matrices do not even have a single term in common.*

We express this by saying that when we are dealing with matrices the operation of multiplication (as distinct from that of addition) is not *commutative*. And since the order in which we multiply matrices is so important, we often specify the order in which we are performing the operation by the use of special terms. AB is described as A post-multiplied by B, and BA is described as A pre-multiplied by B. Then we know exactly what we are doing.

What about Division?

We now know what the operations of addition, subtraction and multiplication are conventionally taken to mean when we are dealing with matrices rather than with single numbers. But what about *division*? What is the division of one matrix by another conventionally taken to mean? The answer is that in matrix algebra division in the commonly accepted sense of the word does not exist. We do not talk about 'dividing' by a matrix A; we talk instead about *multiplying* by a matrix which we call the *inverse* of A.

In order to understand what this means, we must first define an *identity matrix*. In ordinary arithmetic there is a number 1, or unity, such that when we multiply any other number (8, say) by it, then $8 \times 1 = 8$. In the arithmetic of matrices, by analogy, we can define an *identity matrix* (I), such that when we multiply any other matrix A by it, then $AI = A$. Suppose, for example, that A were the following 2×3 matrix:

$$\begin{bmatrix} 6 & 3 & 0 \\ 5 & 0 & -2 \end{bmatrix}.$$

* This should not be taken to imply that AB and BA can *never* be equal. For example:

$$\begin{bmatrix} 3 & 2 \\ 2 & 3 \end{bmatrix} \begin{bmatrix} -1 & 2 \\ 2 & -1 \end{bmatrix} = \begin{bmatrix} 1 & 4 \\ 4 & 1 \end{bmatrix} = \begin{bmatrix} -1 & 2 \\ 2 & -1 \end{bmatrix} \begin{bmatrix} 3 & 2 \\ 2 & 3 \end{bmatrix}.$$

What would the identity matrix, as so defined, look like in this case? It would *not* (as we might be tempted to think at first sight) be another 2×3 matrix with all its components consisting of 1s. Far from it. It would in fact be a 3×3 square matrix with entries of 1 in the diagonal going down from left to right (the *main diagonal*) and entries of 0 everywhere else. Using the definition of matrix multiplication it is easy to show that

$$\begin{bmatrix} 6 & 3 & 0 \\ 5 & 0 & -2 \end{bmatrix} \begin{bmatrix} 1 & 0 & 0 \\ 0 & 1 & 0 \\ 0 & 0 & 1 \end{bmatrix} = \begin{bmatrix} 6 & 3 & 0 \\ 5 & 0 & -2 \end{bmatrix}.$$

If A were a 3×2 matrix, to take another example, the identity matrix I would be a 2×2 square matrix with 1s in the main diagonal and 0s everywhere else. For example:

$$\begin{bmatrix} 2 & 4 \\ 3 & 1 \\ 0 & -3 \end{bmatrix} \begin{bmatrix} 1 & 0 \\ 0 & 1 \end{bmatrix} = \begin{bmatrix} 2 & 4 \\ 3 & 1 \\ 0 & -3 \end{bmatrix}.$$

Putting this in general terms, if A is an $n \times m$ matrix, and AI is always to be equal to A, the I must be an $m \times m$ square matrix with 1s in the main diagonal and 0s everywhere else. Why must it be a *square* matrix? What would the dimensions of I have to be if the multiplication were done the other way round, so that IA, rather than AI, was to be equal to A? Let us stare these questions boldly in the face and walk straight on, in order not to delay our first meeting with the inverse of a matrix.

In ordinary arithmetic, we define the inverse (or reciprocal) of any number a as a number b such that $ab = 1$. Thus the inverse of the number 4 is .25, since $4 \times .25 = 1$. We often write this as 1/4, and sometimes as 4^{-1}. Well, for many purposes in the arithmetic of matrices it is useful to adopt an analogous concept, that of the inverse of a matrix. We define the inverse of a matrix A (usually written as A^{-1}) as a matrix B such that $AB = BA =$ the identity matrix I.* Thus suppose matrix A happens to be

$$\begin{bmatrix} 1 & 2 \\ -2 & -3 \end{bmatrix},$$

---

* We should perhaps note here that it is only *square* matrices which can possibly have inverses, because if A is not square AB and BA cannot possibly be the same. Suppose that A and B are two matrices such that it is possible to carry out both the operation AB and the operation BA. Then if A is an $n \times m$, matrix B must be an $m \times n$ matrix. But in that case AB will be $n \times n$, and BA will be $m \times m$, so that AB and BA cannot be the same unless $n = m$.

we can fairly easily calculate (by a method yet to be disclosed) that its inverse A^{-1} will be

$$\begin{bmatrix} -3 & -2 \\ 2 & 1 \end{bmatrix},$$

because the product of this matrix and matrix A, whichever way round we do the multiplication, is the identity matrix I:

$$\begin{bmatrix} 1 & 2 \\ -2 & -3 \end{bmatrix} \begin{bmatrix} -3 & -2 \\ 2 & 1 \end{bmatrix} = \begin{bmatrix} -3 & -2 \\ 2 & 1 \end{bmatrix} \begin{bmatrix} 1 & 2 \\ -2 & -3 \end{bmatrix}$$

$$= \begin{bmatrix} 1 & 0 \\ 0 & 1 \end{bmatrix} = I.$$

We are now in a position to see how operations analogous to division in ordinary arithmetic can be carried out when we are dealing with matrices, even though 'division' as such has no meaning in matrix algebra. Suppose we are given two matrices, A and B, and told that B is the product of A and some unknown matrix X – where

$$AX = B.$$

How could we work out the unknown matrix X? If A, X and B were single numbers, the answer would be simple: divide each side of the equation by A and the solution would immediately emerge:

$$X = \frac{B}{A}.$$

But in matrix algebra there is no concept of division – so what do we do? The answer (which shows the usefulness of lateral thinking) is that you *premultiply* both sides of the equation $AX = B$ by the *inverse of A* (that is, by A^{-1}), giving

$$A^{-1}AX = A^{-1}B.$$

Since by definition $A^{-1}A = I$, and since $IX = X$,* we then have

$$X = A^{-1}B,$$

* Multiplication involving an identity matrix is commutative; in this case,

$$IX = XI = X.$$

28

so that, provided A in fact has an inverse, the solution is in our pocket. We shall see later that this way of going about things makes much more sense than it may seem to do at first sight. We shall also see later, however, that it is not quite as simple as it may seem at first sight – partly because it is by no means true that all matrices (even when they are square) do have inverses, and partly because inverses when they exist may well be very difficult to calculate, at any rate without the aid of a computer.

Exercises

Try the following exercises to make sure you have understood the matrix techniques of this chapter.

$$A = \begin{bmatrix} 1 & 2 \\ 3 & 4 \end{bmatrix} \qquad B = \begin{bmatrix} 4 & -2 \\ -3 & 1 \end{bmatrix}$$

$$C = \begin{bmatrix} 1 & 0 \\ 0 & -1 \\ 2 & 2 \end{bmatrix} \qquad D = \begin{bmatrix} 1 & 0 & 2 \\ 2 & -1 & 0 \end{bmatrix}$$

Calculate all of the following or explain why they do not exist:
  1. $A + B$;
  2. $A - B$;
  3. $A + C$;
  4. AB;
  5. BA;
  6. AC;
  7. CA;
  8. BD;
  9. DB;
  10. CD;
  11. DC;
  12. ABC;
  13. ABD;
  14. Use your results for AB and BA to calculate the inverse of A and of B.

2
Matrix Inversion

Inverting matrices turns out to be of considerable importance to social scientists, and in the next chapter we shall look at the important role it plays in economic planning. It is necessary, therefore, that you should be happy with the concept, be able to compute simple matrix inverses and understand how one could approach the calculation in more complicated cases.

The inverse of a square matrix A, as we have seen,* is defined as a matrix B such that $AB = BA =$ the identity matrix I. The example we used was of

$$A = \begin{bmatrix} 1 & 2 \\ -2 & -3 \end{bmatrix},$$

where the inverse turned out to be

$$B = \begin{bmatrix} -3 & -2 \\ 2 & 1 \end{bmatrix}$$

because, as we demonstrated,

$$\begin{bmatrix} 1 & 2 \\ -2 & -3 \end{bmatrix} \begin{bmatrix} -3 & -2 \\ 2 & 1 \end{bmatrix} = \begin{bmatrix} -3 & -2 \\ 2 & 1 \end{bmatrix} \begin{bmatrix} 1 & 2 \\ -2 & -3 \end{bmatrix} = \begin{bmatrix} 1 & 0 \\ 0 & 1 \end{bmatrix}.$$

In other words, $AB = BA = I$.

How could we have actually worked out the inverse in this case, if we had not been told what it was? A little bit of very simple conventional algebra would have done it. Consider the inverse B as a matrix in which the four components are unknowns – let us call them e, f, g and h. Then we can write

$$\begin{bmatrix} 1 & 2 \\ -2 & -3 \end{bmatrix} \begin{bmatrix} e & f \\ g & h \end{bmatrix} = \begin{bmatrix} 1 & 0 \\ 0 & 1 \end{bmatrix}.$$

* Above, p. 27.

From this by multiplying out, we can easily derive a system of four simultaneous equations:

(1) $e + 2g = 1$

(2) $f + 2h = 0$

(3) $-2e - 3g = 0$

(4) $-2f - 3h = 1$.

These equations are readily soluble by the methods of conventional algebra. If we double all the terms of (1), and add the resultant equation to (3), the es cancel out and it immediately emerges that $g = 2$. Substituting this value of g in (1), we get $e = -3$. Similarly, from (2) and (4) we can easily work out that $f = -2$ and $h = 1$.

Let us show now that a matrix need not necessarily *have* an inverse. Suppose that we had used the method just described to try to work out the inverse of

$$A = \begin{bmatrix} 3 & 9 \\ -2 & -6 \end{bmatrix}.$$

We would then have written

$$\begin{bmatrix} 3 & 9 \\ -2 & -6 \end{bmatrix} \begin{bmatrix} e & f \\ g & h \end{bmatrix} = \begin{bmatrix} 1 & 0 \\ 0 & 1 \end{bmatrix}$$

and derived the following equations:

(1) $3e + 9g = 1$

(2) $3f + 9h = 0$

(3) $-2e - 6g = 0$

(4) $-2f - 6h = 1$.

But this system of equations fairly obviously cannot be solved, because it is contradictory. For example, if you multiply all the terms of (3) by $-1\frac{1}{2}$, you will get

$$3e + 9g = 0,$$

thus clearly contradicting equation (1), which tells us that

$$3e + 9g = 1.$$

You will find if you experiment with 2×2 matrices that you will always get a contradictory result like this if, in the matrix of which you are trying to find the inverse, the product of the two components in the main diagonal is equal to the product of the two components in the other diagonal. The difference between these two products, in the case of a 2×2 matrix, is defined as the *determinant* of the matrix. So, for the matrix $\begin{bmatrix} a & b \\ c & d \end{bmatrix}$ the determinant is the *number* ad − bc.

The general rule, in the case of a 2×2 matrix, is that it will have an inverse if and only if its determinant, as so defined, is non-zero.

The General 2 × 2 Case

We can show that this general rule is correct and provides a formula that enables us to write down the inverse of a 2×2 matrix (if it exists) by considering a general case.

We have just derived the inverse of a matrix with numerical values for the elements by supposing the inverse to be

$$\begin{bmatrix} e & f \\ g & h \end{bmatrix}.$$

Now, instead of having numerical values in our matrix to be inverted, let the matrix be

$$\begin{bmatrix} a & b \\ c & d \end{bmatrix}.$$

Our job is to find e, f, g and h such that

$$\begin{bmatrix} a & b \\ c & d \end{bmatrix} \begin{bmatrix} e & f \\ g & h \end{bmatrix} = \begin{bmatrix} 1 & 0 \\ 0 & 1 \end{bmatrix}.$$

Proceeding just as before we have

$$(1) \quad ae + bg = 1$$

$$\text{(2)} \quad af + bh = 0$$

$$\text{(3)} \quad ce + dg = 0$$

$$\text{(4)} \quad cf + dh = 1$$

and we must solve these equations for e, f, g and h.
  Now

$$g = \frac{-ce}{d}$$

from (3), so $ae - \dfrac{bce}{d} = 1$ by substituting in (1);
that is

$$ade - bce = d$$
$$e(ad - bc) = d$$

and

$$e = \frac{d}{ad - bc}.$$

Since

$$g = \frac{-ce}{d}$$

we substitute for e and get

$$g = \frac{-c}{ad - bc}.$$

So far we have used equations (1) and (3) to find e and g. The reader should check that by using equations (2) and (4) we can calculate f and h. The results we get are

$$f = \frac{-b}{ad - bc}$$

33

and

$$h = \frac{a}{ad - bc}.$$

This means that we have managed to invert

$$A = \begin{bmatrix} a & b \\ c & d \end{bmatrix}$$

to get

$$\begin{bmatrix} e & f \\ g & h \end{bmatrix} = A^{-1} = \begin{bmatrix} a & b \\ c & d \end{bmatrix}^{-1} = \begin{bmatrix} \dfrac{d}{ad-bc} & \dfrac{-b}{ad-bc} \\ \dfrac{-c}{ad-bc} & \dfrac{a}{ad-bc} \end{bmatrix}.$$

This looks rather clumsy and unpleasant but we can see all the elements of A^{-1} have a common denominator.

So if we say that writing

$$k \begin{bmatrix} a & b \\ c & d \end{bmatrix}$$

means the same as writing

$$\begin{bmatrix} ka & kb \\ kc & kd \end{bmatrix},$$

we could write

$$\begin{bmatrix} a & b \\ c & d \end{bmatrix}^{-1} = \begin{bmatrix} e & f \\ g & h \end{bmatrix} = \frac{1}{ad-bc} \begin{bmatrix} d & -b \\ -c & a \end{bmatrix}$$

and this looks much less daunting.

It enables us to write down the inverse of a 2 × 2 matrix with very little effort. All we have to do is to swap the elements in the main diagonal; multiply the elements in the other diagonal by − 1 but leave them where they are, and then divide all the elements by $ad - bc$.

34

In the numerical example above we had

$$\begin{bmatrix} a & b \\ c & d \end{bmatrix} = \begin{bmatrix} 1 & 2 \\ -2 & -3 \end{bmatrix}.$$

In this case $ad - bc = 1$, so the inverse is

$$\begin{bmatrix} -3 & -2 \\ 2 & 1 \end{bmatrix}.$$

Similarly if we wanted to find the inverse of

$$\begin{bmatrix} a & b \\ c & d \end{bmatrix} = \begin{bmatrix} 6 & 8 \\ 2 & 3 \end{bmatrix},$$

since $ad - bc = 2$,

$$\begin{bmatrix} a & b \\ c & d \end{bmatrix}^{-1} = \frac{1}{2} \begin{bmatrix} 3 & -8 \\ -2 & 6 \end{bmatrix} = \begin{bmatrix} \frac{3}{2} & -4 \\ -1 & 3 \end{bmatrix}.$$

We have already defined the *determinant* of a 2 × 2 matrix as the difference between the product of the two elements in the main diagonal and the product of the elements in the other diagonal. The determinant of

$$\begin{bmatrix} a & b \\ c & d \end{bmatrix}$$

is $ad - bc$, and now we can see why if the determinant of a 2 × 2 matrix is zero the matrix will not have an inverse. Our formula for finding the inverse tells us to divide the elements of the matrix by the value of the determinant, and if this value is zero we have an impossible task. A matrix that does not have an inverse is said to be *singular*.

To check that you understand what is happening, calculate the inverses (if they exist) of the following matrices

$$\begin{bmatrix} 3 & -1 \\ 4 & 2 \end{bmatrix}, \begin{bmatrix} \frac{1}{2} & \frac{1}{2} \\ \frac{1}{4} & \frac{1}{2} \end{bmatrix}, \begin{bmatrix} 6 & 8 \\ -3 & -4 \end{bmatrix}, \begin{bmatrix} 1 & 1 \\ -1 & 1 \end{bmatrix}.$$

Unfortunately, there are no such easy formulae for calculating the inverses of larger matrices, but we can get a flavour of how we might go about such calculations by tackling our original problem from a different angle.

Elementary Row Operations

Let us look at things a slightly different way. We are trying to find out how to turn a matrix like A into I

$$\begin{bmatrix} 1 & 2 \\ -2 & -3 \end{bmatrix} \xrightarrow{\text{HOW?}} \begin{bmatrix} 1 & 0 \\ 0 & 1 \end{bmatrix}.$$

Suppose we were allowed to play about with A as much as we liked using the following rules:

(i) we can swap the rows of A with each other;

(ii) we can multiply all the elements in any row by any non-zero number; and

(iii) we can multiply any row of A by a non-zero number and add the result to the other row.

In fact it would be easy to get from A to I just using rule (iii) by using the following stages:

(a) Multiply the first row by 2 and add it to the second row. We get

$$\begin{bmatrix} 1 & 2 \\ 0 & 1 \end{bmatrix}.$$

(b) Multiply the second row of the new matrix by -2 and add it to the first row. We get

$$\begin{bmatrix} 1 & 0 \\ 0 & 1 \end{bmatrix} = I.$$

To see why we are playing this game, let us try to use the same rules to go from I to $B = A^{-1}$.

$$\begin{bmatrix} 1 & 0 \\ 0 & 1 \end{bmatrix} \xrightarrow{\text{HOW?}} \begin{bmatrix} -3 & -2 \\ 2 & 1 \end{bmatrix}$$

If we felt a little tired or uninspired we might in desperation use the steps (a) and (b) that we have just used. They worked before, could they, as if by magic, work again?

(a) Multiply the first row of I by 2 and add it to the second row. We get

$$\begin{bmatrix} 1 & 0 \\ 2 & 1 \end{bmatrix}.$$

(b) Multiply the second row of this new matrix by -2 and add it to the first row. We get

$$\begin{bmatrix} -3 & -2 \\ 2 & 1 \end{bmatrix} = B = A^{-1}.$$

So the steps (a) and (b) that turned A into I also turn I into A^{-1}.

This is no coincidence, for it can be shown that *if a sequence of row operations turns A into I, then the same sequence turns I into A^{-1}.*

Thus another way of calculating the inverse of a matrix A is to (i) find a sequence of row operations turning A into I and (ii) use the same sequence to turn I into A^{-1}.

Let us see how this makes finding inverses a painless procedure. Suppose we want to find the inverse of

$$A = \begin{bmatrix} 2 & 1 \\ 1 & 3 \end{bmatrix}.$$

Since we are going to apply the same set of operations to I and A we may as well put I and A next to each other in a table.

	I	A	STEP
Tableau 0	$\begin{bmatrix} 1 & 0 \\ 0 & 1 \end{bmatrix}$	$\begin{bmatrix} 2 & 1 \\ 1 & 3 \end{bmatrix}$	(a) Swap rows then we will have 1s on the diagonal $\longrightarrow$ tableau 1
Tableau 1	$\begin{bmatrix} 0 & 1 \\ 1 & 0 \end{bmatrix}$	$\begin{bmatrix} 1 & 3 \\ 2 & 1 \end{bmatrix}$	(b) To get 0 in row 2 column 1, multiply first row by -2 and add to the second row $\longrightarrow$ tableau 2

	I	*A*	STEP
Tableau 2	$\begin{bmatrix} 0 & 1 \\ 1 & -2 \end{bmatrix}$	$\begin{bmatrix} 1 & 3 \\ 0 & -5 \end{bmatrix}$	(c) To get 0 in row 1 column 2 multiply the second row by $+3/5$ and add to the first row $\longrightarrow$ tableau 3
Tableau 3	$\begin{bmatrix} \frac{3}{5} & -\frac{1}{5} \\ 1 & -2 \end{bmatrix}$	$\begin{bmatrix} 1 & 0 \\ 0 & -5 \end{bmatrix}$	(d) To get to *I* we must multiply the second row by $-1/5$ $\longrightarrow$ tableau 4
Tableau 4	$\begin{bmatrix} \frac{3}{5} & -\frac{1}{5} \\ -\frac{1}{5} & \frac{2}{5} \end{bmatrix}$	$\begin{bmatrix} 1 & 0 \\ 0 & 1 \end{bmatrix}$	We are there. *A* has been transformed into *I* through *elementary row operations*

In this particular case, on the route we have chosen, we have used all three types of elementary row operations. We must check that the same operations on *I* as we have made on *A* do give us the inverse.

From tableau 4 we think that

$$A^{-1} = \begin{bmatrix} \frac{3}{5} & -\frac{1}{5} \\ -\frac{1}{5} & \frac{2}{5} \end{bmatrix}.$$

Now

$$A^{-1}A = \begin{bmatrix} \frac{3}{5} & -\frac{1}{5} \\ -\frac{1}{5} & \frac{2}{5} \end{bmatrix} \begin{bmatrix} 2 & 1 \\ 1 & 3 \end{bmatrix}$$

$$= \begin{bmatrix} 1 & 0 \\ 0 & 1 \end{bmatrix} = I.$$

We have indeed found the inverse of *A*.

The Inverse of Larger Matrices

We can use exactly the same technique that we used for 2×2 matrices to find the inverse of larger matrices.

Thus suppose

$$A = \begin{bmatrix} 1 & 2 & 3 \\ 0 & 1 & 4 \\ 0 & 0 & 2 \end{bmatrix}.$$

To find the inverse we must convert A into I by a series of row operations and apply these same operations to I itself. We need another table.

	I	A	STEP
Tableau 0	$\begin{bmatrix} 1 & 0 & 0 \\ 0 & 1 & 0 \\ 0 & 0 & 1 \end{bmatrix}$	$\begin{bmatrix} 1 & 2 & 3 \\ 0 & 1 & 4 \\ 0 & 0 & 2 \end{bmatrix}$	(a) To get 1 in third row third column, divide the third row by 2 $\longrightarrow$ tableau 1
Tableau 1	$\begin{bmatrix} 1 & 0 & 0 \\ 0 & 1 & 0 \\ 0 & 0 & \frac{1}{2} \end{bmatrix}$	$\begin{bmatrix} 1 & 2 & 3 \\ 0 & 1 & 4 \\ 0 & 0 & 1 \end{bmatrix}$	(b) To get 0 in second row third column, multiply the third row by -4 and add to the second row $\longrightarrow$ tableau 2
Tableau 2	$\begin{bmatrix} 1 & 0 & 0 \\ 0 & 1 & -2 \\ 0 & 0 & \frac{1}{2} \end{bmatrix}$	$\begin{bmatrix} 1 & 2 & 3 \\ 0 & 1 & 0 \\ 0 & 0 & 1 \end{bmatrix}$	(c) To get 0 in first row second column, multiply the second row by -2 and add to the first row $\longrightarrow$ tableau 3
Tableau 3	$\begin{bmatrix} 1 & -2 & 4 \\ 0 & 1 & -2 \\ 0 & 0 & \frac{1}{2} \end{bmatrix}$	$\begin{bmatrix} 1 & 0 & 3 \\ 0 & 1 & 0 \\ 0 & 0 & 1 \end{bmatrix}$	(d) To get 0 in first row third column, multiply the third row by -3 and add to first row $\longrightarrow$ tableau 4
Tableau 4	$\begin{bmatrix} 1 & -2 & \frac{5}{2} \\ 0 & 1 & -2 \\ 0 & 0 & \frac{1}{2} \end{bmatrix}$	$\begin{bmatrix} 1 & 0 & 0 \\ 0 & 1 & 0 \\ 0 & 0 & 1 \end{bmatrix}$	Now for checking

From the table we can see that

$$A^{-1} = \begin{bmatrix} 1 & -2 & \frac{5}{2} \\ 0 & 1 & -2 \\ 0 & 0 & \frac{1}{2} \end{bmatrix}$$

is the inverse of A and by multiplying A^{-1} by A we can check that it is indeed correct.

There are other sequences of row operations that would have led us from A to I but of course they would have given us the same answer for A^{-1}. You may like to check this for yourself. Indeed we could have performed what are known as *elementary column operations* rather than row operations. These column operations are defined in the same way as those for rows with the simple substitution of the word *column* for *row*.

Given sufficient patience we can find the inverse (if it exists) of any square matrix by a series of elementary row or column operations, but it turns out that we may need a great deal of patience. The larger the matrix, the more elementary operations we will need to perform; since there are more elements in each row and column we will have to perform more calculations in each operation. Also we have only examined matrices with small whole numbers as elements. Actual data matrices tend to have elements like 99.37 or even if whole numbers, these numbers may be very large. This not only adds to the arithmetic but can lead to what are known as *rounding errors*. If each operation is not calculated exactly but is rounded say to two decimal places, then this minor error may be compounded many times as more and more operations are done on already rounded figures. This could lead to finding 'inverses' which are quite different from the true 'inverse'. As a rule of thumb, unless you really have nothing else to do with your life, it is unwise to embark on inverting a matrix larger than 5×5 unless you have an electronic computer. Numerical analysts have devised efficient computer programmes for inverting large matrices. Why keep a dog and bark yourself?

Exercises

1. Using elementary row operations calculate the inverses (if they exist) of

$$\begin{bmatrix} 3 & -1 \\ 4 & 2 \end{bmatrix}, \begin{bmatrix} \frac{1}{2} & \frac{1}{2} \\ \frac{1}{4} & \frac{1}{2} \end{bmatrix}, \begin{bmatrix} 6 & 8 \\ -3 & -4 \end{bmatrix}, \begin{bmatrix} 1 & 1 \\ -1 & 1 \end{bmatrix}.$$

Check your answers with the answers you gave in the previous exercises (p. 35).

2. Find the inverses of the following matrices

$$\begin{bmatrix} 1 & 0 & 0 \\ 2 & 1 & 0 \\ 3 & 4 & 2 \end{bmatrix}, \begin{bmatrix} 1 & 2 & 3 \\ 0 & -1 & 2 \\ 0 & 1 & -1 \end{bmatrix}, \begin{bmatrix} 1 & 2 & 2 \\ 3 & 2 & 1 \\ 2 & 3 & 2 \end{bmatrix}.$$

Check your results by matrix multiplication.

3
The Ins and Outs of Economic Planning

Industrial Interrelationships

Let us begin our first illustration of the use of matrices in the social sciences by recalling an example used in the first chapter. We imagined, you may remember, a very simple three-industry economy, in which what we may now call the physical *input–output* relationships between the industries could be represented in the following matrix:

$$
\begin{array}{c c}
& \begin{array}{c} \textit{To} \\ \end{array} \\
\textit{From} \quad \begin{array}{c} A \\ B \\ C \end{array} &
\begin{array}{c c c c}
A & B & C & \textit{Final Demand} \\
\left[\begin{array}{c c c c}
50 & 100 & 50 & 100 \\
25 & 70 & 5 & 50 \\
30 & 10 & 60 & 80
\end{array} \right]
\end{array}
\end{array}
$$

Here the *rows* tell us where each industry's output goes to: of the total output of 300 units produced every year by industry *A*, for example, we see that 50 units are used as input in its own production process; 100 units are sold to industry *B* and 50 to industry *C* for use as inputs in their production processes; and the remaining 100 units are sold to final consumers like you and me (and the government, and foreign consumers, and anyone else you would like to include here). The first three columns tell us where each industry's physical inputs come from;* and the fourth column tells us from which industries you and I (and other final consumers) get the various things that we want and need.

By adding up the elements in the rows of this matrix we can see that in order to satisfy final demands of 100 units of *A*, 50 units of *B*, and 80 units of *C*, industries *A*, *B* and *C* must in total produce 300, 150 and 180 units respectively. The question we might ask as an economic planner is 'How much would these industries have to produce if we wanted to satisfy some

---

* *Physical* inputs, because each industry will also have an input of *labour*, which we shall not bring into the picture until a little later on.

42

different level of final demand?' Because industry A uses its own product and the products of B or C to make its goods, it would be necessary, if we wanted to increase the amount of A available for final demand without reducing that of B and C, to increase the output of all three industries. Our job is to discover what exactly such increases would have to be. This is no easy task and it will be wise to start with an even simpler economy than the one we have just pictured.

So let us suppose there are just two industries (F and G standing for food and guns) and that the authorities tell us as planners that they want 300 units of F and 200 units of G for final demand. We have to find out what the total output of F and G must be to satisfy the level of final demand. We shall call these totals f and g.

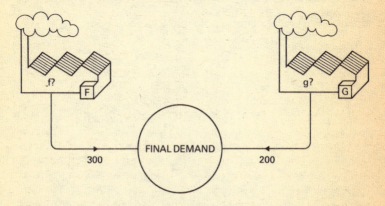

Now we have not as yet got nearly enough information to complete our assignment. We need to know more, or rather something, about the techniques of producing the goods. How much of its own product does F need to produce a unit? How much of industry G's product does F need? Suppose we find this information and it turns out that whatever the level of output F is producing, it always requires $\frac{1}{4}$ of a unit of F and a $\frac{1}{4}$ of a unit of G to produce a unit of F.

This means that if F is producing a total of f units it must use $\frac{1}{4}f$ of its own product and $\frac{1}{4}f$ of G's product in the production process.

We also discover that, again regardless of the level of output of G, to produce each unit of G requires $\frac{1}{2}$ a unit of F and $\frac{1}{3}$ of a unit of G. So to

43

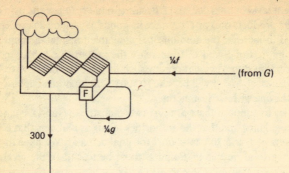

produce g units of G requires $\frac{1}{2}g$ of F and $\frac{1}{3}g$ of G.

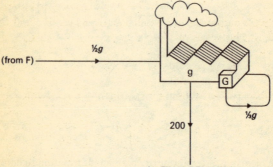

We can combine the three diagrams above to give an overall picture of inputs and outputs in the economy.

The output of industry F must be sufficient to cover its own production requirements, the requirements of G, and final demand. If it is just sufficient then we can see that

$$f = \frac{1}{4}f + \frac{1}{2}g + 300.$$

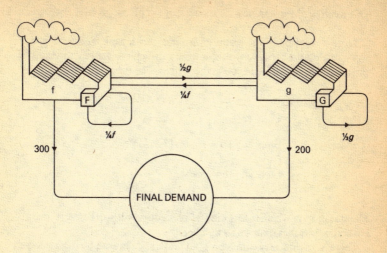

Similarly G's output has to cover the requirements of F and G and final demand, which gives us

$$g = \tfrac{1}{4}f + \tfrac{1}{3}g + 200.$$

Putting these two relationships in matrix form we can write

$$\begin{bmatrix} f \\ g \end{bmatrix} = \begin{bmatrix} \tfrac{1}{4} & \tfrac{1}{2} \\ \tfrac{1}{4} & \tfrac{1}{3} \end{bmatrix} \begin{bmatrix} f \\ g \end{bmatrix} + \begin{bmatrix} 300 \\ 200 \end{bmatrix}.$$

The definitions of matrix multiplication and addition allow us to make this step.

Here we represent the total outputs as a 2×1 column vector (call it X); the total input demands as the product of our 2×2 matrix of input requirements per unit output (A) and the column vector of total outputs X; and the final demands as a 2×1 column vector (call it Y). Instead of writing out the matrices in full, as we have just done, we can use our three symbols A, X and Y and express the interrelationships much more succinctly:

$$X = AX + Y.$$

Our main problem can now be stated very simply as: given A and Y, find X.

Now if we were in the realm of ordinary arithmetic, and A, Y and X were single numbers, we would have no difficulty at all in solving this problem. We could do the job in three steps, like this:

$$\text{If} \qquad X = AX + Y,$$

Step 1:   then $X - AX = Y$

Step 2:   so $(1 - A)X = Y,$

Step 3:   therefore $X = \dfrac{Y}{1 - A}.$

The question is whether this kind of procedure will work if A, Y and X are matrices rather than single numbers.

There is no difficulty with Step 1, and no difficulty with Step 2, *provided* that we substitute for 1 the identity matrix I.[*] The only real problem arises in Step 3, since here we have divided each side of the equation by $1 - A$, and as we already know[†] there is no concept of division (as such) in matrix algebra. But, as we also already know, we can often do the same sort of job with the aid of the inverse of a matrix. Suppose that in the present case, after Step 2, we proceeded to premultiply both sides of the equation by $(I - A)^{-1}$ – that is, by the inverse of the matrix $I - A$.

We would then have

Step 3: $(I - A)^{-1}(I - A)X = (I - A)^{-1}Y.$

Then, since $(I - A)^{-1}(I + A) = I$, and $IX = X$, we could immediately write

Step 4: $X = (I - A)^{-1}Y.$

[*] The so-called distributive law which holds in ordinary algebra also holds in matrix algebra. In other words $A(B + C) = AB + AC$.

[†] See above, p. 26.

Thus we have solved our problem algebraically and just need to put the numbers in. We had

$$A = \begin{bmatrix} \frac{1}{4} & \frac{1}{2} \\ \frac{1}{4} & \frac{1}{3} \end{bmatrix}.$$

So

$$I - A = \begin{bmatrix} 1 & 0 \\ 0 & 1 \end{bmatrix} - \begin{bmatrix} \frac{1}{4} & \frac{1}{2} \\ \frac{1}{4} & \frac{1}{3} \end{bmatrix} = \begin{bmatrix} \frac{3}{4} & -\frac{1}{2} \\ -\frac{1}{4} & \frac{2}{3} \end{bmatrix}$$

and we can immediately find the inverse of this by using the techniques of the last chapter:

$$(I - A)^{-1} = \frac{8}{3} \begin{bmatrix} \frac{2}{3} & \frac{1}{2} \\ \frac{1}{4} & \frac{3}{4} \end{bmatrix}.$$

Hence

$$\text{total outputs} = X = \begin{bmatrix} f \\ g \end{bmatrix} = \frac{8}{3} \begin{bmatrix} \frac{2}{3} & \frac{1}{2} \\ \frac{1}{4} & \frac{3}{4} \end{bmatrix} \begin{bmatrix} 300 \\ 200 \end{bmatrix}$$

$$\begin{bmatrix} f \\ g \end{bmatrix} = \frac{8}{3} \begin{bmatrix} 300 \\ 225 \end{bmatrix} = \begin{bmatrix} 800 \\ 600 \end{bmatrix}.$$

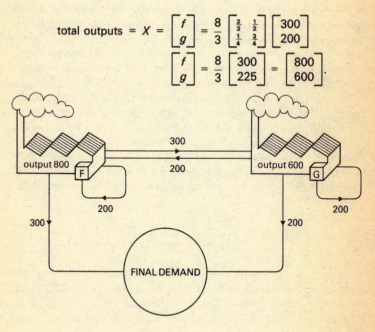

To satisfy a final demand of 300 units of F and 200 units of G we need to produce in total 800 units of F and 600 units of G.

The input–output table giving the physical flows of goods between the industries and to final demand will look like this:

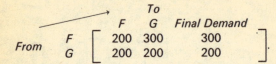

$$\text{From} \begin{array}{c} F \\ G \end{array} \begin{array}{ccc} F & G & \text{Final Demand} \\ \left[\begin{array}{ccc} 200 & 300 & 300 \\ 200 & 200 & 200 \end{array}\right] \end{array}$$

In principle we could solve a problem like this with many more than two industries and we shall work through a slightly more complicated example. But before doing this let us recap what we have done.

Input–output Coefficients

We have been practising *input–output analysis* which was developed in the first instance by Wassily Leontief, who was deservedly given a Nobel prize for his work in this field. Having recognized the importance of industrial or sectoral relationships in an economy and hence the difficulties that arise in analysing a modern economy with many, many industries, Leontief cut through some of these difficulties by making a simple assumption that we made earlier – namely, that the amount of each input required to produce a commodity varies *proportionately* with the total output of that commodity. In other words, if the total output of the commodity doubles, then we assume that the amount of each input required to produce the commodity also doubles; if the total output trebles, then we assume that the required amount of each input also trebles; and so on. To make ten cans of baked beans you need ten times as many beans and ten times as much tin can as you do to make one can. Suppose there are four industries then for industry 1, for example, we might have the following situation:

Total output	Required inputs of commodities 1–4			
of commodity 1	Comm. 1	Comm. 2	Comm. 3	Comm. 4
600	100	50	100	50
1200	200	100	200	100
1800	300	150	300	150

What this means, in effect, is that we are assuming that the amount of each input required to produce *one unit* of commodity 1 (the *input per unit of output*) remains constant, no matter how much or how little of commodity 1 is produced. To produce one unit of commodity 1 in this case, we *always* need as inputs $\frac{1}{6}$ of a unit of commodity 1, $\frac{1}{12}$ of a unit of commodity 2, $\frac{1}{6}$ of a unit of commodity 3, and $\frac{1}{12}$ of a unit of commodity 4, whatever the total output of commodity 1 which we are producing may happen to be.*

Suppose, then, that you are prepared to work on the basis of this simplifying assumption, and that you are able to obtain a complete list of these constant *input–output coefficients*, as they are called. Engineers tell you, for example, that the amount of commodity 1 required as input in order to produce one unit of commodity 1 is some given quantity: in our example it is $\frac{1}{6}$ of a unit, but since we are considering the problem in general terms let us call it a_{11}. They tell you that the amount of commodity 2 is (let us say) a_{21}. And so on and so forth. In all, they supply you with sixteen input–output coefficients of this kind. Putting this data in the form of a matrix (call it matrix A), we have

$$A = \begin{bmatrix} a_{11} & a_{12} & a_{13} & a_{14} \\ a_{21} & a_{22} & a_{23} & a_{24} \\ a_{31} & a_{32} & a_{33} & a_{34} \\ a_{41} & a_{42} & a_{43} & a_{44} \end{bmatrix}.$$

In general terms, a_{jk} is the amount of output of the industry j which is required as input in order to produce one unit of output of industry k.

Let us now reformulate our old problem. We are *given* the final demands for the four products (y_1, y_2, y_3 and y_4); we are *given* the matrix of input–output coefficients which we have just been considering; and our main problem is to work out the total outputs (let us call them x_1, x_2, x_3 and x_4) of the four industries. To deal with this problem, let us first remind ourselves that the total output of any of the industries – industry 1, say – will be equal to the *total input demand* for that product plus the *final demand* for it. From our definition of a_{jk}, it should be easy to see that the *total input demand* for the product of industry 1 will be:

$$a_{11}x_1 + a_{12}x_2 + a_{13}x_3 + a_{14}x_4$$

---

* Remember that the units in terms of which we are dealing here are *physical* units, which are different in the case of each commodity.

The four items in this expression represent respectively the amounts of the output of the industry I which is required as input to produce x_1 units of commodity 1, x_2 units of commodity 2, x_3 units of commodity 3, and x_4 units of commodity 4. Thus, since we know that the final demands for the four products are y_1, y_2, y_3 and y_4, we can write

Total output		Total input demand		Final demand
x_1	$=$	$(a_{11}x_1 + a_{12}x_2 + a_{13}x_3 + a_{14}x_4)$	$+$	y_1
x_2	$=$	$(a_{21}x_1 + a_{22}x_2 + a_{23}x_3 + a_{24}x_4)$	$+$	y_2
x_3	$=$	$(a_{31}x_1 + a_{32}x_2 + a_{33}x_3 + a_{34}x_4)$	$+$	y_3
x_4	$=$	$(a_{41}x_1 + a_{42}x_2 + a_{43}x_3 + a_{44}x_4)$	$+$	y_4

Or, putting this set of interrelationships in matrix form, we can equally write

$$\begin{bmatrix} x_1 \\ x_2 \\ x_3 \\ x_4 \end{bmatrix} = \begin{bmatrix} a_{11} & a_{12} & a_{13} & a_{14} \\ a_{21} & a_{22} & a_{23} & a_{24} \\ a_{31} & a_{32} & a_{33} & a_{34} \\ a_{41} & a_{42} & a_{43} & a_{44} \end{bmatrix} \begin{bmatrix} x_1 \\ x_2 \\ x_3 \\ x_4 \end{bmatrix} + \begin{bmatrix} y_1 \\ y_2 \\ y_3 \\ y_4 \end{bmatrix},$$

just as we did in the two industry example.

Again we can write this equation as

$$X = AX + Y$$

and solve this to get*

$$X = (I - A)^{-1} Y.$$

The matrix A is our *input–output coefficient* matrix. The element in the ith row and jth column is the amount of the output of industry i which is required to produce one unit of output of industry j. Obviously our solution for X is of the same form whether we have two, twenty or two hundred industries.

* See above, p. 46.

A Concrete Example

Let us suppose we are given a matrix of input–output coefficients A and the column vector of final demands.

$$A = \begin{bmatrix} \frac{1}{6} & \frac{1}{6} & \frac{1}{8} & \frac{1}{8} \\ \frac{1}{12} & \frac{1}{3} & \frac{1}{16} & \frac{1}{8} \\ \frac{1}{6} & \frac{1}{6} & \frac{1}{16} & \frac{1}{4} \\ \frac{1}{12} & \frac{1}{6} & \frac{1}{16} & \frac{1}{8} \end{bmatrix} ; \quad Y = \begin{bmatrix} 300 \\ 50 \\ 500 \\ 200 \end{bmatrix}.$$

The numbers in the first column of A, you will note, are those which were used when describing the basic assumption of input–output analysis. The other columns show the necessary inputs into industries 2, 3 and 4 to produce a unit of their respective outputs.

The first step, then, is to subtract A from the identity matrix I. This, as we have already seen, is an easy operation

$$I - A = \begin{bmatrix} 1 & 0 & 0 & 0 \\ 0 & 1 & 0 & 0 \\ 0 & 0 & 1 & 0 \\ 0 & 0 & 0 & 1 \end{bmatrix} - \begin{bmatrix} \frac{1}{6} & \frac{1}{6} & \frac{1}{8} & \frac{1}{8} \\ \frac{1}{12} & \frac{1}{3} & \frac{1}{16} & \frac{1}{8} \\ \frac{1}{6} & \frac{1}{6} & \frac{1}{16} & \frac{1}{4} \\ \frac{1}{12} & \frac{1}{6} & \frac{1}{16} & \frac{1}{8} \end{bmatrix}$$

$$= \begin{bmatrix} \frac{5}{6} & -\frac{1}{16} & -\frac{1}{8} & -\frac{1}{8} \\ -\frac{1}{12} & \frac{2}{3} & -\frac{1}{16} & -\frac{1}{8} \\ -\frac{1}{6} & -\frac{1}{6} & \frac{15}{16} & -\frac{1}{4} \\ -\frac{1}{12} & -\frac{1}{6} & -\frac{1}{16} & \frac{7}{8} \end{bmatrix}.$$

The next step is to ask the computer politely to work out the inverse of $I - A$, which it obligingly tell us is

$$(I - A)^{-1} = \begin{bmatrix} 1.3250 & 0.4690 & 0.2294 & 0.3218 \\ 0.2328 & 1.6793 & 0.1643 & 0.3201 \\ 0.3287 & 0.4884 & 1.1732 & 0.4519 \\ 0.1940 & 0.3994 & 0.1369 & 1.2668 \end{bmatrix}.$$

You can check up that the computer has given us the right answer, if you want to, by getting out your pocket calculator and showing that the sums work out correctly – that when you multiply the $I - A$ matrix by this inverse of it which the computer has churned out, the product is near enough to the identity matrix I. But you will probably want to take this

51

on trust, and rush breathlessly on to the dénouement by multiplying the inverse of $I - A$ by the column vector Y in order to get the necessary total outputs:

$$X = (I - A)^{-1}Y$$

$$= \begin{bmatrix} 1.3250 & 0.4690 & 0.2294 & 0.3218 \\ 0.2328 & 1.6793 & 0.1643 & 0.3201 \\ 0.3287 & 0.4884 & 1.1732 & 0.4519 \\ 0.1940 & 0.3994 & 0.1369 & 1.2668 \end{bmatrix} \begin{bmatrix} 300 \\ 50 \\ 500 \\ 200 \end{bmatrix}$$

$$= \begin{bmatrix} 600 \\ 300 \\ 800 \\ 400 \end{bmatrix}.$$

So you can now go ahead and tell industry 1 to produce 600 units of its product, industry 2 to produce 300 units, industry 3 to produce 800 units and industry 4 to produce 400 units. And in order to prove to your masters that these total outputs will be sufficient to satisfy not only the prescribed final demands for their products but also the input demands, you can refer back to A, work out the actual input demands corresponding to these total outputs, and show that all the sums add up properly by presenting the following complete input–output table:

		To				Final demand	Total output
		1	2	3	4		
	1	100	50	100	50	300	600
From	2	50	100	50	50	50	300
	3	100	50	50	100	500	800
	4	50	50	50	50	200	400

Everything works out very prettily, as you see – although I hasten to confess that the nice round numbers everywhere are not accidental. I cheated, of course, by starting with the end-product and working backwards.

Inputs to Produce Inputs to Produce Inputs to Produce ...

We have seen that the solution to our problem is to premultiply our required vector of final demands by a particular matrix, namely

$$(I-A)^{-1}.$$

Suppose, for no apparent good reason, that A was just a single number and not a matrix. Then we have

$$(I-A)^{-1} = \frac{1}{1-A}.$$

Now also let us suppose that A is a number smaller than one. Those of you familiar with geometric progressions will recognize that you can if you so wish write

$$\frac{1}{1-A} = 1 + A + A^2 + A^3 + A^4 + A^5 + \ldots$$

Thus for instance

$$2 = \frac{1}{1-\frac{1}{2}} = 1 + \tfrac{1}{2} + \tfrac{1}{4} + \tfrac{1}{8} + \tfrac{1}{16} + \ldots$$

$$4 = \frac{1}{1-\frac{3}{4}} = 1 + \tfrac{3}{4} + \tfrac{9}{16} + \tfrac{27}{64} + \tfrac{81}{256} + \ldots$$

Now, why should anyone want to be so perverse as to want to write a short expression as the sum of an infinite series? The answer is that it gives us an explanation of why the formula we have used to calculate total output requirements actually works.

Suppose that with A as a matrix we could still write

$$(I-A)^{-1} = I + A + A^2 + A^3 + A^4 + \ldots$$

The planning formula could then be written

$$X = (I-A)^{-1}Y = (I + A + A^2 + A^3 + A^4 + \ldots)\, Y$$

$$= Y + AY + A^2Y + A^3Y + A^4Y + \ldots$$

In this way the vector X showing the total outputs of the various industries required to satisfy a final demand of Y can be seen to be the sum of an infinite number of terms all of which have a specific interpretation. Let us examine the terms on the right-hand side of the equation in turn. The first term (Y) is easy to explain. The total output must be at least as much as the final demand that has to be satisfied. The remaining terms must represent the input requirements of the industries. Let us write down the second term in full.

$$AY = \begin{bmatrix} a_{11} & a_{12} & a_{13} & a_{14} \\ a_{21} & a_{22} & a_{23} & a_{24} \\ a_{31} & a_{32} & a_{33} & a_{34} \\ a_{41} & a_{42} & a_{43} & a_{44} \end{bmatrix} \begin{bmatrix} y_1 \\ y_2 \\ y_3 \\ y_4 \end{bmatrix}$$

$$= \begin{bmatrix} a_{11}y_1 + a_{12}y_2 + a_{13}y_3 + a_{14}y_4 \\ a_{21}y_1 + a_{22}y_2 + a_{23}y_3 + a_{24}y_4 \\ a_{31}y_1 + a_{32}y_2 + a_{33}y_3 + a_{34}y_4 \\ a_{41}y_1 + a_{42}y_2 + a_{43}y_3 + a_{44}y_4 \end{bmatrix}$$

From our definition of the as, the first element in this column vector is the amount of the product of the first industry required in total by the four industries as input to produce the required final demand. so AY is a vector of the products of the four industries that are directly required as inputs to produce the final demand. But these inputs require inputs to produce them. If we call this direct input requirement vector d then, by the same argument as before, we will require a vector Ad of inputs to produce d.

Now

$$d = AY,$$

so

$$Ad = AAY = A2Y.$$

This is the third term in our expansion of vector X. Similarly the fourth term $A^3 Y$ represents the inputs required to produce the inputs required to produce the direct inputs. We have no need to go further. Our problem is to add this infinite series and we now know that this problem can be expressed by the formula

$$X = (I - A)^{-1}Y.$$

By expressing the matrix multiplier $(I - A)^{-1}$ as an infinite series we can see the economic logic behind this formula. We need inputs to produce inputs to produce inputs to produce ... final outputs. Provided that the system is productive in the sense that we get more output than we require inputs to produce it, then the terms in our infinite series will be getting smaller as we move from left to right. The direct input requirements to produce final output will be greater than the input requirement to produce those direct inputs and so on. This is the same as saying that

$$A^n \longrightarrow \begin{bmatrix} 0 \end{bmatrix} \text{ as } n \longrightarrow \text{ infinity}$$

where $[0]$ is a matrix with zero elements everywhere. Just as if A were a single number we could only write

$$\frac{1}{1-A} = 1 + A + A^2 + A^3 + \dots,$$

if A were less than 1, so we can only write

$$(I - A)^{-1} = I + A + A^2 + A^3 + \dots,$$

if the matrix A satisfies certain conditions. However, as long as the economy is productive in the sense we have outlined above this will always be so.*

---

* In our simple 2×2 case we had

$$A = \begin{bmatrix} \frac{1}{4} & \frac{1}{2} \\ \frac{1}{4} & \frac{1}{3} \end{bmatrix}.$$

By calculating A^2, A^3 etc. see how $A^n \to 0$ as n increases.

Now consider

$$A = \begin{bmatrix} 2 & 1 \\ 1 & 3 \end{bmatrix}$$

(This is definitely an unproductive economy as it requires 2 units of good 1 to make 1 unit of good 1!)

What is $(I - A)^{-1}$?

Calculate A^2, A^3. What is happening?

Will $I + A + A^2 + \dots = (I - A)^{-1}$?

Some Final Problems

As an economic planner, you will of course be concerned not only with working out the appropriate inputs and total outputs which accord with the list of final demands with which you were presented, but also with pronouncing upon the *feasibility* of this programme. People are apt to ask too much of economic planners; and for various reasons it may in fact be impossible for the economy to produce as much – at any rate of some commodities – as the original list of final demands given to you logically implies. There may, for example, be physical limitations on the output of certain industries (coal for example); or the amount of *labour* available in the economy may be insufficient to enable the programme to be carried out without some modification.

Let us suppose that you are worried about whether there is in fact enough labour available to do the job. How would you check up on this? Let us do it in general terms first, and then take a concrete example.

We assume, as we did when we were dealing with *physical* inputs, that required inputs of *labour* also vary proportionately with the total output of the commodity concerned, and that our engineers can obtain for us technical details about the respective amounts of labour which are required (in conjunction with the physical inputs) to produce one unit of each of the four commodities. Imagine that these *labour* input–output coefficients are presented in the form of a 1×4 row vector, which we shall label L for short. Then, if we multiply this 1×4 row vector by X (the 4×1 column vector representing total annual outputs), we will get a 1×1 matrix – a single number, representing the total amount of labour required to fulfil this output programme. Obviously if the amount of labour available in the economy each year is restricted to some given level – call it W for *W*orkers – the programme will be feasible only if LX is less than or equal to W – that is, if

$$LX \leqslant W.$$

Or, if we assume that we have not yet worked out what X is, and that we know only Y, the vector of final demands, we can rewrite this condition as

$$L(I - A)^{-1}Y \leqslant W,$$

since we know from our previous analysis that $X = (I - A)^{-1}Y$.

Suppose, then – going now from the general to the particular – that the total amount of labour (W) available each year is 10,000 man-hours, and the vector of *labour* input–output coefficients (L) turns out to be as follows:

$$L = \begin{bmatrix} 4, 5, 10, 2 \end{bmatrix}.$$

In other words, 4 man-hours are required as input in order to produce one unit of commodity 1; 5 man-hours to produce one unit of commodity 2; and so on. If we were then presented with the original list of final demands which we considered above, namely

$$Y = \begin{bmatrix} 300 \\ 50 \\ 500 \\ 200 \end{bmatrix},$$

we could immediately tell our masters whether the programme implied by these demands was feasible. We have to work out the value of

$$L(I - A)^{-1}Y$$

but we know $X = (I - A)^{-1}Y$ and we have already worked this out for the vector Y we are considering.*

So

$$L(I-A)^{-1}Y = LX = \begin{bmatrix} 4 & 5 & 10 & 2 \end{bmatrix} \begin{bmatrix} 600 \\ 300 \\ 800 \\ 400 \end{bmatrix}$$

$$= 12,700.$$

Since 12,700 is considerably greater than 10,000 the value we have assumed for W, the programme is not feasible, and will have to be scaled down. Conversely, if the situation were such that $L(I - A)^{-1}Y$ worked out at appreciably *less than* W, and full employment of the labour force was one of the aims that the government was pursuing, the programme would

* See p. 52.

have to be scaled up – assuming, of course, that there were no other physical constraints which would prevent this.

Up to this point in the present chapter, we have measured inputs and outputs in terms of the number of *physical units* – tons of steel, gallons of oil, yards of cloth and so on – of the commodities concerned. For some purposes, however, it may be useful to measure them in terms of their *money values*. This enables us, of course, to add up the columns as well as the rows. Take the following simple three-industry economy, for example:

		To			Final demand	Total output
		1	2	3		
From	1	£50	£100	£100	£200	£450
	2	£75	£ 25	£ 50	£300	£450
	3	£30	£ 20	£ 50	£400	£500

Here we see that industry 1 produces a total output worth £450, of which £50 worth goes as input into its own production process; £100 worth as input into that of industry 2; £100 worth as input into that of industry 3; and the remaining £200 worth goes to satisfy final demand. And industry 1, in order to produce this £450 worth of output, uses as physical inputs £50 worth of its own output, £75 worth of the output of industry 2, and £30 worth of the output of industry 3. Now, if we assume that the whole of what remains of the value of industry 1's output, after paying for this £50 + £75 + £30 = £155 worth of physical inputs, is distributed as wages, profit and rent to the labourers, capitalists and landlords who participate actively or passively in the process of production, it is clear that the total paid out in wages, profit and rent in industry 1 must be £450 − £155 = £295. Similarly, the total paid out in wages, profit and rent in industry 2 must be £305, and in industry 3 £300. So we can add a fourth row to our table, thus:

		1	2	3	Final demand	Total output
	1	£ 50	£100	£100	£200	£450
Wages,	2	£ 75	£ 25	£ 50	£300	£450
profit	3	£ 30	£ 20	£ 50	£400	£500
and rent		£295	£305	£300		

If we draw up the table in this way, it is pretty obvious that the *sum* of the wages, profit and rent paid out in the economy must be equal to the *sum* of the final demands (£900 in each case). This means that if we were given, say, only the vector of total outputs and the matrix of input–output coefficients (both of them, this time, in *value* terms), we would have no difficulty in working out the vector of wages, profit and rent.

My last word to you about all this is that on no account should you allow yourself to be deluded that it is all actually as easy as this in the real world. Imagine, for example, what the components of the matrix of input–output coefficients might look like if we were not able to make that simplifying assumption about the proportionality of inputs to outputs. Imagine, again, that your masters told you that several alternative technological methods of meeting the prescribed final demands were available, and that they asked you, as part of the problem, to determine which of these methods ought to be used. Imagine, finally, that they told you that during the next few years some of these methods were likely to change, or that the relative *prices* of (say) machinery and labour were likely to change. What would you do then? For answers to these questions you would have to consult accounts of input-output analysis* which are a little more complicated than this simplified one.

Exercises

1. Calculate $(I - A)^{-1}$ when

(i) $$A = \begin{bmatrix} \frac{1}{5} & \frac{1}{5} \\ \frac{1}{5} & \frac{1}{5} \end{bmatrix};$$

(ii) $$A = \begin{bmatrix} \frac{1}{2} & \frac{2}{5} \\ \frac{1}{4} & \frac{1}{5} \end{bmatrix};$$

(iii) $$A = \begin{bmatrix} 0 & \frac{1}{2} \\ \frac{1}{2} & 0 \end{bmatrix};$$

(iv) $$A = \begin{bmatrix} \frac{1}{2} & 0 \\ 0 & \frac{1}{4} \end{bmatrix}.$$

* Readers interested in pursuing this topic might first look at Chiou-shuang Yan, *Introduction to Input–Output Economics*, Holt, Rinehart and Winston, New York, 1969; or Richard Stone, *Input–Output and National Accounts*, OEEC, Paris, 1961.

2. An economy is represented by the following input–output table:

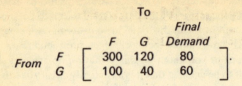

$$\begin{array}{c} & & \text{To} \\ & & \begin{array}{ccc} & & \text{Final} \\ & F & G & \text{Demand} \end{array} \\ \text{From} \begin{array}{c} F \\ G \end{array} & \left[\begin{array}{ccc} 300 & 120 & 80 \\ 100 & 40 & 60 \end{array} \right]. \end{array}$$

(i) What is the matrix A of input–output coefficients for this economy?
(ii) What is $(I - A)^{-1}$.
(iii) Suppose you wanted to produce enough of F and G so that 100 units of each could go to final demand. What would the total output of F and G have to be?
(iv) To produce a unit of F and G you need to use 10 units and 20 units of labour respectively. How much labour is needed to allow 100 units of both F and G to go to final demand?
(v) There are actually 1500 units of labour in the economy. You want the amounts of F and G going to final demand to be equal to each other. How much of F and G could go to final demand if all the labour was used? What would be the total outputs of F and G?

4
Matrices and Matrimony
in Tribal Societies

Kinship Systems

In the first chapter of this book we were introduced to a type of matrix in which the components were all either 1s or 0s, representing not different *quantities* of something or other, but rather the presence ($= 1$) or the absence ($= 0$) of some particular *quality* or *relationship*. What we are going to do in the present chapter is to see how matrices of this kind can be used to throw light on certain kinds of *kinship systems* – such as those existing for example among Australian aboriginal tribes – which lie at the centre of the studies of many anthropologists. My account here will be based very largely upon the influential analysis of kinship structures developed by H. C. White.*

What do we mean by a 'kinship system' exactly? A kinship system is a particular kind of social structure which represents a fusion of a set of *social* relations and a set of *biological* relations. The idea is that in such a system the roles which people adopt in their relationships with one another in society are built on the basis of certain primary kinship relations (brother, sister, father, mother, son, daughter and so on), extended cumulatively as in a family tree. The mutual social relations between a certain woman and myself, for example, may be based on the fact that she happens to be the daughter of the sister of my father's mother.

Now, imagine that you were given the task, starting from scratch, of transforming a set of cumulatively extended biological relations of this kind into a viable set of social or role relations suitable, say, for a group of Australian aboriginal tribes. You would soon find yourself faced with a number of rather difficult problems. For one thing, there is the obvious fact that family trees proliferate very rapidly. Suppose that you began by constructing a kind of ideal family tree, starting from a particular individual (usually called *ego* by the anthropologists) and tracing the tree

* Harrison C. White, *An Anatomy of Kinship*, Prentice-Hall, New Jersey, 1963. I shall also in places be drawing quite heavily on the excellent summary of White's analysis given in R. K. Leik and B. F. Meeker, *Mathematical Sociology*, Prentice-Hall, New Jersey, 1975, Chapter 5.

upwards to his grandparents and downwards to his children. Using the symbols employed by the anthropologists (males, Δ; females, 0; marriage relationship, =; parent–child relationship, vertical line; sibling, horizontal line), you would presumably draw a picture something like this:

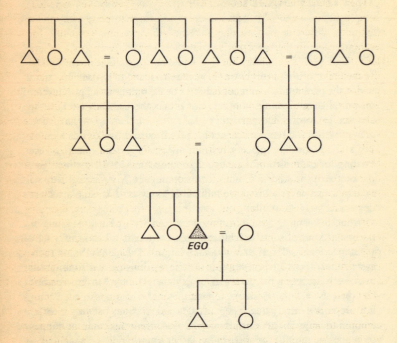

Here, although we have not gone very far either up or down the tree, a large number of distinct biological relationships is revealed. Ego has two parents, each of whom has (or may have) brothers and sisters – a total of six distinct relationships. He has four grandparents, each of whom also has brothers and sisters – twelve more distinct relationships. He has himself brothers and sisters; he has a wife; and he has sons and daughters. And if we went up the tree one further step, to great-grandparents, and down one further step, to grandchildren, it is clear that the total number of distinct relationships would be greatly increased. Obviously, it would be very difficult to transform *each* of these different biological relationships into a single type of social relationship: we would necessarily have to simplify our system by collapsing at least *some* of these different biological relationships into a single type of social relationship. In Western societies, for example, ego's father's brother, his mother's brother, his father's sister's husband and his mother's sister's husband, are all regarded as being related to him in the same way – namely, as uncles.

Then again, you would soon find that as your family tree ramified, complications would arise because ego would come to be related in two (or more) different ways to one and the same person. Normally, for example, ego's mother's brother's daughter will be a different person from his father's sister's daughter. But this would not be so if, as might well be the case, his mother's brother was in fact the husband of his father's sister. Obviously, in order to avoid conflicting role expectations in such a case, you would have to set up your role categories very carefully, so that the roles implied were consistent.

Actual kinship systems in the real world solve these problems (to quote Leik and Meeker) 'by placing restrictions on the establishment of the two basic relationships of marriage and parenthood'.* All such systems operate one or another form of incest taboo, usually by laying it down that a man can never marry a woman of his own group or clan; and there is very often a rule prescribing one and only one other clan where the man must find his wife. Quite often, too, marriages with particular kinds of relatives are preferred or encouraged – for example, cross-cousin marriages in certain Papua New Guinean societies. In addition to these *marriage rules*, most actual kinship systems operate *descent rules* which lay down, for a father in any clan, the particular clan to which his children will belong (which may or may not be his own clan).

A prescribed marriage system of the general type just described is common to many actual kinship systems, but within this common framework a large number of distinct kinship structures is to be found – depending, for example, on the kinds of first cousins who are permitted (or encouraged) to marry. Since, as White puts it, 'the combinatorial possibilities are too rich to keep straight verbally or even with diagrams',† matrix algebra has been called into service for the purpose of analysing these systems and differentiating them from one another. What a number of quantitatively inclined anthropologists have done, in effect, is to build a kind of general or 'ideal' model, in matrix form, of a society based on a prescribed marriage system, and then to work out its logical implications. This exercise has proved to be extremely interesting and instructive; and

* Leik and Meeker, *op cit.*, p. 77. *Cf.* White, *op. cit.*, pp. 15–16 and 28.
† White, *op. cit.*, p. 2.

some analysts (including White himself) have claimed that it has certain applications to modern Western society as well as to the more 'primitive' societies of the Australian aborigines and the peoples of Papua New Guinea.

The first thing to do, if we are to build a model of this kind, is to lay down a set of properties which all the prescribed marriage systems to be covered by the general model or 'typology' of such systems must necessarily possess. White* delineates eight such properties, or 'Axioms', as he calls them:

1. The entire population of the society is divided into mutually exclusive groups, which we call *clans*. The identification of a person with a clan is permanent. Hereafter n denotes the number of clans.

2. There is a permanent rule fixing the single clan among whose women the men of a given clan must find their wives.

3. In rule 2, men from two different clans cannot marry women of the same clan.

4. All children of a couple are assigned to a single clan, uniquely determined by the clans of their mother and father.

5. Children whose fathers are in different clans must themselves be in different clans.

6. A man can never marry a woman of his own clan.

7. Every person in the society has some relative by marriage and descent in each other clan: i.e., the society is not split into groups not related to each other.

8. Whether two people who are related by marriage and descent links are in the same clan depends only on the kind of relationship, not on the clan either one belongs to.'

The next problem is the really crucial one – how to translate this collection of properties or axioms into mathematical form. The most useful method† has turned out to be the one used by White, whose model is based on two very simple square matrices, the first reflecting the marriage restrictions and the second the parenthood restrictions. Both of these matrices are $n \times n$, reflecting the number of clans assumed in axiom 1.

The rows of the first matrix (usually labelled W) represent the clans of males and the columns the clans of females. If a particular component – that in row i and column j, for example – is 0, this means that a man in

---

* *Op. cit.*, pp. 34–5.

† But not the only possible method: *cf.* White, *op. cit.*, pp. 31–2.

clan *i* is prohibited from marrying a woman in clan *j*. If the component in row *i* and column *j* is 1, this means that a man in clan *i* is permitted to marry a woman in clan *j*. Suppose there were five clans, for example. In that case matrix *W* might (but need not necessarily) look like this:

Wife's clan

		P	Q	R	S	T
	P	0	1	0	0	0
Husband's	Q	0	0	1	0	0
clan	R	1	0	0	0	0
	S	0	0	0	0	1
	T	0	0	0	1	0

Here men of clan *P* can take their wives from clan *Q* but not from clans *P*, *R*, *S* or *T*, – and so on for the other rows.

The rows of the second matrix used by White (usually labelled *C*) represent the clans of fathers and the columns the clans of children. If a particular component – that in row *i* and column *j*, for example – is 0, this means that a father in clan *i* does not have children in clan *j*. If the component in row *i* and column *j* is 1, this means that a man in clan *i* does have children in clan *j*. In our five-clan case, matrix *C* might (but need not necessarily) look like this:

Child's clan

		P	Q	R	S	T
	P	0	0	0	0	1
Father's	Q	1	0	0	0	0
clan	R	0	1	0	0	0
	S	0	0	1	0	0
	T	0	0	0	1	0

Axioms 2 and 3 impose certain fairly obvious constraints upon the number and distribution of the 1s in the *W* matrix. Axiom 2 means in effect that each row of the *W* matrix must contain one and only one entry of 1, all the rest of the components in the row being 0s; and Axiom 3 means that each column of the matrix must also contain one and only one entry of 1. Axioms 4 and 5 in effect place the same constraints upon the number and distribution of the 1s in the *C* matrix. In the hypothetical examples just given, it will be seen that these constraints have been duly applied.

Axiom 6 – 'A man can never marry a woman of his own clan' – imposes a further constraint upon the distribution of the 1s in the W matrix: it means that none of the 1s can appear on the main diagonal of the matrix. This constraint, it should be noted, does *not* apply to the C matrix, since a child's clan may be the same as its father's. A little thought will show, however, that Axiom 8 implies that if fathers of one clan have children in their own clan, this must be true of all fathers in all clans. In other words, if *any* of the entries on the main diagonal of the C matrix is a 1, then *all* the entries must be 1s – in which case, of course, the C matrix would be the identity matrix I.

Excursus on Permutation Matrices

A matrix with exactly one entry of 1 in each row and one entry of 1 in each column, all the other entries being 0, is known as a *permutation matrix*. Why? Because if you multiply a row vector by a permutation matrix (assuming of course that the two are in fact multipliable) the resulting product will be another row vector containing the same components as the first but in a different order. For example:

$$\begin{bmatrix} 1 & 2 & 3 & 4 & 5 \end{bmatrix} \begin{bmatrix} 0 & 1 & 0 & 0 & 0 \\ 0 & 0 & 1 & 0 & 0 \\ 1 & 0 & 0 & 0 & 0 \\ 0 & 0 & 0 & 0 & 1 \\ 0 & 0 & 0 & 1 & 0 \end{bmatrix} = \begin{bmatrix} 3 & 1 & 2 & 5 & 4 \end{bmatrix}.$$

If the permutation matrix as so defined happened to be an identity matrix, however, and you performed the same multiplicative operation with it, the order of the components in the row vector would necessarily remain the same.

Another feature of a permutation matrix is that it is very easy to find its inverse. Consider the permutation matrix (W) above – we can find its inverse using the elementary row operation approach we developed in Chapter 2.

In this way we can calculate the inverse of any permutation matrix in one step. Let us consider the row-swapping process in general. If the 1 in the first row of W is in column j then the first row must move to row j to get I. Necessarily, therefore, column 1 of the inverse has 1 in its jth row. This

	I	W	STEP
Tableau 0	$\begin{bmatrix} 1 & 0 & 0 & 0 & 0 \\ 0 & 1 & 0 & 0 & 0 \\ 0 & 0 & 1 & 0 & 0 \\ 0 & 0 & 0 & 1 & 0 \\ 0 & 0 & 0 & 0 & 1 \end{bmatrix}$	$\begin{bmatrix} 0 & 1 & 0 & 0 & 0 \\ 0 & 0 & 1 & 0 & 0 \\ 1 & 0 & 0 & 0 & 0 \\ 0 & 0 & 0 & 0 & 1 \\ 0 & 0 & 0 & 1 & 0 \end{bmatrix}$	To get from W to I is simply a matter of swapping rows. We need Row 1 → row 2 Row 2 → row 3 Row 3 → row 1 Row 4 → row 5 Row 5 → row 4
Tableau 1	$\begin{bmatrix} 0 & 0 & 1 & 0 & 0 \\ 1 & 0 & 0 & 0 & 0 \\ 0 & 1 & 0 & 0 & 0 \\ 0 & 0 & 0 & 0 & 1 \\ 0 & 0 & 0 & 1 & 0 \end{bmatrix}$	$\begin{bmatrix} 1 & 0 & 0 & 0 & 0 \\ 0 & 1 & 0 & 0 & 0 \\ 0 & 0 & 1 & 0 & 0 \\ 0 & 0 & 0 & 1 & 0 \\ 0 & 0 & 0 & 0 & 1 \end{bmatrix}$	

means that the first column of the inverse of W is the same as the first row of W itself. Similarly the second column of W^{-1} is the same as the second row of W and likewise for the third, fourth and any further columns and rows.

To get the inverse of a permutation matrix all we need do is transpose the rows and columns. The inverse of a permutation matrix is identical with what is called its *transpose*. We shall write the transpose of a matrix W as W' and we have the result that if W is a permutation matrix then

$$W' = W^{-1}.$$

Back to the Kinship System

If we express the marriage and descent rules of a prescribed marriage system in the form of the two permutation matrices W and C described above, we shall find ourselves in possession of a very handy tool for unravelling complex kinship relations. In particular, by combining the W and C matrices in various ways, we shall be able to specify, for a man of any given clan, what the clan of any given relative of his will necessarily be.

Suppose, for example, that the W and C matrices are in fact those which

I used as illustrations on p. 65 above, and that we want to find out, for a male ego of any given clan (clan Q, let us say), what the clan of his mother's brother's daughter must be. There are three steps in the investigation. The first step is to find out the clan of the man's father, which we may do very easily by transposing the C matrix, thereby in effect changing it from a matrix which describes, for a man in each clan, what the clan of his child will be, to a matrix which describes, for a child in each clan, what the clan of his father will be:

$$
\begin{array}{c}
\textit{Father's} \\
\textit{clan}
\end{array}
$$

From this transpose of the C matrix we can see directly that if the son is in clan Q, his father must be in clan R.

There is another way of describing what we have just done, which may seem unnecessarily complicated but whose usefulness will shortly become clear. *In effect*, what we have done is to start with a 1×5 row vector (call it A) in which the *second* entry, corresponding to ego's clan Q, is 1 and the other entries are 0s, and then to multiply this by the transpose (= the inverse) of the C matrix (that is, C^{-1}), obtaining as the product another 1×5 row vector with an entry of 1 in the *third* place, corresponding to ego's father's clan R:

$$
AC^{-1} = \begin{bmatrix} 0 & 1 & 0 & 0 & 0 \end{bmatrix} \begin{bmatrix} 0 & 1 & 0 & 0 & 0 \\ 0 & 0 & 1 & 0 & 0 \\ 0 & 0 & 0 & 1 & 0 \\ 0 & 0 & 0 & 0 & 1 \\ 1 & 0 & 0 & 0 & 0 \end{bmatrix}
$$

$$
= \begin{bmatrix} 0 & 0 & 1 & 0 & 0 \end{bmatrix}.
$$

Now for the second step. We know that ego's father's clan is R, and we can easily deduce what his mother's clan must be by inspecting the marriage rule matrix W:

$$W = \begin{array}{c} \\ P \\ Q \\ R \\ S \\ T \end{array} \begin{array}{c} \begin{array}{ccccc} P & Q & R & S & T \end{array} \\ \left[\begin{array}{ccccc} 0 & 1 & 0 & 0 & 0 \\ 0 & 0 & 1 & 0 & 0 \\ 1 & 0 & 0 & 0 & 0 \\ 0 & 0 & 0 & 0 & 1 \\ 0 & 0 & 0 & 1 & 0 \end{array} \right] \end{array},$$

from which it is obvious that his mother's clan must be P. Once again, we can say that what we have *in effect* done is to multiply the 1×5 row vector AC^{-1} by the matrix W, obtaining as the product another 1×5 row vector with an entry of 1 in the first place:

$$(AC^{-1})W = \begin{bmatrix} 0 & 0 & 1 & 0 & 0 \end{bmatrix} \begin{bmatrix} 0 & 1 & 0 & 0 & 0 \\ 0 & 0 & 1 & 0 & 0 \\ 1 & 0 & 0 & 0 & 0 \\ 0 & 0 & 0 & 0 & 1 \\ 0 & 0 & 0 & 1 & 0 \end{bmatrix}$$

$$= \begin{bmatrix} 1 & 0 & 0 & 0 & 0 \end{bmatrix}.$$

We know from Axiom 4 that ego's mother's brother must be in the same clan as his mother – namely in clan P. So we are now ready for the third and final step – to find out the clan of ego's mother's brother's daughter. To do this, as should now be pretty obvious, we must refer again to matrix C, from which we can see by inspection that the child of a man in clan P must be in clan T. In other words, when we multiply the 1×5 row vector $(AC^{-1})W$ by the matrix C, we obtain as the product another 1×5 row vector with an entry of 1 in the fifth place.

$$[(AC^{-1})W]C = \begin{bmatrix} 1 & 0 & 0 & 0 & 0 \end{bmatrix} \begin{bmatrix} 0 & 0 & 0 & 0 & 1 \\ 1 & 0 & 0 & 0 & 0 \\ 0 & 1 & 0 & 0 & 0 \\ 0 & 0 & 1 & 0 & 0 \\ 0 & 0 & 0 & 1 & 0 \end{bmatrix}$$

$$= \begin{bmatrix} 0 & 0 & 0 & 0 & 1 \end{bmatrix}.$$

Now since $[(AC^{-1})W]C = A(C^{-1}WC)$,* we can construe the matrix

---

* This follows from the fact that matrices obey what is called the *associative law* under multiplication. If A, B and C are three multipliable matrices, it can be shown that $ABC = A(BC) = (AB)C$.

$C^{-1}WC$ as a matrix which shows, for a man in each clan, what the clan of his mother's brother's daughter will be:

$$
C^{-1}WC =
\overset{C^{-1}}{\begin{bmatrix} 0 & 1 & 0 & 0 & 0 \\ 0 & 0 & 1 & 0 & 0 \\ 0 & 0 & 0 & 1 & 0 \\ 0 & 0 & 0 & 0 & 1 \\ 1 & 0 & 0 & 0 & 0 \end{bmatrix}}
\overset{W}{\begin{bmatrix} 0 & 1 & 0 & 0 & 0 \\ 0 & 0 & 1 & 0 & 0 \\ 1 & 0 & 0 & 0 & 0 \\ 0 & 0 & 0 & 0 & 1 \\ 0 & 0 & 0 & 1 & 0 \end{bmatrix}}
\overset{C}{\begin{bmatrix} 0 & 0 & 0 & 0 & 1 \\ 1 & 0 & 0 & 0 & 0 \\ 0 & 1 & 0 & 0 & 0 \\ 0 & 0 & 1 & 0 & 0 \\ 0 & 0 & 0 & 1 & 0 \end{bmatrix}}
$$

$$
=
\overset{C^{-1}W}{\begin{bmatrix} 0 & 0 & 1 & 0 & 0 \\ 1 & 0 & 0 & 0 & 0 \\ 0 & 0 & 0 & 0 & 1 \\ 0 & 0 & 0 & 1 & 0 \\ 0 & 1 & 0 & 0 & 0 \end{bmatrix}}
\overset{C}{\begin{bmatrix} 0 & 0 & 0 & 0 & 1 \\ 1 & 0 & 0 & 0 & 0 \\ 0 & 1 & 0 & 0 & 0 \\ 0 & 0 & 1 & 0 & 0 \\ 0 & 0 & 0 & 1 & 0 \end{bmatrix}}
$$

	Mother's brother's daughter's clan				
Man's clan	P	Q	R	S	T
P	0	1	0	0	0
Q	0	0	0	0	1
R	0	0	0	1	0
S	0	0	1	0	0
T	1	0	0	0	0

Given the $C^{-1}WC$ matrix, then, there is no need to bring A into the picture at all: you can simply read off the answer you want from the matrix itself – and you can read it off, of course, for a man in any clan, not merely for one in clan Q. So $C^{-1}WC$ is what we can call the 'mother's brother's daughter' matrix; it defines the permutation which in effect transforms a man's clan into his mother's brother's daughter's clan.

Similar permutation matrices can be worked out to transform a man's clan into the clan of any of his other relatives, simply by multiplying W, W^{-1}, C and C^{-1} in the appropriate order. It can readily be shown, for example, that the 'wife's brother's child' matrix is WC; and so on. One of the uses of the model, then, is that it provides us with a remarkably convenient way of describing all the kinship relations in a society characterized by White's eight Axioms.

Exercises

1. Calculate WC and C^2.
2. A man is in clan P. What clan is his son's daughter in? What clan is his wife's brother's daughter in?
3. A woman is in clan Q. In what clan is her brother's son? In what clan is her sister's daughter?
4. What matrix product tells us the clan of a man's
   (i) daughter's child;
   (ii) wife's mother?
5. What matrix product tells us the clan of a woman's
   (i) daughter's child;
   (ii) husband's mother?
6. What do the following matrix products tell us about:
   (i) $C^{-1}C^{-1}$;
   (ii) $C^{-1}W$;
   (iii) $W^{-1}C^{-1}$;
   (iv) $W^{-1}CC$?

First-cousin Marriages

The model also provides us with the method of classifying different kinship systems on the basis ('logically and empirically appropriate', according to White*) of the kinds of first cousins allowed to marry. The main question which has to be asked here is this: given a society to which the eight Axioms apply, under what conditions will first cousins be permitted to marry, if at all?

---

* *Op. cit.*, p. 39. The discussion which follows in the text is based fairly closely on White's analysis.

Let us consider four distinct types of first-cousin relationship, which we may symbolize as follows:

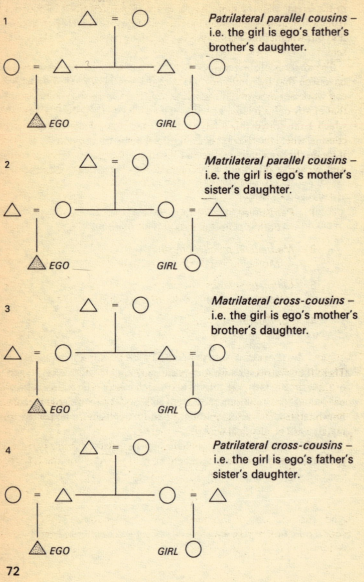

1 *Patrilateral parallel cousins* – i.e. the girl is ego's father's brother's daughter.

2 *Matrilateral parallel cousins* – i.e. the girl is ego's mother's sister's daughter.

3 *Matrilateral cross-cousins* – i.e. the girl is ego's mother's brother's daughter.

4 *Patrilateral cross-cousins* – i.e. the girl is ego's father's sister's daughter.

Now if an ego belonging to a particular clan is going to be permitted to marry *any* of these four types of first cousin, the girl must obviously be in the 'right' clan for him, that is, in the clan (prescribed in matrix W) from which men of ego's clan have to select their wives. How then can we find out whether these four girls are or are not in the 'right' clans in this sense?

The analysis of the previous section can help us on our way here. We have seen that by combining the W and C matrices in various ways we can work out a permutation matrix which transforms a man's clan into that of any of his relatives – and you may have noticed that the case with which I illustrated this analysis was in fact one of matrilateral cross-cousins, where the relevant permutation matrix turned out to be $C^{-1}WC$. If we do the same job in respect of the three other types of first cousin as well, we arrive at the following complete list of permutation matrices:

		Matrix
1.	*Patrilateral parallel cousins* 'Father's brother's daughter' matrix =	CC^{-1}
2.	*Matrilateral parallel cousins* 'Mother's sister's daughter' matrix =	$C^{-1}WW^{-1}C$
3.	*Matrilateral cross-cousins* 'Mother's brother's daughter' matrix =	$C^{-1}WC$
4.	*Patrilateral cross-cousins* 'Father's sister's daughter' matrix =	$C^{-1}W^{-1}C$

These four matrices tell us, for a male ego in any of the n clans, in which of these n clans the particular types of girl cousin concerned will in fact be located. The condition for the girl to be located in the 'right' clan can now be stated in a very simple and striking way: the relevant permutation matrix must be identical with the W matrix.

Thus the condition which would have to be satisfied if ego's patrilateral parallel cousin was to be a legitimate marriage partner for him is simply

$$CC^{-1} = W.$$

And from this way of formulating it we can see immediately that this condition can never be satisfied in a society characterized by the eight Axioms. For CC^{-1} necessarily equals I, the identity matrix, and we already know* that Axiom 6 implies that the W matrix can never be the identity matrix.

By a similar process of reasoning we may deduce that matrilateral parallel cousins can never marry in such a society. The condition for their marriageability is

$$C^{-1}WW^{-1}C = W.$$

But $C^{-1}WW^{-1}C = I$, the identity matrix;† and once again, since $W \neq I$, this condition can never be satisfied.

In the case of matrilateral cross-cousins, however, where the condition for marriageability is

$$C^{-1}WC = W,$$

there is no inherent reason why it should not be fulfilled. (It was not in fact fulfilled in the particular case we considered above when we were working out the $C^{-1}WC$ matrix, but there are certainly W and C matrices for which it *could* conceivably be fulfilled.) The condition can be expressed in a more convenient form if we premultiply both sides by C, so that we have

$$(CC^{-1})WC = CW$$

or, more simply,

$$WC = CW.$$

In the case of patrilateral cross-cousins, similarly, the condition for marriageability is

$$C^{-1}W^{-1}C = W$$

---

* See above, p. 66, where we saw that no 1s can appear on the main diagonal of the W matrix.

† To establish this result, we make use of the associative law which as we have seen (p. 69 above) governs matrix multiplication. The chain of reasoning goes as follows:

$$C^{-1}WW^{-1}C = C^{-1}(WW^{-1})C = C^{-1}(IC) = C^{-1}C = I.$$

or (again premultiplying both sides by C)

$$W^{-1}C = CW.$$

We can thus make a preliminary distinction between societies in which marriage between matrilateral cross-cousins is permitted (that is, societies where $WC = CW$), and those in which marriage between patrilateral cross-cousins is permitted (societies where $W^{-1}C = CW$). To take us a little further, let us ask ourselves in what kind of society *both* these types of marriage would be permitted. Fairly clearly, its W and C matrices would have to be such that WC was equal to CW *and* that $W^{-1}C$ was equal to CW. Or, combining these two equations together, it would have to be such that

$$WC = W^{-1}C.$$

If we postmultiply both sides of this by C^{-1}, it reduces immediately to

$$W = W^{-1},$$

but we know

$$W^{-1} = W'$$

and so

$$W = W'.$$

In a society where marriage between both matrilateral and patrilateral cousins is permitted the W matrix must equal its transpose. This means that the first row of W must be the same as the first column of W, the second row the same as the second column and so on. Such a matrix is said to be *symmetric*; and the condition that W be symmetric has a startlingly simple real-world interpretation. It means that in effect pairs of clans exchange wives. For example consider

$$W = \begin{array}{c} \\ P \\ Q \\ R \\ S \end{array} \begin{array}{c} \begin{array}{cccc} P & Q & R & S \end{array} \\ \left[\begin{array}{cccc} 0 & 1 & 0 & 0 \\ 1 & 0 & 0 & 0 \\ 0 & 0 & 0 & 1 \\ 0 & 0 & 1 & 0 \end{array} \right] \end{array}.$$

This is symmetric and this ensures that if a man from Q takes a wife from P then a man from P takes a wife from Q; similarly if a man from R takes a wife from S then symmetry means a man from S takes a wife from R.

But a society based on paired clans – one where $W = W^{-1}$ – is only a *necessary* condition for the marriageability of both patrilateral and matrilateral cross-cousins. To arrive at the necessary and *sufficient* condition for this dual marriageability, one must postulate not only that $W = W^{-1}$ but also that $WC = CW$, whence it would follow that $W^{-1}C = CW$ (that is, that patrilateral as well as matrilateral cross-cousins were marriageable). This is White's Type I society – one where both patrilateral and matrilateral cross-cousins are marriageable, and thus one where pairs of clans exchange wives (symbolically, $W = W^{-1}$ and $WC = CW$).*

White's Type II, Type III and Type IV societies follow logically from this. A Type II society is one where matrilateral cross-cousins are marriageable but patrilateral cross-cousins are not (symbolically, $WC = CW$, but $W \neq W^{-1}$; so that $W^{-1}C \neq CW$). A Type III society is one where patrilateral cross-cousins are marriageable but matrilateral cross-cousins are not (symbolically, $W^{-1}C = CW$, but $W \neq W^{-1}$, so that $WC \neq CW$). Finally, a Type IV society is one where pairs of clans exchange wives, but no first cousins of any kind, whether patrilateral or matrilateral, are marriageable (symbolically, $W = W^{-1}$, but $WC \neq CW$, so that $W^{-1}C \neq CW$).

That is about as far as we can follow White's argument in this relatively elementary introduction to his method. From here on things become much more complicated. For example, you may think that the analysis of first-cousin relationships which we have just gone over is difficult enough. But, as White proceeds to point out, 'in some of the more common kinds of societies satisfying Axioms 1–8, no first cousins may marry and the marriage prescription is formulated in terms of a whole set of types of *second* cousins'.† There are sixteen distinct possible types of second cousins (as opposed to four basic types of first cousins); and the formulae for the relevant permutation matrices converting ego's clan into the clan of his second cousin can become very involved. For example, if his second cousin is ego's mother's mother's brother's son's daughter the relevant matrix is defined by $C^{-1}WC^{-1}WCC$.

Just how one *tests* a model of this kind against reality is rather difficult

---

* White, *op. cit.*, p. 47.

† *Op. cit.*, pp. 42–3 (my italics).

to determine. White suggests that one method might be to have a look at the kinship terms applied by an individual to different relatives. If the individual applies the same kinship term to, say, his mother's brother's daughter and his mother's mother's brother's son's daughter, then it would seem reasonable to assume that both these women are in the same clan, implying that

$$C^{-1}WC = C^{-1}WC^{-1}WCC.$$

If we were able to obtain a number of descriptions of the kinds of relatives who are classed together in this way, we might be able to derive the relevant W and C matrices. If we then found that these W and C matrices obeyed the eight Axioms – and White claims that the matrices which he has thus derived do in fact obey them – we could perhaps take this as a test of the 'validity' (in some meaningful sense) of the model. Another possible test would be to look at the W matrix derived from the kinship terminology and to try to discover whether marriages in the society concerned actually followed the pattern of this matrix.*

However, I am not concerned here with the question of how one ought to test the model. Nor, as a non-anthropologist, am I competent to pronounce upon its actual or potential utility, whether in the field to which White actually applies it or in the wider field to which he suggests that it *may* be applicable. All I have tried to do, by explaining how a brilliant investigator has deployed matrix methods to deal with these fascinating problems, is to give a further illustration of the remarkable power and versatility of these methods.

Exercises

Consider the following societies. Decide for each society whether it is White Type I, II, III or IV.

1.

$$W = \begin{array}{c} \\ P \\ Q \\ R \\ S \end{array} \begin{array}{cccc} P & Q & R & S \\ \left[\begin{array}{cccc} 0 & 1 & 0 & 0 \\ 1 & 0 & 0 & 0 \\ 0 & 0 & 0 & 1 \\ 0 & 0 & 1 & 0 \end{array}\right] \end{array} \qquad C = \begin{array}{c} \\ P \\ Q \\ R \\ S \end{array} \begin{array}{cccc} P & Q & R & S \\ \left[\begin{array}{cccc} 0 & 0 & 1 & 0 \\ 0 & 0 & 0 & 1 \\ 0 & 1 & 0 & 0 \\ 1 & 0 & 0 & 0 \end{array}\right] \end{array}.$$

* See Leik and Meeker, *op. cit.*, pp. 84–5.

2.

$$
W = \begin{array}{c} \\ P \\ Q \\ R \\ S \end{array}
\begin{array}{cccc}
P & Q & R & S \\
\left[\begin{array}{cccc}
0 & 1 & 0 & 0 \\
1 & 0 & 0 & 0 \\
0 & 0 & 0 & 1 \\
0 & 0 & 1 & 0
\end{array}\right]
\end{array}
\qquad
C = \begin{array}{c} \\ P \\ Q \\ R \\ S \end{array}
\begin{array}{cccc}
P & Q & R & S \\
\left[\begin{array}{cccc}
0 & 0 & 0 & 1 \\
1 & 0 & 0 & 0 \\
0 & 1 & 0 & 0 \\
0 & 0 & 1 & 0
\end{array}\right]
\end{array}.
$$

3.

$$
W = \begin{array}{c} \\ P \\ Q \\ R \\ S \end{array}
\begin{array}{cccc}
P & Q & R & S \\
\left[\begin{array}{cccc}
0 & 0 & 1 & 0 \\
0 & 0 & 0 & 1 \\
0 & 1 & 0 & 0 \\
1 & 0 & 0 & 0
\end{array}\right]
\end{array}
\qquad
C = \begin{array}{c} \\ P \\ Q \\ R \\ S \end{array}
\begin{array}{cccc}
P & Q & R & S \\
\left[\begin{array}{cccc}
0 & 1 & 0 & 0 \\
1 & 0 & 0 & 0 \\
0 & 0 & 0 & 1 \\
0 & 0 & 1 & 0
\end{array}\right]
\end{array}.
$$

4.

$$
W = \begin{array}{c} \\ P \\ Q \\ R \\ S \end{array}
\begin{array}{cccc}
P & Q & R & S \\
\left[\begin{array}{cccc}
0 & 0 & 1 & 0 \\
0 & 0 & 0 & 1 \\
0 & 1 & 0 & 0 \\
1 & 0 & 0 & 0
\end{array}\right]
\end{array}
\qquad
C = \begin{array}{c} \\ P \\ Q \\ R \\ S \end{array}
\begin{array}{cccc}
P & Q & R & S \\
\left[\begin{array}{cccc}
0 & 0 & 1 & 0 \\
1 & 0 & 0 & 0 \\
0 & 0 & 0 & 1 \\
0 & 1 & 0 & 0
\end{array}\right]
\end{array}.
$$

5
Dominance in Coops and Courts

Farmer Brown's Hens

Farmer Brown keeps five hens. He calls them by pet names, but we shall call them simply A, B, C, D and E. He notices, as caring hen-keepers apparently do, that there is a strict pecking order between his five charges. In the case of each of the ten possible pairs of hens (AB, AC, AD, AE, BC, BD, BE, CD, CE and DE), one of the hens is the pecker and the other is the pecked. Farmer Brown also notes that the pecking relationship is not necessarily *transitive*, in the sense that (for example) hen A may peck hen B, and hen B may peck hen C, but it does not necessarily follow from this that hen A will peck hen C. On the contrary, hen C may – and in the imaginary case we are about to consider in fact does – peck hen A.

Farmer Brown, who for some inexplicable and probably perverted reason is interested in this matter, draws a diagram of the particular pecking relationships which he observes between his five hens. He does not know that he is drawing a *directed graph* (*digraph* for short), but this is what he is in fact doing, and here it is:

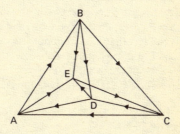

From the direction of the arrows, each of which means 'pecks', we can see that in the case of the ten possible pairs of hens (*A*B, *A*C. *A*D, *A*E, *B*C, *B*D, *B*E, *C*D, *C*E and *D*E, the pecker is the hen whose name is in italics and the pecked is of course the other member of the pair.

The digraph is rather complicated, so Farmer Brown decides to display the observed pecking relationships between his hens in the much simpler form of a 5 × 5 matrix, like this:

Pecked

	A	B	C	D	E
A	0	1	0	0	1
B	0	0	1	1	1
C	1	0	0	1	0
D	1	0	0	0	1
E	0	0	1	0	0

Pecker

Once again, he does not know exactly what he is doing: he is in fact drawing a *dominance matrix*. In such a matrix, the entries of 1 and 0 represent respectively the presence and absence of a relationship of dominance by one individual – or hen – over another. From the first row of Farmer Brown's matrix, for example, we see that hen A dominates (or pecks) hens B and E, but does not dominate (or is pecked by) hens C and D. The fact that hen A is pecked by hens C and D is more directly indicated by the two 1s which appear at the appropriate places in the first column of the matrix. The reader should check before going any further that the relationships expressed in the dominance matrix are in fact identical with those expressed in the digraph.

You will notice that the components of the main diagonal of the dominance matrix are all 0s. This reflects, of course, the fact that hens do not dominate (or peck) themselves. You will also notice that the components of the matrix are *complementary* (if the component in row i and column j is 1, then the component in column i and row j is 0, and vice versa). This reflects the fact that mutual dominance within any pair of hens is ruled out: one hen in each pair, we assume, must dominate the other. It can also be seen – although not quite so easily – that if the pecking relationships were *transitive* (so that A dominating B and B dominating

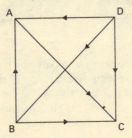

C implied that A dominated C, and so on), we could arrange the hens in an order that would make the dominance matrix one in which all the entries to the right of the main diagonal were 1s.

For instance, suppose with four hens we have the digraph above. You can check that the pecking relationships are transitive. The dominance matrix is

$$
\text{Pecker}\quad
\begin{array}{c}
\\ A \\ B \\ C \\ D
\end{array}
\begin{array}{c}
\textit{Pecked} \\
\begin{array}{cccc}
A & B & C & D \\
\end{array} \\
\left[
\begin{array}{cccc}
0 & 0 & 1 & 0 \\
1 & 0 & 1 & 0 \\
0 & 0 & 0 & 0 \\
1 & 1 & 1 & 0 \\
\end{array}
\right].
\end{array}
$$

Clearly D is the most powerful hen and C the weakest hen. A is the next to weakest since it only pecks C. Let us rearrange the order of the hens in the matrix with the strongest at the top and the weakest at the bottom. This gives us

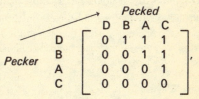

$$
\text{Pecker}\quad
\begin{array}{c}
\\ D \\ B \\ A \\ C
\end{array}
\begin{array}{c}
\textit{Pecked} \\
\begin{array}{cccc}
D & B & A & C \\
\end{array} \\
\left[
\begin{array}{cccc}
0 & 1 & 1 & 1 \\
0 & 0 & 1 & 1 \\
0 & 0 & 0 & 1 \\
0 & 0 & 0 & 0 \\
\end{array}
\right],
\end{array}
$$

and this is a matrix with 1s above the main diagonal and 0s everywhere else.

If we have transitive pecking relationships there is no difficulty in deciding on the order of power, but with non-transitive pecking relationships things are more difficult. We return to Farmer Brown's coop of non-transitive hens and ask, 'What is the pecking order?' One possible – and very simple – way of deciding this would be to sum the numbers in each of the rows of the dominance matrix, obtaining the following authority vector:

$$
\begin{array}{c}
A \\ B \\ C \\ D \\ E
\end{array}
\left[
\begin{array}{c}
2 \\ 3 \\ 2 \\ 2 \\ 1
\end{array}
\right].
$$

This clearly puts hen B in the lead, pecking as she does three of the other hens; hens A, C and D tie for second place, with two pecks apiece; and poor hen E is at the bottom, being the most hen-pecked of the five.

This measure of power may be all right for hens. But if we imagine that A, B, C, D and E constitute a group of *people*, in which one member of each pair in some sense dominates or has influence over the other, it might not be sufficient, when gauging the power of each member, to measure only his or her *direct* influence on the other members. If A has a direct influence over B, and B has a direct influence over C, then there is a sense in which A has an *indirect* influence over C, through B; and this indirect 'second-order' influence of A over C ought somehow to be taken into account when we are measuring the degree of A's power.

How then, in working out the relative degrees of power possessed by the different individuals in a group, can we take account of any second-order (or third-, or fourth-, or nth-order) influences which they may be able to exert. The answer is simple: you can read off the number of the nth-order influences from the nth power of the original dominance matrix. The explanation of this answer is not quite as simple as the answer itself.

Consider the original matrix relating to Farmer Brown's hens (call it D):

$$
D = \begin{array}{c} \\ A \\ B \\ C \\ D \\ E \end{array}
\begin{array}{c}
\begin{array}{ccccc} A & B & C & D & E \end{array} \\
\left[\begin{array}{ccccc}
0 & 1 & 0 & 0 & 1 \\
0 & 0 & 1 & 1 & 1 \\
1 & 0 & 0 & 1 & 0 \\
1 & 0 & 0 & 0 & 1 \\
0 & 0 & 1 & 0 & 0
\end{array}\right].
\end{array}
$$

Suppose now that we square this matrix, thus:

$$
D^2 = \left[\begin{array}{ccccc}
0 & 1 & 0 & 0 & 1 \\
0 & 0 & 1 & 1 & 1 \\
1 & 0 & 0 & 1 & 0 \\
1 & 0 & 0 & 0 & 1 \\
0 & 0 & 1 & 0 & 0
\end{array}\right]
\left[\begin{array}{ccccc}
0 & 1 & 0 & 0 & 1 \\
0 & 0 & 1 & 1 & 1 \\
1 & 0 & 0 & 1 & 0 \\
1 & 0 & 0 & 0 & 1 \\
0 & 0 & 1 & 0 & 0
\end{array}\right]
$$

$$
= \begin{array}{c} \\ A \\ B \\ C \\ D \\ E \end{array}
\begin{array}{c}
\begin{array}{ccccc} A & B & C & D & E \end{array} \\
\left[\begin{array}{ccccc}
0 & 0 & 2 & 1 & 1 \\
2 & 0 & 1 & 1 & 1 \\
1 & 1 & 0 & 0 & 2 \\
0 & 1 & 1 & 0 & 1 \\
1 & 0 & 0 & 1 & 0
\end{array}\right].
\end{array}
$$

Have a look at the entry in any particular row and column of D^2 – that in the third row and second column, say. To arrive at this entry ($= 1$), we have multiplied the components of the third row of the matrix D by the corresponding components of the second column, and have added up the five products, thus:

$$(1 \times 1) + (0 \times 0) + (0 \times 0) + (1 \times 0) + (0 \times 0) = 1.$$

Now products of this kind can be non-zero only if both the factors are equal to 1, as here in the case of the first of the five products. And since the first 1 in this first product indicates that C dominates A, and the second 1 indicates that A dominates B, we can therefore deduce, from the fact that this particular product is non-zero, that C has an indirect second-order influence over B, through A. One can see this also on the digraph, of course: one line points along from C to A, and another points up from A to B.

To make the point clearer, let us take another example. Consider the entry of 2 in the second row and first column of D^2. To arrive at this entry, we have multiplied the components of the second row of the matrix D by the corresponding components of the first column, and have added up the five products, thus:

$$(0 \times 0) + (0 \times 0) + (1 \times 1) + (1 \times 1) + (1 \times 0) = 2.$$

The fact that the third of these products is non-zero indicates that B dominates C and that C dominates A – that is; that B has an indirect second-order influence over A, through C. The fact that the fourth of the products is non-zero indicates that B dominates D and that D dominates A – that is, that B has an indirect second-order influence over A not only through C but also through D. Thus the number 2 in the second row and first column of D^2 indicates that B has *two* indirect second-order influences over A. Once again this can be quite clearly seen on the digraph.

By a similar argument, it can easily be shown that D^3 will give us the number of *third*-order indirect influences exercised by each member of the group:

$$D^3 = (D^2)D = \begin{bmatrix} 0 & 0 & 2 & 1 & 1 \\ 2 & 0 & 1 & 1 & 1 \\ 1 & 1 & 0 & 0 & 2 \\ 0 & 1 & 1 & 0 & 1 \\ 1 & 0 & 0 & 1 & 0 \end{bmatrix} \begin{bmatrix} 0 & 1 & 0 & 0 & 1 \\ 0 & 0 & 1 & 1 & 1 \\ 1 & 0 & 0 & 1 & 0 \\ 1 & 0 & 0 & 0 & 1 \\ 0 & 0 & 1 & 0 & 0 \end{bmatrix}$$

$$= C \begin{array}{c} A \\ B \\ C \\ D \\ E \end{array} \left[\begin{array}{ccccc} A & B & C & D & E \\ 3 & 0 & 1 & 2 & 1 \\ 2 & 2 & 1 & 1 & 3 \\ 0 & 1 & 3 & 1 & 2 \\ 1 & 0 & 2 & 2 & 1 \\ 1 & 1 & 0 & 0 & 2 \end{array} \right].$$

Here, for example, the entry of 3 in the second row and fifth column of D^3 indicates that there are three indirect third-order influences exercised by B over E. And one can indeed trace out these three indirect routes from B to E on the digraph – BCDE, BCAE and BDAE. The entries on the main diagonal of D^3, however, can be ignored: the fact that there are two third-order routes from B back to B, for example, is irrelevant, since we are assuming that a person (or a hen) cannot dominate (or peck) itself.

If we now add up D, D^2 and D^3, we shall get a matrix showing the total number of direct first-order and indirect second- and third-order influences exercised by each member of the group:

$$D + D^2 + D^3 = \left[\begin{array}{ccccc} 0 & 1 & 0 & 0 & 1 \\ 0 & 0 & 1 & 1 & 1 \\ 1 & 0 & 0 & 1 & 0 \\ 1 & 0 & 0 & 0 & 1 \\ 0 & 0 & 1 & 0 & 0 \end{array} \right] + \left[\begin{array}{ccccc} 0 & 0 & 2 & 1 & 1 \\ 2 & 0 & 1 & 1 & 1 \\ 1 & 1 & 0 & 0 & 2 \\ 0 & 1 & 1 & 0 & 1 \\ 1 & 0 & 0 & 1 & 0 \end{array} \right] +$$

$$\left[\begin{array}{ccccc} 3 & 0 & 1 & 2 & 1 \\ 2 & 2 & 1 & 1 & 3 \\ 0 & 1 & 3 & 1 & 2 \\ 1 & 0 & 2 & 2 & 1 \\ 1 & 1 & 0 & 0 & 2 \end{array} \right] = \left[\begin{array}{ccccc} 3 & 1 & 3 & 3 & 3 \\ 4 & 2 & 3 & 3 & 5 \\ 2 & 2 & 3 & 2 & 4 \\ 2 & 1 & 3 & 2 & 3 \\ 2 & 1 & 1 & 1 & 2 \end{array} \right].$$

The authority vector which we now get when we add up the rows of the matrix $(D + D^2 + D^3)$, omitting the elements on the main diagonal of D^3, is as follows:

$$\begin{array}{c} A \\ B \\ C \\ D \\ E \end{array} \left[\begin{array}{c} 10 \\ 15 \\ 10 \\ 9 \\ 5 \end{array} \right],$$

and this can perhaps be claimed to give us a rather more reliable indicator of the relative powers of the five members than the one which we derived solely from D. Certainly, at any rate, one of the ties has been eliminated.

Two questions immediately arise, however. First, where should we stop when we are adding up successive powers of a dominance matrix in this way? The answer is simply that stopping at any particular number of powers (for example, three, as we have just done) is more or less arbitrary: the investigator will simply stop at the point where it seems safe and convenient to stop, given the nature of the problem he is trying to solve.

Second, in working out the authority vector, should we not give less weight to indirect second-order influences than to direct first-order ones, to third-order ones than to second-order ones, and so on? The answer, broadly speaking, is yes. One might decide, for example, when adding up the matrices, to divide each element of D^2 by 2, of D^3 by 3, of D^4 (if we use it) by 4 and so on. But the particular divisors which we use in order to give less and less weight to less and less direct influences are bound to be fairly arbitrary.

Exercises

1.

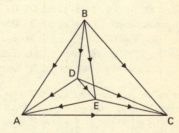

What is the dominance matrix for this digraph? Rearrange the order of A, B, C, D and E in your dominance matrix to give a matrix for which the elements above the main diagonal are all 1s.

2. (a)   (b)

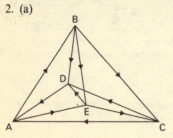
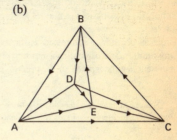

For both the above digraphs work out the dominance matrix, D, D^2 and D^3. Allowing for second- and third-order influences what do you consider to be the pecking order in each case?

Dominant Judges

The pecking order between hens is not likely to be of great interest to anyone except a farmer or an ornithologist. But the pecking order between certain groups of humans being is, or ought to be, of considerable interest to everyone. Take a bench of justices, for example. One would not of course expect to find these justices pecking one another in the literal sense (in spite of the fact that they might be beaks). But one might find that some of them were more influential, or dominant, than others, and it would be useful to be able to measure and compare the degree of their dominance. Professor S. Sidney Ulmer, of Michigan State University, has endeavoured to do precisely this for the eight justices who constituted the bench of Michigan Supreme Court at the end of the 1950s, and what I am going to say in the remainder of the present chapter is based more or less directly upon his fascinating article on this subject.[*]

In the Michigan Supreme Court, Professor Ulmer tells us,[†] 'each judge ... is given a number, and individual cases are assigned to justices by number on a rotation basis'. After arguments by counsel, and a certain amount of preliminary discussion among the judges themselves,

the justice to whom the case is assigned writes an opinion for the case, which is circulated among the other justices at least ten days prior to a conference set for the decision. At the same time any other justice may write an opinion if he chooses to do so. On conference day justices as a group review all the opinions written, having previously done so individually. If differences can be reconciled, an unanimous opinion results; otherwise, all opinions are circulated for signature. No formal vote is taken. The writer signs first and the opinion goes around the table at which justices sit according to number. The majority opinion, in a given case, is simply the one obtaining a majority of the signatures. Authors of majority opinions, therefore, are not known until the process of suggestion and compromise that precedes decision is completed. Justices of the court are free to support or oppose any opinion and often do so, not knowing whether the opinion will ultimately be a dissent, a concurrence, or the opinion of the court.

[*] S. Sidney Ulmer, 'Leadership in the Michigan Supreme Court', in Glendon Schubert (ed.), *Judicial Decision-making*, Free Press of Glencoe, New York, 1963, pp. 13–28.

[†] *Op. cit.*, pp. 16–17.

Professor Ulmer examined all the opinions produced in this way in 500 successive cases in the period 1958–60, and on this basis worked out an index of the extent to which the eight judges supported the opinions of each other during this period – an 'inter-individual solidarity index', as he calls it. Here it is:

Inter-individual solidarity index, Michigan Supreme Court, 1958–1960

Targets				INITIATORS				
	Ka	Vo	De	Sm	Ca	Ed	Bl	Ke
Kavanagh		76	80	85	81	88	83	77
Voelker	81		60	90	59	86	99	63
Dethmers	66	65		75	99	77	72	95
Smith	78	79	63		57	81	84	64
Carr	63	58	100	66		70	61	100
Edwards	61	68	66	76	65		70	65
Black	75	84	48	77	44	68		55
Kelly	60	53	86	63	91	61	62	

Each number in this table represents the degree of support given by each individual judge (as 'initiator') to each of the other judges (as 'target'). Suppose, for example, that Judge Dethmers had agreed with 72 of Judge Voelker's written opinions (whether these were majority, concurring or dissenting opinions), but had failed to agree with 48. The inter-individual solidarity index (ISI) in that case would be

$$ISI = \frac{72}{72 + 48} \times 100 = 60 \text{ per cent,}$$

which is in fact the figure appearing in the Dethmers column and Voelker row of the table.* Similarly, the figure of 77 in the Kelly column and Kavanagh row indicates in effect that Kelly agreed with 77 per cent of Kavanagh's opinions and disagreed with the remaining 23 per cent. Note particularly that the index does not reveal *equal* reciprocal support in the case of any of the pairs of judges. Kelly may have agreed with 77 per cent of Kavanagh's opinions, but the entry in the Kavanagh column and Kelly row indicates that Kavanagh did not by any means fully reciprocate: he supported only 60 per cent of Kelly's opinions.

The ISI, Ulmer goes on to argue, not only furnishes interesting infor-

---

* The figures of 72 and 48 which I have used to arrive at this figure of 60 per cent, unlike this figure itself, are purely hypothetical.

mation about relationships between pairs of justices, but also enables us to speculate concerning 'influence structure' in the court. The numbers in each column of the table can be regarded as a kind of rating, by the judge whose name appears at the head of the column (as 'initiator'), of each of his seven colleagues (as 'targets'). If we now proceed to 'rank order' these column entries (putting the highest = 1, the next highest = 2, and so on), we get a table of ISI ranks, which comes out as follows:

ISI Ranks, Michigan Supreme Court, 1958–1960

Targets	INITIATORS								Σ Rows	Average Rank
	Ka	Vo	De	Sm	Ca	Ed	Bl	Ke		
Ka		3	3	2	3	1	3	3	18	1
Vo	1		6	1	5	2	1	6	22	2
De	4	5		5	1	4	4	2	25	3.5
Sm	2	2	5		6	3	2	5	25	3.5
Ca	5	6	1	6		5	7	1	31	5.5
Ed	6	4	4	4	4		5	4	31	5.5
Bl	3	1	7	3	7	6		7	34	7
Ke	7	7	2	7	2	7	6		38	8

Adding up the numbers in each row, and ranking these sums (as is done on the right-hand side of the table), we see that Kavanagh emerges as the judge receiving the highest amount of support and Kelly as the one receiving the lowest, with the other judges being spaced out at various points in between. Kavanagh is given a pretty high rating by all the other judges, whereas Kelly is given a very low one by all the others except Dethmers and Carr – which may possibly not be unconnected with the fact that Kelly, Dethmers and Carr are the three Republican members of the court (the other five being Democrats).

These solidarity tables are of course limited to first-order relationships between pairs of justices. But, as Ulmer points out (and as we already know from our study of Farmer Brown's hens), influence can be exerted not only directly, but also indirectly. From the ISI table, for example, we can see that Kavanagh seems to exercise a considerable direct or first-order influence on Carr – at any rate if we can deduce this from the fact that Carr supports 81 per cent of Kavanagh's opinions whereas Kavanagh supports only 63 per cent of Carr's. But Carr, for similar reasons, can be said to exercise a considerable direct influence on Black. Therefore we can perhaps say that Kavanagh exercises an indirect, second-order influence on Black, through the medium of his influence on Carr. How are we to take these second-order (and, maybe, third-, fourth-, et cetera order) influences into account?

Well, we know the answer to this one already. If we can derive a plausible *dominance matrix* from the information in the ISI table, we can take these indirect influences into account by calculating successive powers of this matrix. And a possible way of deriving a plausible dominance matrix readily presents itself. If Carr supports more of Kavanagh's opinions than Kavanagh does of Carr's, we can assume that Kavanagh dominates Carr, entering a 1 in the Kavanagh row and Carr column, and a 0 in the Carr row and Kavanagh column. If Black supports more of Carr's opinions than Carr does of Black's, we can say that Carr dominates Black, entering a 1 in the Carr row and Black column, and a 0 in the Black row and Carr column. The result of doing this across the board is the following matrix (call it *D*):

Dominance matrix D: first-order relationships

	Vo	Ka	De	Ca	Sm	Ed	Ke	Bl	Σ Rows	Average Rank
Vo	0	1	0	1	1	1	1	1	6	1.5
Ka	0	0	1	1	1	1	1	1	6	1.5
De	1	0	0	0	1	1	1	1	5	3.5
Ca	0	0	1	0	1	1	1	1	5	3.5
Sm	0	0	0	0	0	1	1	1	3	5
Ed	0	0	0	0	0	0	1	1	2	6
Ke	0	0	0	0	0	0	0	1	1	7
Bl	0	0	0	0	0	0	0	0	0	8

If we sum the rows of this *D* matrix, and rank these sums as we did before,* we find that Kavanagh is no longer clearly in the lead: he and Voelker now tie for first place. Nor is Kelly any longer at the bottom: Black has now usurped that position.

The next job is to bring the second-, third- and later order relationships into the picture, which we do by working out D^2, D^3 and so on, and summing these successive powers. And here, of course, the two problems which we mentioned at the end of our study of the hens rear their ugly heads once again – what weights ought we to attach to the successive

---

* Note that in the case of the dominance matrix the *highest* row sum wins, whereas in the case of the table of ISI ranks it was of course the *lowest* row sum which won.

powers, and where ought we to call a halt to the process of adding them up? Ulmer's formula for what he calls the 'weighted summary matrix' (S) was

$$S = D + \frac{D^2}{2} + \frac{D^3}{3} + \frac{D^4}{4} + \frac{D^5}{5} + \frac{D^6}{6}.$$

The weights here attached to the successive powers ($\frac{1}{2}$, $\frac{1}{3}$, $\frac{1}{4}$, $\frac{1}{5}$ and $\frac{1}{6}$) were presumably more or less arbitrary, but the point at which a halt was called to the process of summation (D^6) was determined, Ulmer tells us, by the fact that at that point the rank order which emerged from the sum of the matrices was (a) free of ties and (b) the same for three successive stages. The weighted summary matrix S, thus calculated, turned out as follows:

Weighted summary matrix S for matrices D–D^6

	Vo	Ka	De	Ca	Sm	Ed	Ke	Bl	Σ Rows	Average Rank
Vo	0	1.91	2.46	2.65	6.16	9.11	17.96	23.16	63.41	1
Ka	1.56	0	2.40	2.38	4.21	8.15	13.48	20.88	53.06	2
De	1.50	1.35	0	1.76	4.54	6.31	10.89	19.15	45.50	3
Ca	1.06	1.03	1.50	0	3.59	5.32	8.60	13.48	34.58	4
Sm	0	0	0	0	0	1	1.50	2.33	4.83	5
Ed	0	0	0	0	0	0	1	1.5	2.5	6
Ke	0	0	0	0	0	0	0	1	1	7
Bl	0	0	0	0	0	0	0	0	0	8

When we sum the rows of this S matrix, and rank the sums as we have done twice before, Voelker for the first time emerges as the clear winner. It is clear from a comparison of S with D, however, that apart from the elimination of ties the introduction of orders of influence beyond the first does not (at any rate in this case) make all that much difference so far as the ranking of the degrees of influence is concerned.

One final point which has probably already occurred to you should be mentioned. In order to make use of a dominance matrix, with its felicitous properties, complete dominance has to be stipulated for one member of each pair. But clearly in the present case the difference in the degrees of reciprocal support given by one justice to another is sometimes much too small to warrant the assumption of anything like complete dominance of one by the other. For example (looking back at the table on p. 87), we see that Dethmers supports Carr 100 per cent of the time and Carr supports

Dethmers 99 per cent of the time – but this difference of 1 per cent is hardly great enough to warrant our saying (as we do in effect in matrix *D*) that Carr 'dominates' Dethmers! Ulmer shows, however, with considerable ingenuity, that even if we exclude those support differentials which are not 'significant' (in a particular sense which he duly defines), the rank order of the justices in fact remains more or less the same. Maybe he has been lucky here: obviously this would not always be the case. But one can at any rate agree with his claim that the matrix method, with all its fairly obvious limitations, is capable of throwing at least *some* light on the patterns of power and influence in the small group under consideration – and, by implication, in many other small groups as well.

6
The Simple Mathematics of Markov Chains

The Case of the Eccentric Professor

There is a professor in one of our universities who has three pet questions – let us call them A, B and C – one of which always turns up in every examination he sets his students. He never uses the same question twice in succession. If he used question A last time, he decides on the question he will use this time by tossing a coin; if it comes up heads he uses question B; if tails, he uses question C. If he used question B last time, he decides on the question he will use this time by tossing *two* coins: if at least one of them comes up heads he uses question C; otherwise he uses question A. If he used question C last time, he decides on the question he will use this time by tossing *three* coins; if at least one of them comes up heads he uses question A; otherwise he uses question B.*

Suppose we know which question he used last time. What can we say about the one he will use this time? We obviously cannot say *for certain* which one he will use this time, but, on the assumption that the coins he tosses have not been fixed by his students, we can easily work out the relevant *probabilities*. If he used A last time, there is clearly a 50 per cent chance that he will use B this time, and a 50 per cent chance that he will use C: that is, the relevant probabilities are $\frac{1}{2}$ for B and $\frac{1}{2}$ for C. If he used B last time, the relevant probabilities are $\frac{1}{4}$ for A and $\frac{3}{4}$ for C. And if he used C last time, the relevant probabilities (although not quite so obviously) are $\frac{7}{8}$ for A and $\frac{1}{8}$ for B.†

---

*This delightful professor is, alas, a mythical character. I discovered him in one of the brilliant problems set by J. G. Kemeny, J. L. Snell and G. L. Thompson in their remarkable *Introduction to Finite Mathematics*, third edition, Prentice-Hall, New Jersey, 1974, p. 213.

† If three coins are tossed together, there are eight possible combinations of heads and tails (HHH, HHT, HTT, HTH, THH, THT, TTT and TTH), each of which has an equal probability of occurring. Thus at least one head will come up, on the average, in seven out of every eight throws.

We can represent these facts about the relevant probabilities of the different outcomes diagrammatically:

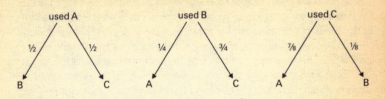

Alternatively we can express these facts in the form of a matrix (call it *P*) as follows.

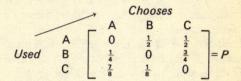

Here the numbers in row A, for example, indicate the respective probabilities of the professor choosing question A, question B and question C this time, given that he chose question A last time – and similarly for the other two rows of the matrix.

The square matrix which we have just constructed is an example of a matrix of *transition probabilities*, which is defined as a matrix whose components are all non-negative and in which the sum of the components of each row is 1. A matrix of this kind plays a crucial role in a special kind of process which has been claimed to have a wide degree of applicability in the social (and natural) sciences – a *Markov chain process*. We can explain what this means by carrying on with the example of the professor.

The professor, we shall assume, never deviates one iota from the procedure we have described. Thus if we know the particular question he used *last* time – or, to put it in the jargon, if we know what the particular *state* of the process was last time – and if we also know the matrix of transition probabilities, we can easily work out, even if only in probabilistic terms, what is likely to happen *this* time. We can calculate, in other words, the respective probabilities that the process will this time be in state A, state B and state C. Similarly, if we know the particular question which the professor in fact chooses *this* time, we can work out, although again only in probabilistic terms, what is likely to happen *next* time; and so on for all subsequent times. The two important assumptions we are making here are, first, that the matrix of transition probabilities does not change as the process moves from one stage to the next; and, second, that the state of the process at any given stage depends *only* on this constant set of transition probabilities *and on the state of the process at the immediately preceding stage*. In determining the probable state of the process at any given stage, in other words, we assume that information about its state at any stage earlier than the immediately preceding one is superfluous. A process which carries on over time on the basis of these two assumptions is called a Markov chain process.

In the study of a real-world Markov chain process, the question we are usually most interested in is this: given that the process *starts* in some particular state i, what is the probability that after a given number of stages it will find itself in some particular state j? Suppose for instance that some students look at the examination paper for this year (call it year 0), see which question was set and try to predict which question is likely to be set in two years' time (year 2) when they will be sitting the exams. They will not be able to make a certain prediction but we want to know how they should go about making the best possible probabilistic prediction.

We enlist the aid of what is called a *tree diagram* to set out the possible

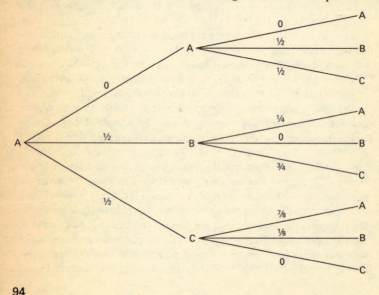

states of the process in years 0, 1 and 2. Every path from one state to another is labelled with the probability that this path will be taken.* We have just drawn the tree diagram for the case where the process is in state A in year 0. The reader should draw the tree diagrams for the process starting in states B and C.

Suppose that question A is set in year 0. The probability that it will be set again in year 2 will be the probability that the path of the process goes A to A to A or A to B to A or A to C to A. There are no other routes to A in our tree diagram. Hence the probability that the process will be in state A in year 2 is

$$(0 \times 0) + (\tfrac{1}{2} \times \tfrac{1}{4}) + (\tfrac{1}{2} \times \tfrac{7}{8}) = \tfrac{9}{16}.$$

In vector notation we would write this

$$\begin{bmatrix} 0 & \tfrac{1}{2} & \tfrac{1}{2} \end{bmatrix} \begin{bmatrix} 0 \\ \tfrac{1}{4} \\ \tfrac{7}{8} \end{bmatrix} = \tfrac{9}{16}.$$

Similarly if the process starts in A the probability that it will be in state B in year 2 is

$$(0 \times \tfrac{1}{2}) + (\tfrac{1}{2} \times 0) + (\tfrac{1}{2} \times \tfrac{1}{8}) = \tfrac{1}{16},$$

that is,

$$\begin{bmatrix} 0 & \tfrac{1}{2} & \tfrac{1}{2} \end{bmatrix} \begin{bmatrix} \tfrac{1}{2} \\ 0 \\ \tfrac{1}{8} \end{bmatrix} = \tfrac{1}{16}.$$

Finally the probability of C being the question set in year 2 is

$$(0 \times \tfrac{1}{2}) + (\tfrac{1}{2} \times \tfrac{3}{4}) + (\tfrac{1}{2} \times 0) = \tfrac{3}{8}$$

---

* We could in this diagram have omitted the one-step paths from A to A, B to B and C to C since there is a zero probability of the process going on these paths. However, we want to use the tree diagram to illustrate some general results, and not particular ones that apply only to processes that cannot stay in the same states.

or, in vector notation,

$$\begin{bmatrix} 0 & \frac{1}{2} & \frac{1}{2} \end{bmatrix} \begin{bmatrix} \frac{1}{2} \\ \frac{3}{4} \\ 0 \end{bmatrix} = \frac{3}{8}.$$

As a guidance to a work-plan the students would take it that there was only a small chance (1 in 16) of having to answer question B and much larger chances of having to answer A (9 in 16) and C (3 in 8).

Likewise we can work out the probabilities of the process being in the various states in year 2 if it starts in B or C by drawing the relevant tree diagrams. However tree diagrams get very large and cumbersome if there are a large number of states or if we want to analyse the likely outcome of the process after many years. Using matrix algebra helps to avoid a lot of work. Looking back at the matrix of transition probabilities P, and comparing it with our calculations written in vector notation, we can see that the probability, starting in state A, of being in states A, B and C after two years has been calculated by multiplying the row vector associated with A of P by the column vector of P associated with A, B and C respectively. Similarly, to calculate the probabilities of being in states A, B and C if the process started in B or C, we could multiply the relevant row vector of P by the columns of P in turn. These are the same calculations as those performed when the matrix P is multiplied by itself.

$$P.P = P^2 = \begin{bmatrix} 0 & \frac{1}{2} & \frac{1}{2} \\ \frac{1}{4} & 0 & \frac{3}{4} \\ \frac{7}{8} & \frac{1}{8} & 0 \end{bmatrix} \begin{bmatrix} 0 & \frac{1}{2} & \frac{1}{2} \\ \frac{1}{4} & 0 & \frac{3}{4} \\ \frac{7}{8} & \frac{1}{8} & 0 \end{bmatrix} \begin{matrix} A \\ B \\ C \end{matrix} \begin{matrix} A & B & C \\ \frac{9}{16} & \frac{1}{16} & \frac{3}{8} \\ \frac{21}{32} & \frac{7}{32} & \frac{1}{8} \\ \frac{1}{32} & \frac{7}{16} & \frac{17}{32} \end{matrix}$$

The element in the ith row and the jth column of P^2 gives the probability that the process will be in state j in year 2 given that it started in state i in year 0.

Immediately a suspicion must arise that elements of P^3, P^4 and so on will be the probabilities of being in the various states in years 3, 4 and so on, given the starting state, and in general P^n will yield probabilities for year n. Such a suspicion is correct, and it is straightforward to see why this is so.

Starting in year 0 in state A we can write the probabilities of being in the various states in year 2 as a vector.

$$\begin{matrix} A & B & C \\ \begin{bmatrix} \frac{9}{16} & \frac{1}{16} & \frac{3}{8} \end{bmatrix} \end{matrix}$$

This is the first row of P^2 – if the process had been in state B in year 0 the vector we should want would be the second row of P^2. Such a vector is known as a *probability vector* (formally defined as a vector with no negative components and whose elements add up to one). We know the probabilities of going from any state to any state in one year from P so we can calculate the probability of being in the various states in year 3. For instance the probability of going from A to A is 0, from B to A is $\frac{1}{4}$ and from C to A is $\frac{7}{8}$, so the probability of being in state A in year 3 if we were in state A in year 0 is

$$\left(\tfrac{9}{16}\times 0\right)+\left(\tfrac{1}{16}\times\tfrac{1}{4}\right)+\left(\tfrac{3}{8}\times\tfrac{7}{8}\right)=\tfrac{22}{64}.$$

The probability of being in state B in year 3 is

$$\begin{bmatrix} \frac{9}{16} & \frac{1}{16} & \frac{3}{8} \end{bmatrix} \begin{bmatrix} \frac{1}{2} \\ 0 \\ \frac{1}{8} \end{bmatrix} = \frac{21}{64},$$

and the probability of being in state C is

$$\begin{bmatrix} \frac{9}{16} & \frac{1}{16} & \frac{3}{8} \end{bmatrix} \begin{bmatrix} \frac{1}{2} \\ \frac{3}{4} \\ 0 \end{bmatrix} = \frac{21}{64}.$$

Thus if we start in state A in year 0 our probability vector for year 3 (call it v_3) is

$$\begin{bmatrix} \frac{22}{64} & \frac{21}{64} & \frac{21}{64} \end{bmatrix}$$

and we have obtained it by premultiplying P by the probability vector for year 2 (v_2).

$$v_3 = v_2 P.$$

By the same argument in calculating the probability vector for any year we have

$$v_n = v_{n-1} P,$$

and since

$$v_{n-1} = v_{n-2}P$$
$$v_n = v_{n-2}P^2.$$

Working back until we reach year 0 we obtain

$$v_n = v_0 P^n.$$

The vector v_0 is the probability vector at year 0; so if we are assuming the process starts in state A in year 0, v_0 will be the vector $[1 \quad 0 \quad 0]$ implying there is a probability of one that the process will be in state A in year 0.

In this case

$$v_n = v_0 P^n = \begin{bmatrix} 1 & 0 & 0 \end{bmatrix} P^n$$

and matrix arithmetic tells us that this means v_n is simply the first row of P^n. If we had started in state B then v_n would be the second row of P^n. Thus the elements of P^n give us the probabilities of being in the various states in year n given the starting state, the element in the ith row and jth column being the probability of being in state j given that the process started in state i. Thus if we know the starting state of a process we can predict the probabilities of it being in the various states n years later.

An Important Theorem

Indeed we can go further than the last statement. It turns out that if we look far enough ahead the probabilities of the process being in the various states become *independent* of the state in which the process started. This has an intuitive appeal. In our example the way the professor chooses questions will determine the relative frequency with which the questions are set. As we move in time further from the starting date our probability vectors will reflect increasingly the nature of this choice process and less and less the starting state of the process. Since the row vectors of P^n indicate the probabilities of being in the various states for their corresponding starting states we should, therefore, expect the rows of this matrix to become more alike as n gets larger. This idea is the subject of an important theorem in the mathematics of Markov chains. It states that if you keep raising a transition matrix P to successively higher and higher powers, the resulting matrices become more and more like each other and approach a particular matrix W the rows of which are identical.*

For example, routine calculation for the transition matrix in our example yields

$$P^8 = \begin{bmatrix} .3805 & .2471 & .3723 \\ .3740 & .2428 & .3832 \\ .4011 & .2309 & .3680 \end{bmatrix},$$

and multiplying this matrix by itself gives

$$P^{16} = \begin{bmatrix} .3865 & .2400 & .3734 \\ .3868 & .2398 & .3733 \\ .3866 & .2401 & .3732 \end{bmatrix}.$$

The rows of P^8 look quite similar to each other and by the time we reach P^{16} they are identical to three places of decimals.

The process thus approaches some kind of equilibrium. After a certain time the probability of being in any state remains constant and this probability is independent of the starting state of the process. We can estimate these probabilities for our example very easily, since the matrix P^{16} is obviously very near to the limiting equilibrium because its rows are almost identical. In general, however, it may be rather tedious keeping multiplying a matrix by itself and there is a quicker method.

We have shown that if the probability vector for year n is v_n then the probability vector for year $n + 1$ is

$$v_{n+1} = v_n P.$$

Now if we have reached equilibrium our theorem tells us that the probability vector is the same, regardless of our starting state, and will be the same for all future time periods. If we call this equilibrium probability vector w where

$$w = \begin{bmatrix} w_1 & w_2 & w_3 \end{bmatrix},$$

* This theorem applies only to transition matrices which are 'regular'. A transition matrix is 'regular' if some power of the matrix has only positive components. The one we have been using is 'regular' as we can readily see from our calculation of P^2.

then

$$w = wP.$$

In the example

$$\begin{bmatrix} w_1 & w_2 & w_3 \end{bmatrix} = \begin{bmatrix} w_1 & w_2 & w_3 \end{bmatrix} \begin{bmatrix} 0 & \frac{1}{2} & \frac{1}{2} \\ \frac{1}{4} & 0 & \frac{3}{4} \\ \frac{7}{8} & \frac{1}{8} & 0 \end{bmatrix}.$$

Performing the multiplication we have

$$w_1 = \tfrac{1}{4}w_2 + \tfrac{7}{8}w_3$$
$$w_2 = \tfrac{1}{2}w_1 + \tfrac{1}{8}w_3$$
$$w_3 = \tfrac{1}{2}w_1 + \tfrac{3}{4}w_2.$$

Remembering that from the nature of the probability vector

$$w_1 + w_2 + w_3 = 1,$$

we can solve these simultaneous equations to obtain

$$w = \begin{bmatrix} w_1 & w_2 & w_3 \end{bmatrix} = \begin{bmatrix} \frac{58}{150} & \frac{36}{150} & \frac{56}{150} \end{bmatrix}$$
$$= \begin{bmatrix} .3867 & .2400 & .3733 \end{bmatrix}.$$

All the row vectors of P^n will approach this vector as n gets larger and larger.

How should one *interpret* this interesting result? Let us look at it from the point of view of a student who, twenty or thirty years after our professor obtained his chair, is trying to predict which of the three questions, A, B and C the professor will ask this year. The student, we shall assume, knows the matrix of transition probabilities P, which the professor has either unwittingly disclosed when in his cups, or has deliberately revealed in order to encourage his students to acquire a little knowledge about the mathematics of Markov chain processes. The student, we assume, knows nothing more than this; in particular, he does not know which of the three questions the professor actually asked either in his first year in the chair or in any of the subsequent years. The best that the student can do under these circumstances is to assume that by now the process is bound to have reached equilibrium, and that the probability vector must therefore be [.3867 .2400 .3733]. What this equilibrium probability vector indicates in the present case is simply the *fraction of times* that the professor uses question A, B and C respectively. Taking one year with another, question A crops up 39 per cent of the time, question B 24 per cent, and question C 37 per cent. If, as we are assuming, the process has been going on for twenty or thirty years, the values of these fractions will now have become quite independent of their values during the first few years of the professor's occupancy of his chair.

This suggests another, rather more useful, interpretation of our result. Suppose that all the professors in the country are exactly like our professor in the relevant respects. They *all* have the same three pet questions A, B and C; and they *all* employ the same slightly crazy coin-tossing method of selecting the question they are going to use this year. What one can then say, with some degree of confidence, is that in 39 per cent of the examination papers in any given year question A will appear; that in 24 per cent question B will appear; and that in 37 per cent question C will appear. After the process has been going on for some time, in other words, the relative frequency with which each of the questions appears in examination papers (over the country as a whole) is very likely to be that indicated by the equilibrium probability vector, quite irrespective of what the frequency was when the process started.

Rumour and Truth

It is useful, at this stage, to illustrate the use of this theorem by another example. The spread of gossip, rumour and news through a population has been a very popular field of study for social scientists. We take as our example a famous simple model of the consequences of rumour-mongering. Suppose the Prime Minister tells a confidant that he or she has the intention of either calling or not calling a general election in the next few months. This confidant passes the message to one other person who in turn passes it to a different person and so on. Let us suppose that, because of malice or bad telephone lines or something else, there is a chance that an individual will change the message before passing it on. In particular we assume that if a person is told there is to be an election there is a probability of p_1 that he or she will pass on the message that there will be no election and that if someone is told there is to be no election there is a probability of p_2 that they will reverse the rumour when spreading it. We can set up a simple Markov chain model of the process where the states 'election' and 'no election' indicate the message being passed on.

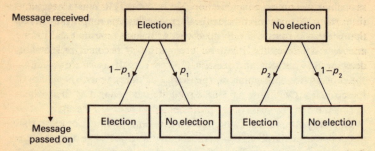

(Since there are only two states, if the probability of going from state 'election' to 'no election' is p_1 the probability of going from 'election' to 'election' is $1 - p_1$. Likewise the probability of going from 'no election' to 'no election' is $1 - p_2$.)

Combining the two diagrams above gives us a picture of the message moving round and round:

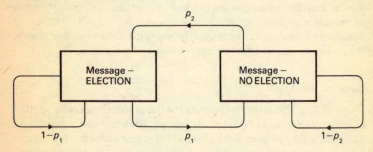

We can summarize the process in a transition matrix:

$$
\text{\textit{Message received}} \quad
\begin{array}{c}
\\
\text{Election} \\
\text{No election}
\end{array}
\begin{array}{cc}
\textit{Message passed on} \\
\begin{array}{cc}
\text{Election} & \text{No election} \\
\end{array} \\
\left[
\begin{array}{cc}
1 - p_1 & p_1 \\
p_2 & 1 - p_2
\end{array}
\right] = P.
\end{array}
$$

From the mathematics earlier in the chapter, we know that the first row of the matrix P^n will give the probabilities of the nth person being told that there is to be an election or not given that the PM said there was to be one. The second row of P^n gives these probabilities assuming that the PM said there was not to be an election. We know that as n gets larger and the rumour, in one form or the other, spreads throughout the population that these two rows will tend to become constant and identical to one another. Whatever the PM said originally will become irrelevant in determining what state the message is in.

Let us suppose, then, that as n gets larger P^n approaches

$$ w = \begin{bmatrix} w_1 & 1-w_1 \\ w_1 & 1-w_1 \end{bmatrix}. $$

When the process has reached this stage the probability of the process being in the two states is given by the equilibrium probability vector

$$ w = \begin{bmatrix} w_1 & 1-w_1 \end{bmatrix}, $$

regardless of the starting state of the process. After another step the probabilities of the process being in the two states will still be the same since P^n remains unchanged and hence

$$ w = wP. $$

That is,

$$ \begin{bmatrix} w_1 & 1-w_1 \end{bmatrix} = \begin{bmatrix} w_1 & 1-w_1 \end{bmatrix} \begin{bmatrix} 1-p_1 & p_1 \\ p_2 & 1-p_2 \end{bmatrix}. $$

Performing the matrix multiplication we have

$$ w_1(1-p_1) + (1-w_1)p_2 = w_1. $$

Solving this equation for w_1 yields

$$ w_1 = \frac{p_2}{(p_1+p_2)}. $$

Thus our equilibrium probability vector is

$$ \begin{bmatrix} w_1 & 1-w_1 \end{bmatrix} = \begin{bmatrix} \dfrac{p_2}{(p_1+p_2)} & \dfrac{p_1}{(p_1+p_2)} \end{bmatrix}. $$

When the process has gone on for some time, this gives us the proportion of people who hear one version of the rumour and the proportion who hear the other. Taking some particular numerical examples let us first suppose $p_1 = p_2$, so that the chance of the message being reversed is the same for both possible messages. We have, then, that $w = [\frac{1}{2} \; \frac{1}{2}]$. In this case, in the long run, regardless of what the PM whispered to the confidant, half of the population will hear there is to be an election and half that there is not. This result depends on the equality of p_1 and p_2 and not on their size. As long as there is some chance of the message being reversed we shall get this result.

If p_2 is twice as large as p_1 so that there is a greater chance of the message 'no election' being changed than that of 'election' we shall have

$$w = \left[\frac{p_2}{(p_1 + p_2)} \quad \frac{p_1}{(p_1 + p_2)} \right] = \left[\frac{2}{3} \quad \frac{1}{3} \right],$$

which means that we can expect two thirds of the population will hear that there is to be an election whether the PM declared there was to be one or not.

This model, famous probably because it appeals to our cynical natures, shows clearly that the long-run outcome of a Markov process is determined by the values of the components of the transition matrix and is independent of the starting state of the process. We can learn that if we want to spread a rumour we have no need to worry whether it be true or false, but should try to estimate the transition matrix to see whether we should speak at all.

Exercises

1. In a certain country it is found that if it rains one day, the probability that it will rain the next day is $\frac{1}{2}$; if it does not rain on a certain day the probability that it will rain the next day is $\frac{1}{3}$. Using 'rain' and 'no rain' as states write down a transition probability matrix to illustrate the process of weather change from one day to the next.

   If it rained on January 1st what is the probability that it will rain on (i) January 3rd (ii) January 5th (iii) January 9th?

   How many rainy days will there be on average during a year?

2. Suppose after studying the foreign-exchange market you discovered the following information about the behaviour of the pound sterling against the dollar.

If the pound went up against the dollar one day, the probability of it going up again the next day is $\frac{1}{4}$ and the probability of the value remaining unchanged is $\frac{3}{4}$. If the pound remains unchanged against the dollar the probability, the next day, of it going up in value is $\frac{1}{3}$ and the probability of it going down is $\frac{2}{3}$. If the pound goes down against the dollar any day, the probability that next day it will remain unchanged in value is $\frac{1}{2}$ and the probability that it will fall in value is also $\frac{1}{2}$.

Construct a transition probability matrix to illustrate this process.

If the pound falls in value one day what is the probability that it will rise in value two days later? Three days later? Show that on average the pound will be rising 16 per cent of the time and falling 48 per cent of the time.

7
Models of Mobility

Our examples in the last chapter were rather frivolous – and designedly so, because frivolity is often a good teacher. But suppose that our subject of study were not the question which some absurd professor was going to ask in an exam paper, but the division of the population of a nation between town and country. Suppose one could work out a matrix of transition probabilities which showed the probability of a town-dweller moving to the country, and that of a country-dweller moving to the town in a particular period of time – a year, say. One ought to be able to construct such a matrix, at any rate in principle, by finding out what proportion of town-dwellers have in fact moved to the country, and what proportion of country-dwellers have in fact moved to the town, in each year over the past five or six years. Striking an average, one might find that in each year approximately 2 per cent of the people in the country move to towns, and 5 per cent of the people in the towns move to the country.

We can show this migration process as a picture.

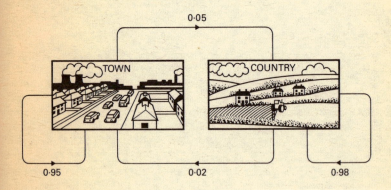

Alternatively we can construct a simple matrix of transition probabilities.

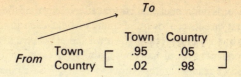

$$\begin{array}{cc} & \text{To} \\ & \begin{array}{cc} \text{Town} & \text{Country} \end{array} \\ \begin{array}{c} \text{From} \\ \end{array} \begin{array}{c} \text{Town} \\ \text{Country} \end{array} & \begin{bmatrix} .95 & .05 \\ .02 & .98 \end{bmatrix} \end{array}$$

Suppose, again, that at the present time 40 per cent of the population live in the country and 60 per cent in the towns, and suppose also that the total population of the nation remains constant from year to year. We could then build on this basis a Markov chain model which would enable us to predict the relative proportions of people who would be living in town and country in one year, two years, or n years. Such a model would predict that after one year the relative proportions would be given by

$$\begin{matrix} & \text{Town} & \text{Country} \end{matrix}$$
$$\begin{bmatrix} .60 & .40 \end{bmatrix} \begin{bmatrix} .95 & .05 \\ .02 & .98 \end{bmatrix} = \begin{bmatrix} .578 & .422 \end{bmatrix};$$

after two years by

$$\begin{matrix} & & \text{Town} & \text{Country} \end{matrix}$$
$$\begin{bmatrix} .60 & .40 \end{bmatrix} \begin{bmatrix} .95 & .05 \\ .02 & .98 \end{bmatrix} \begin{bmatrix} .95 & .05 \\ .02 & .98 \end{bmatrix} = \begin{bmatrix} .558 & .442 \end{bmatrix};$$

and after n years ($n \to \infty$) by

$$\begin{bmatrix} .60 & .40 \end{bmatrix} \begin{bmatrix} .95 & .05 \\ .02 & .98 \end{bmatrix}^n.$$

If n is large this approaches

$$\begin{bmatrix} .60 & .40 \end{bmatrix} \begin{bmatrix} .286 & .714 \\ .286 & .714 \end{bmatrix}$$

and this equals

$$\begin{bmatrix} .286 & .714 \end{bmatrix}.$$

In other words our model predicts that after a long time the distribution of the population between town and country would reach an equilibrium,* with approximately 29 per cent in the town and 71 per cent in the country, quite independent of the proportions initially in the town and country.

Take another example, rather closer to reality. We are interested, let us say, in the question of the extent to which the occupational class of the father affects the occupational class of the son. To throw light on this question, attempts have sometimes been made to construct a matrix of transition probabilities representing the probabilities of movement by a son from his father's occupational class to another, and to build on this basis a Markov chain model from which predictions may be made about future changes in the occupational structure of the population.

Here, for example, is a matrix of transition probabilities constructed by Kemeny and Snell† from data collected by Glass and Hall from England and Wales for 1949:

Son

		Upper	Middle	Lower
	Upper	.448	.484	.068
Father	Middle	.054	.699	.247
	Lower	.011	.503	.486

The numbers in the first row of this matrix (P) indicate that of the total numbers of sons whose fathers were in upper-class occupations 44.8 per cent went to upper-class occupations, 48.4 per cent to middle-class occupations, and 6.8 per cent to lower-class occupations. The numbers in the second row indicate that of the sons whose fathers were in middle-class occupations 5.4 per cent went to upper-class occupations, 69.9 per cent to middle-class occupations, and 24.7 per cent to lower-class occupations, and similarly for the third row. The time period concerned is of course one generation.

If we want to set up a Markov chain model on the basis of this matrix, we must make the usual assumptions – that the matrix does not change

---

* The 'equilibrium' situation would not be one in which movement ceased, but one in which the fraction of the population moving from town to country (.286 × .05 = .014) was exactly equal to the fraction moving from country to town (.714 × .02 = .014).

† J. C. Kemeny and J. L. Snell, *Finite Markov Chains*, Van Nostrand, Princeton, New Jersey, 1962, p. 191.

as the process moves from one stage to the next, and that the state of the process at any given stage depends only on these constant transition probabilities and its state at the immediately preceding stage. It is also convenient to assume, in the present case, that changes in the distribution of the population between the different occupational classes from one generation to the next are due solely to the movements predicted by the matrix: we ignore, for example, the fact that fathers in one occupational class may have more children than those in another.

As Kemeny and Snell point out, there are two different purposes for which we may want to set up a Markov chain model on this basis. We may be interested, first, in the future history of *an individual family* (assuming that each family has exactly one son). Suppose, for example, that the head of a particular family starts off in an upper-class occupation, so that the initial probability vector is [1, 0, 0]. The probabilities that it will be in the upper, middle and lower classes respectively after two generations will then be given by

$$f^{(2)} = f^{(0)}p^2$$

$$= \begin{bmatrix} 1 & 0 & 0 \end{bmatrix} \begin{bmatrix} .448 & .484 & .068 \\ .054 & .699 & .247 \\ .011 & .503 & .486 \end{bmatrix}^2$$

$$= \begin{bmatrix} 1 & 0 & 0 \end{bmatrix} \begin{bmatrix} .228 & .589 & .183 \\ .065 & .639 & .296 \\ .038 & .601 & .361 \end{bmatrix}$$

$$= \begin{bmatrix} .228 & .589 & .183 \end{bmatrix}.$$

The upper-class family, it would appear, is not very likely to find itself in the working class after two generations, but it is more than twice as likely to move to the middle class than it is to remain in the upper class.

Second, we may be interested in predicting the proportion of *the total population* which is likely to be in each of the occupational classes after a certain number of generations. Suppose, for example, that when the process begins 10 per cent are in the upper class, 40 per cent in the middle class, and 50 per cent in the lower class. The relative proportions which are likely to be found in the three occupational classes after three generations will then be given by:

$$\begin{bmatrix} .1 & .4 & .5 \end{bmatrix} \begin{bmatrix} .448 & .484 & .068 \\ .054 & .699 & .247 \\ .011 & .503 & .486 \end{bmatrix}^{3}$$

$$= \begin{bmatrix} .1 & .4 & .5 \end{bmatrix} \begin{bmatrix} .136 & .614 & .250 \\ .067 & .627 & .306 \\ .053 & .620 & .327 \end{bmatrix}$$

$$= \begin{bmatrix} .067 & .622 & .311 \end{bmatrix}.$$

What about the equilibrium situation towards which, as we know, Markov chain processes of this kind inevitably tend? Clearly the rows even of the third power of the basic matrix of transition probabilities are already getting quite close to one another; by raising the matrix to higher power – or by using the alternative method outlined on p. 99 above – we can fairly easily show that in equilibrium the constant probability vector will be

$$\begin{bmatrix} .067 & .624 & .309 \end{bmatrix}.$$

Looking at this from an unborn individual's point of view, we can say that it represents the best we can do today by way of predictions for the occupation of *any* individual in the distant future – predictions which are quite independent of the occupation of the individual's present-day ancestor. Looking at the vector from the point of view of the total population, it tells us what the proportions in the different occupational classes are likely to be – and to remain – when the process has reached an equilibrium. These proportions will be quite independent of those which existed at the beginning of the process.*

A Markov Model of Industrial Mobility

Attempts to apply stochastic models to the question of probability as

* If the process we are analysing has already been going on for a long time, it may of course be near to equilibrium *now*. The actual proportions in the different occupational classes which were disclosed in the 1949 data from which the matrix of transition probabilities on p. 108 was derived were [.076 .634 .290] – remarkably close to the constant probability vector [.067 .624 .309].

110

between one generation and another have been many and various, but it is always difficult to get clear-cut conclusions from them: the problems of measurement of the data and interpretation of the results are often pretty intractable. In this section we are going to look at a much more modest – but very interesting – attempt to apply a Markov chain model to the question of mobility of workers between one industry and another – *intra*generational mobility rather than *inter*generational mobility, if you like. This is the famous model built by I. Blumen, M. Kogan and P. J. McCarthy* (hereafter B K M) to analyse the movement between industries of American workers, on the basis of government statistics, collected at one-quarter intervals between 1947 and 1949, showing the current occupation of a 1 per cent sample of all workers covered by social security since 1937.

The government statistics used a very detailed classification of industries, and one of the first things that B K M did was to combine a number of the official categories into broader ones, arriving in the end at ten 'industry code groups', A,B, ... K, with an extra one (U) added to represent being outside the system (for example, by entering an occupation not covered by social security, or by ceasing to work because of retirement or death). So there were eleven possible 'states' in any one of which an individual could theoretically find himself at each of the twelve times at which the quarterly returns were made; and the statistics gave complete information about the particular 'state' occupied by each individual covered by the sample at each of these twelve different times.

The next job was to construct a matrix of transition probabilities, representing (to put it in general terms) the probability of a worker who was in state i at time n moving to state j at time $n + 1$. The time-interval used was one quarter (that is, three months), but the probabilities were worked out by taking a kind of average of the changes from one state to another which occurred during all the pairs of consecutive quarters during the period. Thus, to take an arbitrary and completely theoretical illustration, suppose we were dealing with only three industries (A, B and C) and that our observations covered four quarters. In quarter 1, let us say, we find that there were 100 people in industry A; in quarter 2, 50 of these 100 were still in industry A, but 25 of them had moved to industry B and 25 to industry C. In quarter 2, we find that there were, say, 110 people in industry A; in quarter 3, 60 of these 110 were still in industry A, but 30 had moved to B and 20 had moved to C. In quarter 3, there were, say, 105

* I. Blumen, M. Kogan and P. J. McCarthy, *The Industrial Mobility of Labour as a Probability Process*, Cornell University, Ithaca, New York, 1955.

people in industry A; in quarter 4, 50 of these 105 were still in industry A, but 25 had moved to B and 30 had moved to C. So the average *proportion* of workers who moved between two quarters from state A to state B is given by the fraction

$$\frac{25 + 30 + 25}{100 + 110 + 105} = .254;$$

the proportion who moved to state C is

$$\frac{25 + 20 + 30}{100 + 110 + 105} = .238;$$

and the proportion who stayed in state A is

$$\frac{50 + 60 + 50}{100 + 110 + 105} = .508.$$

Thus if we wanted to construct a matrix of transition probabilities, based on the sum of all one-quarter observations, we would now be able to fill in the first row

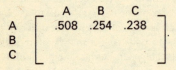

Similar calculations would enable us to fill in the other two rows and thus complete the matrix.

B K M worked out in this way matrices of transition probabilities for a number of separate groups of workers divided by age and sex. Let us consider, however, only one of these matrices – the one they worked out for males aged 20 to 24. Here it is:

One-quarter transition matrix for males, 20–24
(based on the sum of all one-quarter observations)

Code group or origin	Code group of destination										
	A	B	C	D	E	F	G	H	J	K	U
A	.407	.035	.081	.012	.046	.023	.081	.000	.035	.000	.279
B	.001	.727	.021	.009	.022	.012	.036	.004	.011	.002	.155
C	.001	.016	.761	.008	.022	.009	.038	.003	.010	.002	.129
D	.000	.014	.019	.815	.021	.011	.027	.003	.011	.001	.077
E	.000	.016	.015	.010	.827	.011	.032	.002	.008	.002	.078
F	.001	.021	.012	.008	.018	.777	.030	.004	.011	.002	.116
G	.001	.020	.020	.008	.019	.012	.788	.004	.016	.002	.112
H	.000	.019	.016	.006	.015	.012	.048	.787	.015	.003	.079
J	.001	.024	.018	.007	.023	.012	.054	.005	.704	.002	.151
K	.000	.052	.052	.022	.073	.009	.082	.017	.030	.468	.197
U	.002	.039	.037	.012	.033	.017	.065	.006	.028	.002	.760

Source: I. Blumen, M. Kogan and P. J. McCarthy, *op. cit.*, p. 59.

Each of the components obviously enough lies between zero and one; and the sum of the components in any row adds up to one, or at any rate very nearly to one.

Given this matrix of transition probabilities (call it P) it is easy to set up a Markov chain model. If we make the two basic Markovian assumptions, and if we are able to start with a row vector $f^{(0)}$ which represents the actual proportions in which the workers in the particular group we are concerned with are initially divided between the eleven possible states, we know that the probability vector relating to any later time t will be given by

$$f^{(t)} = f^{(0)} P^t.$$

Suppose, for example, that we know the proportions in which male workers aged 20 to 24 are distributed between the eleven states today ($f^{(0)}$), and we are interested in predicting the probable proportions in which they will be distributed between them in two years' time – that is, after eight quarters have elapsed ($f^{(8)}$). If the general process actually operates as a Markov process – that is, if the Markovian assumptions fit the facts – then we can safely use the formula

$$f^{(8)} = f^{(0)} P^8.$$

The matrix P^8, of course, shows us the probability of a worker's moving from any given state to any other state in eight quarters; and it is obvious that if we premultiply P^8 by a row vector representing the present proportionate distribution of the workers between the states, the product will be a row vector representing their probable proportionate division between the states eight quarters hence.

The great question here is whether the Markovian assumptions *do* fit the facts. How could we test this in the present case from the data available to us? One way, obviously, would be to take a particular quarter's distribution as the starting-point ($f^{(0)}$), to work out the distribution we would *expect* (assuming the Markovian assumptions hold) eight quarters later ($f^{(8)}$) by using the formula $f^{(8)} = f^{(0)} P^8$; and then to compare this expected distribution with the actual distribution eight quarters later. Or we could simply take the matrix P^8, which shows us the probability of a worker moving from any given state to any other state in eight quarters (if the Markovian assumptions hold), and compare it with another matrix showing the *actual observed* fractions of workers who moved from any given state to any other state in a particular (or average) eight-quarter period. B K M concentrate on the latter method, calculating expected and observed eighth-order matrices (and, for good measure, fourth-order matrices as well) for males aged 20–24, and males aged 40–44.

Here are the eighth-order matrices (put together for ease of comparison) for males aged 20 to 24.

The 'exp.' (expected) figures are those in P^8; the 'obs.' (observed) figures show the fractions of workers who were actually observed, in the period of three years covered by the data, to move from any given state to any other state during a time period of eight years.

Compare first the expected and observed figures in the main diagonal of this combined matrix. The expected figure in the E E slot, for example, tells us that if the Markov assumptions were valid we would expect a fraction .276 (= 27.6 per cent) of the workers who were in state E in a particular quarter to be still in state E eight quarters later. The observed figure shows us, however, that of the workers who were in state E in a particular quarter a much larger percentage than this – 48.9 per cent – were actually observed to be still in state E eight quarters later. This considerable underestimation of the proportion of workers who stay in a given state is true all along the (main diagonal) line.* Given this we also

---

* Except for the A A slot, and the very small number of observations (32) on which the figures in row A are based renders this particular result of little significance.

Comparison of expected and observed eighth-order matrices for males, 20–24

Code group or origin		A	B	C	D	E	F	G	H	J	K	U	Number of observations
A	Exp.	.002	.086	.105	.042	.116	.053	.181	.016	.058	.004	.337	
	Obs.	.000	.062	.062	.000	.125	.156	.312	.000	.000	.000	.281	(32)
B	Exp.	.002	.144	.087	.040	.104	.050	.163	.018	.052	.004	.336	
	Obs.	.003	.449	.039	.020	.048	.035	.079	.014	.023	.006	.284	(1,448)
C	Exp.	.002	.077	.176	.039	.103	.046	.163	.016	.050	.004	.324	
	Obs.	.002	.037	.461	.023	.046	.021	.101	.007	.022	.002	.278	(2,017)
D	Exp.	.001	.070	.080	.218	.099	.046	.141	.015	.047	.003	.279	
	Obs.	.000	.064	.044	.459	.083	.024	.091	.011	.030	.002	.192	(1.081)
E	Exp.	.001	.072	.075	.040	.276	.046	.147	.013	.044	.004	.279	
	Obs.	.002	.045	.042	.034	.489	.031	.094	.010	.023	.002	.227	(2,777)
F	Exp.	.002	.081	.076	.038	.097	.166	.152	.017	.050	.004	.316	
	Obs.	.003	.056	.033	.022	.054	.440	.090	.020	.026	.010	.245	(1,016)
G	Exp.	.002	.080	.084	.039	.098	.049	.261	.017	.053	.004	.314	
	Obs.	.002	.047	.051	.025	.046	.038	.491	.020	.044	.002	.235	(3,259)
H	Exp.	.001	.077	.077	.035	.090	.048	.170	.158	.052	.004	.287	
	Obs.	.000	.044	.007	.015	.026	.085	.096	.439	.074	.000	.214	(271)
J	Exp.	.002	.084	.085	.038	.105	.049	.178	.018	.105	.004	.333	
	Obs.	.002	.061	.033	.018	.054	.035	.145	.019	.339	.000	.294	(1,083)
K	Exp.	.002	.089	.096	.047	.130	.048	.179	.023	.056	.006	.325	
	Obs.	.000	.113	.097	.032	.121	.048	.137	.032	.024	.048	.347	(124)
U	Exp.	.002	.090	.095	.042	.112	.052	.179	.019	.058	.004	.346	
	Obs.	.001	.069	.068	.035	.077	.040	.153	.018	.055	.004	.482	(7,820)

Source: I. Blumen, M. Kogan and P. J. McCarthy, *op. cit.*, p. 61.

find of course that the expected movement into the various states other than the state of origin (indicated by the expected entries which are not on the main diagonal) is usually larger than the observed movement into these states.

On the other hand, as BKM state, 'the code groups of distribution do seem to maintain approximately the same relative positions as "receivers" of movement, whether one uses the observed or expected matrices' (I. Blumen, M. Kogan and P. J. McCarthy, *op. cit.*, p. 63) – but this is rather cold comfort.

Another approach to the problem of testing the Markovian assumptions, however, leads to a much happier result. Since movement between industries had been taking place for a long time before 1947–9, it would seem reasonable to suppose – if the process were in fact Markovian in character – that by 1947–9 it might have reached an 'equilibrium', in the sense in which we used this term in the preceding chapter. In this equilibrium situation, as we know, the rows of P^n (n being large) would be identical, and each of them would itself be identical to the constant probability vector representing the distribution of workers between the different states. Suppose, then, that in the present case we calculated P^n ($n \to \infty$), and found that the actual present-day distribution of workers corresponded to the common row vector. We should then obviously want to think twice before deciding that the Markov chain model was completely inapplicable to the process of movement between industries.

B K M did this job, but because computers were not as powerful as they are today, they did it on the basis of a reduced (5×5 instead of 11×11) matrix of transition probabilities constructed by combining certain of the code groups together. The reduced transition matrix P, for males aged 20–24, became

$$
P = \begin{array}{c} \\ (C,D,E) \\ (G) \\ (F,H) \\ (A,B,J,K) \\ (U) \end{array}
\begin{array}{ccccc}
(C,D,E) & (G) & (F,H) & (A,B,J,K) & (U) \\
.832 & .033 & .013 & .028 & .095 \\
.046 & .788 & .016 & .038 & .112 \\
.038 & .034 & .785 & .036 & .107 \\
.054 & .045 & .017 & .728 & .156 \\
.082 & .065 & .023 & .071 & .759
\end{array}
$$

Source: I. Blumen, M. Kogan and P. J. McCarthy, op. cit., p. 64.

and the common row vector of P^n ($n \to \infty$) was calculated to be

(C,D,E)	(G)	(F,H)	(A,B,J,K)	(U)
.27	.18	.08	.15	.32

The actual average percentage of male workers aged 20–24 in these five industry groups for 1947–9 was as follows:

(C,D,E)	(G)	(F,H)	(A,B,J,K)	(U)
28.2	17.0	6.8	13.7	34.3

The degree of congruity here is rather surprising – if not downright spooky – and it suggests, as BKM put it, that 'something "regular" is going on in the observed industrial movement'.

Movers and Stayers

Something 'regular' may be going on – but it's pretty clear from what has been said above that a simple Markov chain model cannot fully explain it. It unfortunately remains true that the model seriously and consistently underestimates the extent to which workers will remain in the same industry over a long period. The expected entries on the main diagonal of P^4 and P^8 are too small, and the other expected entries are usually too large. BKM made a very ingenious attempt to get over this difficulty by building a revised Markov-type model in which it is assumed that there are two different kinds of workers – stayers and movers. The stayers are those who never move at all from their original industries; the movers are those who do (or may) move. The movements of the mover, it is supposed, are governed, in accordance with the usual Markovian assumptions, by a matrix of transition probability (M) applying to them alone.

Suppose, then, that we know the proportions in which the workers in each industry are divided between movers and stayers. It is convenient to use matrix notation for these quantities, entering the proportion of stayers on the main diagonal of a matrix S (*not* a transition matrix), and entering zeros in all the other slots, as in this simple three-industry example:

$$S = \begin{bmatrix} \frac{1}{4} & 0 & 0 \\ 0 & \frac{1}{2} & 0 \\ 0 & 0 & \frac{1}{3} \end{bmatrix}.$$

The proportions of *movers* in each industry will then be given by the matrix $I - S$. Thus in our simple example:

$$(I-S) = \begin{bmatrix} 1 & 0 & 0 \\ 0 & 1 & 0 \\ 0 & 0 & 1 \end{bmatrix} - \begin{bmatrix} \frac{1}{4} & 0 & 0 \\ 0 & \frac{1}{2} & 0 \\ 0 & 0 & \frac{1}{3} \end{bmatrix} = \begin{bmatrix} \frac{3}{4} & 0 & 0 \\ 0 & \frac{1}{2} & 0 \\ 0 & 0 & \frac{2}{3} \end{bmatrix}.$$

Given that we also know the movers' matrix of transition probabilities M, it is fairly easy to show that the matrix of transition probabilities (P) for the workers as a whole (that is, movers plus stayers) will be given by:

$$P = S + (I-S)M.$$

For example, if we suppose in our simple case that

$$M = \begin{bmatrix} .90 & .05 & .05 \\ .10 & .80 & .10 \\ .20 & .20 & .60 \end{bmatrix},$$

then the matrix of transition probabilities for all workers will be:

$$P = S + (I - S)M$$

$$= \begin{bmatrix} .25 & 0 & 0 \\ 0 & .50 & 0 \\ 0 & 0 & .33 \end{bmatrix} + \begin{bmatrix} .75 & 0 & 0 \\ 0 & .50 & 0 \\ 0 & 0 & .67 \end{bmatrix} \begin{bmatrix} .90 & .05 & .05 \\ .10 & .80 & .10 \\ .20 & .20 & .60 \end{bmatrix}$$

$$= \begin{bmatrix} .25 & 0 & 0 \\ 0 & .50 & 0 \\ 0 & 0 & .33 \end{bmatrix} + \begin{bmatrix} .675 & .0375 & .0375 \\ .05 & .40 & .05 \\ .133 & .133 & .40 \end{bmatrix}$$

$$= \begin{bmatrix} .925 & .0375 & .0375 \\ .05 & .90 & .05 \\ .133 & .133 & .73 \end{bmatrix}.$$

To see that this makes sense, consider the first item in the first row of P. The probability that a worker who starts in A will finish up in A at the end of the time interval concerned will be the probability that he is a stayer (.25), so that he remains in A with a probability of one, *plus* the probability that he is a mover (.75) multiplied by the probability that despite the fact that he is a mover he actually remains in A (.90). These arithmetical operations,

$$(.25)1 + (.75)(.90) = .925,$$

are in effect those that are performed in arriving at the first element in the first row of P.

Consider, again, the third element in the second row of P. The probability that a worker who starts in B will finish up in C at the end of the time interval will be the probability that he is a stayer (.50) so that he moves to C with a probability of zero, *plus* the probability that he is a mover (.50) multiplied by the probability that he will move to C (.10).

These arithmetical operations,

$$(.50)0 + (.50)(.10) = .05,$$

are those that are performed in arriving at the third element in the second row of P. And so on.

The important new feature about this matrix P is that if we want to make higher-order comparisons, we must raise to the appropriate power *matrix M* and not *matrix P*, for the obvious reason that the only movements that take place are those governed by matrix M – only movers move. Thus the transition probability matrix applying to all workers showing the probabilities of moving between industries in two time periods will be

$$P^{(2)} = S + (I - S)M^2.$$

In our illustration this is

$$P^{(2)} = \begin{bmatrix} .25 & 0 & 0 \\ 0 & .5 & 0 \\ 0 & 0 & .33 \end{bmatrix} + \begin{bmatrix} .75 & 0 & 0 \\ 0 & .5 & 0 \\ 0 & 0 & .67 \end{bmatrix} \begin{bmatrix} .90 & .05 & .05 \\ .10 & .8 & .1 \\ .2 & .2 & .6 \end{bmatrix}^2$$

$$= \begin{bmatrix} .25 & 0 & 0 \\ 0 & .5 & 0 \\ 0 & 0 & .33 \end{bmatrix} + \begin{bmatrix} .75 & 0 & 0 \\ 0 & .5 & 0 \\ 0 & 0 & .67 \end{bmatrix} \begin{bmatrix} .825 & .095 & .080 \\ .190 & .665 & .145 \\ .320 & .290 & .390 \end{bmatrix}$$

$$= \begin{bmatrix} .869 & .071 & .060 \\ .095 & .832 & .073 \\ .214 & .194 & .590 \end{bmatrix}.$$

Similarly it is easy to compute the probability matrices applying to longer time periods.

Now compare matrix P with matrix M and matrix $P^{(2)}$ with M^2. One thing stands out immediately. All the elements on the main diagonal of both P and $P^{(2)}$ are greater than the the corresponding elements in M and M^2, while all the non-diagonal elements of the P matrices are smaller than the corresponding elements of the M matrices. This is, of course, no accident. We have already examined the relationship between P and M. To compute a non-diagonal element of P we simply have to multiply the corresponding element of M by $1-s_i$, where s_i is the proportion of stayers

119

in industry i, and so long as there are some stayers (s_i greater than zero) then this means that to get P we are multiplying the elements of M by numbers that are less than one. To compute an element on the main diagonal of P (say p_{ii}, the element in the ith row and ith column) we multiply the corresponding element of $M(m_{ii})$ by $1-s_i$ and then add s_i to this product. In algebra

$$p_{ii} = (1 - s_i)m_{ii} + s_i.$$

This implies

$$p_{ii} - m_{ii} = s_i(1 - m_{ii}).$$

Provided that m_{ii} is less than one (which just means that there is at least one stayer in the industry) the right-hand side of this equation is always positive and so the diagonal elements of P are greater than those of M. By the same reasoning the diagonal elements of $P^{(n)}$ will be greater than those of M^n while the off-diagonal elements will be smaller.

This is a happy characteristic, since the original model underestimated the diagonal entries and overestimated the others. Possibly the reason for this was that it assumed that the same transition matrix applied to everyone. If we divide the workers up into stayers and movers, and assume that the transition matrix that applies to the latter does not apply to the former, might we get better results? BKM tested this hypothesis by estimating S and M from the 1947–9 data, and compared the expected probabilities over various time periods with the observed probabilities.

The results were up to a point quite encouraging. The degree of agreement between expected and observed probabilities in eighth-order matrices was pretty high in the case of all four of the age and sex groups considered. Unfortunately, however, this good 'fit' did not hold up too well for either shorter or longer periods of time. The model fairly consistently underestimated the items on the main diagonal in the case of fourth-order matrices, and overestimated them in the case of eleventh-order matrices. So although the overall 'fit' of the new model was appreciably better than that of the old, it too seems to contain a kind of built-in systematic error – although a rather different one.

What is to be done? BKM argue that the overestimation of the diagonal entries in the eleventh-order matrices is due to the non-existence of stayers (in the strict sense) in the real world, and they try to amend their Markov-type model to take account of this. Other researchers in different fields, trying to apply Markovian methods to processes in which they happen to be interested and coming face to face with similar discrepancies, have followed a whole number of methods in order to get a better fit. The difficulty is that generally speaking you cannot get a good fit unless you reject or modify one or both of the two basic Markovian assumptions – and once you do this a large number of alternative paths open up, between which it is very difficult to make a choice. Here one need only say that one of these alternatives that may be fruitful in producing more realistic Markovian models of such processes is to view the processes not as *simple* but as *absorbing* Markov chains. Absorbing Markov chains will be our subject in the next chapter.

Exercises

1. Consider a group of 200 people, 100 of whom at the moment support the Labour Party and 100 of whom support the Conservative Party. Assume that the probability of a Labour supporter changing to a Conservative supporter any month is .015 and the probability of a Conservative supporter becoming a Labour supporter is .01. After a long period of time how would you expect the group of 200 to divide their support between the two parties?

2. Now suppose that in the group there are 80 Labour supporters and 60 Conservative supporters who will never change their allegiance. The rest are floating voters. The probability of a Labour supporting floating voter changing allegiance in a month is .075 and that of a Conservative supporting floating voter is .025.

   Check that in the first month you would expect the same number of Labour and Conservative supporters to change allegiance as you would under the assumptions of question 1.

   What is the long-run distribution of party support?

8
The Mathematics of Absorbing Markov Chains

In the Markov chains we have been considering processes which never come to a stop. We reach an equilibrium in the sense that the probabilities of the process being in each state remains constant as the process goes through further stages. No process gets stuck in a particular state because there is always a definite probability that it will leave that state. To study processes that do come to an end we need to look at the mathematics of a different kind of chain – an *absorbing Markov chain*.

Let us suppose we post a letter from Leicester to an address in London and watch its progress: it may be delayed on the route at Leicester or London sorting houses, completely lost in either place or eventually delivered. Without implying anything about the efficiency of the Post Office let us suppose that the transition probability matrix for the letter's progress during a day in its journey is

$$
\begin{array}{c}
\textit{BEGINS}
\end{array}
\begin{array}{cc}
 & \xrightarrow{\hspace{2cm}} \\
\begin{array}{l}
\text{Lost} \quad 1 \\
\text{Delivered} \quad 2 \\
\text{Leicester} \quad 3 \\
\text{London} \quad 4
\end{array}
\end{array}
\begin{array}{c}
\textit{ENDS} \\
\begin{array}{cccc}
1 & 2 & 3 & 4
\end{array} \\
\left[
\begin{array}{cccc}
1 & 0 & 0 & 0 \\
0 & 1 & 0 & 0 \\
\frac{1}{8} & \frac{1}{8} & \frac{1}{2} & \frac{1}{4} \\
\frac{1}{8} & \frac{3}{8} & 0 & \frac{1}{2}
\end{array}
\right] = P.
\end{array}
$$

The first two rows are called absorbing states. Once the letter is either lost or delivered that is the end of the matter. It is impossible to leave either of these two states and hence the probability of remaining in each is one. The third and fourth rows show the transition probabilities if the letter starts the day in a sorting house. For instance, if it starts the day in London there is a probability of $\frac{1}{2}$ that it still will be there at the end of the day, $\frac{3}{8}$ that it will have been delivered and $\frac{1}{8}$ that it will have been lost. The sorting houses are non-absorbing states. We imagine that eventually the letter will arrive at an absorbing state – it will be either delivered or lost.

There are some obvious questions to ask. What proportion of letters will be delivered and lost? How long on average will it take to deliver a

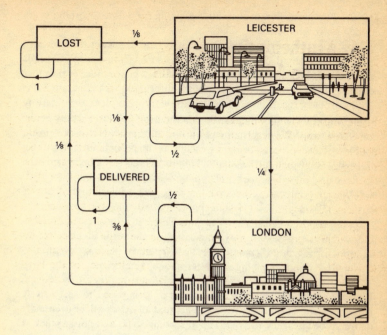

letter? How long is it likely that letters will be stuck in Leicester and London? To answer these questions and to turn them into general results we first look more closely at matrix P.

If we break (*partition* in more correct language) the matrix into four by drawing a horizontal and a vertical line between the two absorbing and two non-absorbing states, we can see that the top left-hand segment is an identity matrix and the top right-hand segment has all zero elements. This is why the states were ordered with all the absorbing states first.

$$P = \begin{bmatrix} 1 & 0 & 0 & 0 \\ 0 & 1 & 0 & 0 \\ \frac{1}{8} & \frac{1}{8} & \frac{1}{2} & \frac{1}{4} \\ \frac{1}{8} & \frac{3}{8} & 0 & \frac{1}{2} \end{bmatrix} = \begin{bmatrix} I & O \\ R & Q \end{bmatrix}.$$

R is a matrix (in this case 2×2) of the transition probabilities of going from the non-absorbing states to the absorbing states. Q is a matrix, also

2×2, of the transition probabilities of going from non-absorbing states to non-absorbing states.

How does this partitioning of the matrix help to answer the questions we posed? The length of time the letter is in a sorting house simply depends on Q, which gives the probabilities of being stuck in one office or the other or going between the two. The rest of the information is redundant as far as this problem is concerned. Now we know from chapter 6 that, starting from one of the states, if Q represents the probabilities of being in the various states after one step, then Q^2 gives us the probabilities of being in these states after two steps, and Q^3 gives us the probabilities after three steps and so on. We can calculate Q raised to higher and higher powers;

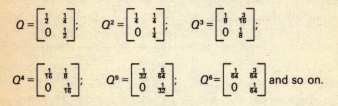

$$Q = \begin{bmatrix} \frac{1}{2} & \frac{1}{4} \\ 0 & \frac{1}{2} \end{bmatrix}; \quad Q^2 = \begin{bmatrix} \frac{1}{4} & \frac{1}{4} \\ 0 & \frac{1}{4} \end{bmatrix}; \quad Q^3 = \begin{bmatrix} \frac{1}{8} & \frac{3}{16} \\ 0 & \frac{1}{8} \end{bmatrix};$$

$$Q^4 = \begin{bmatrix} \frac{1}{16} & \frac{1}{8} \\ 0 & \frac{1}{16} \end{bmatrix}; \quad Q^5 = \begin{bmatrix} \frac{1}{32} & \frac{5}{64} \\ 0 & \frac{1}{32} \end{bmatrix}; \quad Q^6 = \begin{bmatrix} \frac{1}{64} & \frac{3}{64} \\ 0 & \frac{1}{64} \end{bmatrix} \text{ and so on.}$$

The size of the elements are diminishing as Q is raised to successively higher powers. This fits in with our belief that all letters will be eventually delivered or lost (they will reach an absorbing state) and not be stuck at a sorting house for ever.

To find out how long a letter is likely to remain further in the London office if it starts there, we simply add the elements in the bottom right-hand corner of all these matrices because each element gives the probability of remaining in London after each successive step. Thus the average time we would expect a letter to remain in the office is

$$1 + \tfrac{1}{2} + \tfrac{1}{4} + \tfrac{1}{8} + \tfrac{1}{16} + \tfrac{1}{32} + \tfrac{1}{64} + \ldots \text{days}.$$

The 1 at the beginning of the series is because the letter is definitely in London for the first step of the process by assumption. This series is a familiar geometrical progression and elementary arithmetic tells us that the sum as we take more and more terms gets closer and closer to 2. So if the letter is not immediately delivered but goes to the London office we can expect it to be there on average for two days.

It is a little more difficult to find out how long a letter may be expected to be stuck in London if it starts the day in Leicester. The same logic as before tells us that the answer will be obtained by adding all the elements in the first row and second column of the matrices Q, Q^2, Q^3 etc. This sum is

$$\tfrac{1}{4}+\tfrac{1}{4}+\tfrac{3}{16}+\tfrac{1}{8}+\tfrac{5}{64}+\tfrac{3}{64}\dots \text{ days}$$

but this is not a geometrical progression. However, the terms do seem to be getting smaller and we might conjecture that their sum does approach 1. An excursion into matrix algebra will persuade us that this is true.

Let n_{ij} be the expected time spent in the non-absorbing state j if we start in state i (labelling Leicester as state 1 and London as state 2 we know that $n_{22} = 2$ and conjecture that $n_{12} = 1$). Our argument tells us that

$$N = \begin{bmatrix} n_{11} & n_{12} \\ n_{12} & n_{22} \end{bmatrix} = \begin{bmatrix} 1 & 0 \\ 0 & 1 \end{bmatrix} + \begin{bmatrix} \tfrac{1}{2} & \tfrac{1}{4} \\ 0 & \tfrac{1}{2} \end{bmatrix} + \begin{bmatrix} \tfrac{1}{4} & \tfrac{1}{4} \\ 0 & \tfrac{1}{4} \end{bmatrix} + \dots$$

$$N = I + Q + Q^2 + Q^3 + Q^4 + \dots$$

The identity matrix at the beginning of the sum notes that if we start in Leicester or London we are automatically there for one step.

The right-hand side of the equation is another geometrical progression even though the Qs are matrices and not simply single numbers. In addition since all the elements of the Q matrices are probabilities they are numerically less than 1, and indeed the sum of the components in any row cannot be greater than 1. If we had a series

$$s = 1 + r + r^2 + r^3 + \dots,$$

and we knew that r was less than 1, then a quick look at an arithmetic text would tell us that

$$s = \frac{1}{1-r} = (1-r)^{-1}.$$

In exactly the same fashion we may write

$$N = (I - Q)^{-1},$$

where the superscript -1 again means that the matrix $I - Q$ has to be inverted.* N is known grandly as *the fundamental matrix* of the Markov chain.

* We met a matrix of exactly the same form as N in chapter 3 on input-output analysis, where we gave an economic interpretation of why $(I - A)^{-1} = I + A + A^2 + A^3 + \dots$

Now in our particular example

$$I - Q = \begin{bmatrix} \frac{1}{2} & -\frac{1}{4} \\ 0 & \frac{1}{2} \end{bmatrix}$$

and, using the simple techniques developed in chapter 2,

$$N = (I - Q)^{-1} = \begin{bmatrix} 2 & 1 \\ 0 & 2 \end{bmatrix}.$$

Thus we have a general answer to the question of how long we can expect a process to be in any non-absorbing state starting from any non-absorbing state. In our particular case we can see that our hunch was right and that the sum of the series we were doubtful about is 1, and hence that if a letter starts in Leicester sorting office we can expect it to be stuck in London for an average of one day before it is absorbed.

It is now a simple matter to find out the average length of time it takes before a letter is delivered or lost. We know that starting in Leicester a letter will on average be stuck there for two days and for one day in London, making a total of three days. Adding the elements of N in the row appropriate to our particular starting non-absorbing state gives us the average time to go from this state to absorption.

There is a neat mathematical way of expressing this row addition. If we postmultiply a matrix by a column vector with all elements equal to one (call it e) we get a new vector that has as elements the sums of the individual rows of the matrix,

$$\begin{bmatrix} 2 & 1 \\ 0 & 2 \end{bmatrix} \begin{bmatrix} 1 \\ 1 \end{bmatrix} = \begin{bmatrix} 3 \\ 2 \end{bmatrix}.$$

This may be written as

$$Ne = t,$$

where t is a vector of the average time taken to go from the various non-absorbing states to absorption.

Finally we want to find out what proportion of letters get lost and what proportion delivered, or in general what is the probability of a chain being absorbed in a particular absorbing state if it starts in a particular non-absorbing state. To solve this problem we now need more information than is contained in the matrix Q. We also need to know the probabilities of going in one step from the various non-absorbing states to the absorbing states. These probabilities are contained in R, the bottom left segment of the original transition probability matrix P that we partitioned into four segments:

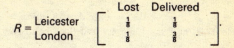

$$R = \begin{matrix} \text{Leicester} \\ \text{London} \end{matrix} \begin{bmatrix} \frac{1}{8} & \frac{1}{8} \\ \frac{1}{8} & \frac{3}{8} \end{bmatrix}.$$

We know from the fundamental matrix N that if a letter starts in Leicester it can be expected to be there for two days and in London for one day. The probability of it being delivered is, then, the sum of the chance of it being delivered in one step from Leicester given it is there for two days, and the chance of it being delivered from London given that it is there for one day. Matrix R tells us that it has a probability of $\frac{1}{8}$ of being delivered from Leicester and $\frac{3}{8}$ from London in one step. Thus the chance of it being delivered is

$$2 \times \tfrac{1}{8} + 1 \times \tfrac{3}{8} = \tfrac{5}{8}.$$

Since the chance of being lost in Leicester and London in one step is $\frac{1}{8}$, the probability overall for loss is

$$2 \times \tfrac{1}{8} + 1 \times \tfrac{1}{8} = \tfrac{3}{8}.$$

Note that $\frac{5}{8} + \frac{3}{8} = 1$ and this gives us a check on the sense of our argument since the probability of a letter being eventually lost or delivered must be one.

This argument can also be expressed conveniently in matrix form. Consider the product of the matrices N and R.

$$NR = \begin{bmatrix} 2 & 1 \\ 0 & 2 \end{bmatrix} \begin{bmatrix} \frac{1}{8} & \frac{1}{8} \\ \frac{1}{8} & \frac{3}{8} \end{bmatrix}.$$

The calculation we have made of the probability of the letter being delivered from Leicester is identical to multiplying the elements in the first row of N by the corresponding elements in the second column of R and then adding. This is the normal process of matrix multiplication.

Performing this multiplication we have

$$NR = B = \begin{matrix} \text{Leicester} \\ \text{London} \end{matrix} \begin{array}{c} \overset{\text{Lost}}{} \quad \overset{\text{Delivered}}{} \\ \left[\begin{matrix} \frac{3}{8} & \frac{5}{8} \\ \frac{1}{4} & \frac{3}{4} \end{matrix} \right] \end{array}.$$

The first row of B gives us the probabilities of going to each of the absorbing states starting from Leicester and the second row these same probabilities starting from London.

We have now answered all the original questions and turn to some examples of where these general methods and results can be applied.

Exercises

1. This is a simple board game. You place a counter on square 1; spin a coin and if it comes down heads you move on one square to 2, but if it's tails you stay still. You repeat the tossing of the coin always moving on one square if heads turns up and staying still if tails turns up. When you reach square 5 you stop.

   Write down the transition probability matrix using squares 1, 2, 3, 4 and 5 as 'states' (square 5 is an absorbing state).

   Starting at square 1 work out the probability of being on the various squares after (i) four tosses of the coin and (ii) ten tosses of the coin.

1 START	2	3	4	5 END

2. The following diagram represents the progress of students trying to qualify for some profession. They can take a maximum of three years to qualify and some drop out on the way. Qualifying and dropping out are absorbing states.

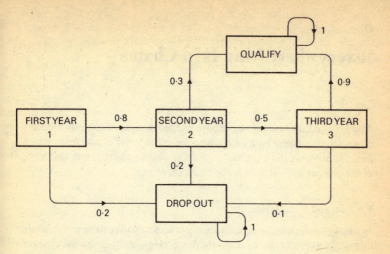

Fill in the transition probability matrix.

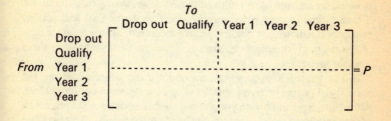

Calculate the fundamental matrix for this absorbing Markov chain. Show that a student beginning the course will be a student for an average 2.2 years and that on average 60 per cent of the students eventually qualify.

9
'Everywhere Man Is in Chains'

Absorbing Markov chains have been and are being used to study a variety of social processes. In this chapter we consider two examples which indicate not only the possible fruitfulness of the approach but also some of the difficulties that such studies may encounter.

Prisons and Recidivism

In order to estimate the prison facilities a society will require in the future one needs to predict many different things. How many and what types of crime will be committed? How effective will the police be at arresting suspects and bringing them to trial? What will be the likelihood of courts finding the accused guilty, and what will be the sentencing policy of judges? It would be no surprise, given the difficulty of answering such questions, if such estimates were based merely on extrapolating past and present prison populations into the future. We shall look at one aspect of the problem for which absorbing Markov chains may help in making more sensible guesses.

In the United Kingdom, and no doubt many other countries, the majority of people receiving gaol sentences have been in custody before. Knowing the present prison population, the release dates of the prisoners, the probability of them 'going straight' or the time that was likely to elapse before they returned to prison, would very much help in forecasting future prison populations. Data collected by the Indiana State Reformatory and reported by Mahoney and Blozan* will help to illustrate this.

Of prisoners released in Indiana, on average 19 per cent of them are back in gaol within a year; 12 per cent of the remainder are back within two years; 7 per cent of those left are inside within three years and a mere 3 per cent of the survivors are put in gaol between three and four years after release. We can use these figures as transition probabilities of going from the state of being free in one year to the state of being in gaol the

---

* W. M. Mahoney and C. F. Blozan, *Cost Benefit Evaluation of Welfare Demonstration Projects*, Resources Management Corporation, Bethesda, Maryland, 1968.

next year. Also we can regard going to gaol as reaching an absorbing state, and if we are interested only in prison requirements for the next four years (for ease of arithmetic rather than shortsightedness) we can regard reaching the fifth year of freedom also as an absorbing state. If a released prisoner survives without another gaol sentence for four years we forget about him and regard him as permanently free. Indeed the evidence suggests that there is a negligible chance of recidivism if an individual is not reconvicted within five years of release.* A diagram will help to illustrate the chain.

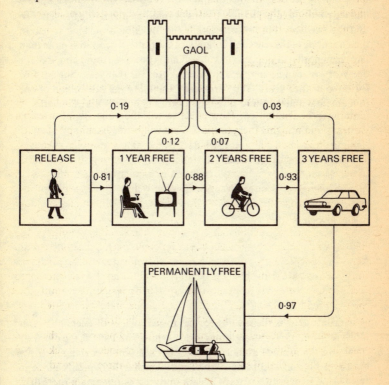

From this the transition probability matrix for convicts and ex-convicts in Indiana can be drawn

*See for instance R. F. Sparks, *Local Prisons: The Crisis in the English Penal System*, Heinemann, London, 1971.

$$
\begin{array}{cc}
 & \begin{array}{cccccc} G & F & 0 & 1 & 2 & 3 \end{array}
\end{array}
$$

		G	F	0	1	2	3
Gaol	G	1	0	0	0	0	0
Permanently free	F	0	1	0	0	0	0
Released	0	.19	0	0	.81	0	0
Free for one year	1	.12	0	0	0	.88	0
Free for two years	2	.07	0	0	0	0	.93
Free for three years	3	.03	.97	0	0	0	0

$$
= \left[\begin{array}{c|c} I & 0 \\ \hline R & Q \end{array} \right],
$$

and we partition it, as in the previous chapter, by arranging the states so that the two absorbing states precede the four non-absorbing states. In this case none of the rows and columns of the Q matrix contains more than one element that is not zero in value. This is because from being free for one year you can go in one step to being free for two years but not free for three or four years. This turns out to simplify the calculation of our fundamental matrix N and save the batteries of our pocket calculators.

We have

$$
I - Q = \begin{bmatrix} 1 & -.81 & 0 & 0 \\ 0 & 1 & -.88 & 0 \\ 0 & 0 & 1 & -.93 \\ 0 & 0 & 0 & 1 \end{bmatrix}.
$$

The inverse is

$$
N = (I - Q)^{-1} = \begin{bmatrix} 1 & .81 & .71 & .66 \\ 0 & 1 & .88 & .82 \\ 0 & 0 & 1 & .93 \\ 0 & 0 & 0 & 1 \end{bmatrix}
$$

– or rather, that is the inverse correct to two places of decimals.* Our interpretation of N is straightforward. We have shown that the elements of N give the average number of times in each non-absorbing state for each possible non-absorbing starting state. Since an individual cannot go from being free for two years to free for one year, or remain for more than the starting step at being free for two years, the elements below the

* Readers are recommended to calculate the inverse matrix for themselves and note why it is easy to do so when a matrix has all zero elements below the main diagonal running from the top left to the bottom right-hand corner.

diagonal are all zero and those on the diagonal are all one. After release
an ex-convict has, reading along the top row of N, a .81 chance of being
free for one year, .71 chance for two years and a .66 chance for three years.

Next we can calculate the mean number of steps to absorption. We
have shown that this is given for all possible non-absorbing starting states
by the vector t where $t = Ne$:

$$
t = \begin{bmatrix} 1 & .81 & .71 & .66 \\ 0 & 1 & .88 & .82 \\ 0 & 0 & 1 & .93 \\ 0 & 0 & 0 & 1 \end{bmatrix} \begin{bmatrix} 1 \\ 1 \\ 1 \\ 1 \end{bmatrix} = \begin{bmatrix} 3.18 \\ 2.70 \\ 1.93 \\ 1.00 \end{bmatrix}.
$$

Thus the average length of time from release that we can expect to elapse
before an ex-convict is back in gaol or permanently free is 3.18 steps; for
an individual who has survived a year outside, this time is 2.70 steps and
so on. Since after four steps from release all individuals will have reached
an absorbing state the vector t must lie numerically between the vectors

$$
\begin{bmatrix} 1 \\ 1 \\ 1 \\ 1 \end{bmatrix} \text{ and } \begin{bmatrix} 4 \\ 3 \\ 2 \\ 1 \end{bmatrix}.
$$

The first vector would correspond to the case where all ex-convicts are
back in gaol within a year of release, and the second where they all have
become reformed characters or at least not caught by the police. The
larger is t the less is the degree of recidivism.

We have shown earlier that the matrix B ($= NR$) will give us the
probability that an absorbing chain will end in a particular absorbing
state for all possible non-absorbing starting states.

$$
B = NR = \begin{matrix} 0 \\ 1 \\ 2 \\ 3 \end{matrix} \begin{bmatrix} 1 & .81 & .71 & .66 \\ 0 & 1 & .88 & .82 \\ 0 & 0 & 1 & .93 \\ 0 & 0 & 0 & 1 \end{bmatrix} \begin{bmatrix} .19 & 0 \\ .12 & 0 \\ .07 & 0 \\ .03 & .97 \end{bmatrix} = \begin{matrix} G \quad\;\; F \\ \begin{bmatrix} .36 & .64 \\ .21 & .79 \\ .10 & .90 \\ .03 & .97 \end{bmatrix} \end{matrix}
$$

This tells us that we can expect 36 per cent of released prisoners to be
back in gaol within the next four years, that of those that are free for at
least one year we can still expect 21 per cent to return to gaol and so on.

It is a simple matter to calculate the mean length of freedom for those that are going to serve another sentence. We have shown that the mean length of time from release to absorption is 3.18 years; we know that if an individual does not return to gaol it takes 4 steps to absorption and that we can expect 36 per cent of the population to return to gaol.

Hence

$$3.18 = (.64)\,4 + .36x,$$

where x is the mean length of time that recidivists are free, and therefore

$$x = 1.72.$$

The model predicts that 36 per cent of all released prisoners will return to gaol and the mean time after release to this return is 1.72 years.

Of course this model would only be of use in planning prison facilities if we could assume that the transition probabilities would remain constant through time or if we knew how they were likely to change. In this latter case we might be able to use such a model to simulate what would happen to prison populations if the police became more or less efficient, or judges' sentencing policies were to become more lenient or more severe.

It is also quite likely that prisoners are not sufficiently alike for the Markov assumptions to give reasonable results. Just as Blumen *et al.* thought that the presence of two distinct groups of people (movers and stayers) might explain the deficiencies of their social-mobility model so it is likely that there may be groups of prisoners with very different probabilities of being recidivists. This can be seen by looking at the recidivism rates associated with different offences. We would guess that some crimes, perhaps an example might be the murder or manslaughter of one's spouse, might be one-off jobs. The police might put more effort into the discovery of culprits for certain types of crime rather than others. The *modus operandi* of criminals in certain types of crime may be very recognizable and hence re-arrest more likely.

Exercise

The reader may like to compare the results we obtained above, which were derived from data on prisoners released after serving sentences for all kinds of offences, to those which can be obtained from more detailed data from Indiana. It seems that forgers and embezzlers have relatively high recidivism rates while robbers have below-average recidivism rates. The transition probability matrices for this exercise are: for embezzlement and forgery

	G	F	0	1	2	3
G	1	0	0	0	0	0
F	0	1	0	0	0	0
0	.30	0	0	.70	0	0
1	.16	0	0	0	.84	0
2	.07	0	0	0	0	.93
3	.04	.96	0	0	0	0

;

and for robbery

	G	F	0	1	2	3
G	1	0	0	0	0	0
F	0	1	0	0	0	0
0	.09	0	0	.91	0	0
1	.01	0	0	0	.99	0
2	.12	0	0	0	0	.88
3	.04	.96	0	0	0	0

.

While there would be a lot of work to do before a model like this could usefully portray the immense complexities of the penal system, many researchers think that this kind of approach may well prove very fruitful.

Conformity to Group Pressure

Our second example of absorbing Markov chains in action is probably the most famous example of the use of these chains to describe a social process. This is a study undertaken by Cohen,* a social psychologist, of the behaviour of individuals when subjected to group pressure. His experiment started by sitting an innocent human guinea-pig at the end of a row of seven well-trained liars. Two cards were held up in front of this group. On one of these cards was a single black line, the standard line, and on the other there were three black lines including one of obviously the same length as the standard line. All members of the group were asked

* B. P. Cohen, *Conflict and Conformity: A Probability Model and its Application*, MIT Press, Cambridge, Mass., 1963.

to name out loud which of the three lines they thought was of equal length to the standard line. The stooges answered in turn and before the innocent, and gave a unanimous wrong answer, thus supposedly subjecting the naive person to group pressure. After the answers had been given, a new identical set of cards was produced and the experiment repeated. Cohen noticed that well within thirty-five repetitions of the experiment all his innocent subjects settled down to giving consistently the same answer. In the end they were always non-conformist, standing out against the group pressure by answering correctly, or else they became conformist, bowed to the pressure of the group, and always gave the same wrong answer as the stooges. Before this stage was reached many of the subjects changed answers from the correct one to the majority verdict and vice versa several times. For instance one subject gave the following series of answers TTTMMTTTMMMTTTTMTTTTTTTTTTTTTTTTTTT where T stands for the true answer and M for the false majority verdict.

Cohen tried to view the process as an absorbing Markov chain. Eventually everybody is a permanent conformist or a permanent non-conformist so there are two absorbing states. At first, however, individuals are only temporary non-conformists or conformists and can change states. Thus we can draw a transition probability matrix for the chain.

		1	2	3	4
Permanent non-conformist	1	1	0	0	0
Permanent conformist	2	0	1	0	0
Temporary non-conformist	3	p_{31}	0	p_{33}	p_{34}
Temporary conformist	4	0	p_{42}	p_{43}	p_{44}

The zeros in the bottom left-hand segment (R) indicate that Cohen assumed reasonably that an individual could not go straight from being a temporary non-conformist to a permanent conformist without passing through the stage of temporary conformist.

The model creates a difficult problem because the experiments do not give direct observations of which state an individual is in. The states in the transition matrix are states of mind and all that is observed is the subject's answers to questions. This difficulty can be illustrated by attempting to translate the particular sequence of answers written out above into the subject's state of mind. The first part of the sequence is easy because his state of mind must obviously be temporary since the answer changes several times. Thus we know that for the first seventeen experiments he moves from state to state in the following way,

33344333444333343, where 3 stands for being a temporary non-conformist and 4 for being a temporary conformist. We do not know what happens after this. We presume that eventually he arrives in state 1, as a permanent non-conformist, but cannot tell when the transition to this state takes place. This is a common problem for many models of human behaviour because the concepts used are often not directly observable. Indeed it is more pervasive than might first be thought. In the fictitious example we used to explain the mathematics of absorbing chains of the letter travelling from Leicester to London we assumed we knew when a letter was lost. To estimate the transition probabilities all we can do is to see whether on any day the letter is delivered or observable in either of the two sorting houses. If it is not delivered after a long period of time we may presume it is lost but we cannot know exactly when it was lost.

The problem is not insurmountable but it requires a good deal of ingenuity to get round it. Certainly we cannot use the model in the same way that Blumen and friends used their model of social mobility. If we cannot recognize which state the process is in then we cannot estimate transition probabilities from what happens in the first step and then test the model by examining what would happen if these probabilities remained constant in the future and compare these predictions to what actually happened. We shall not go into the technicalities here but will try to give a crude indication of one way round the problem. Basically we use all the information, the whole sequence of answers for all the guinea-pigs in Cohen's experiments rather than just the first step, to get estimates for the transition probabilities. Thus, for instance, rather than predicting the proportions of chains finishing in the various absorbing states (matrix B) from transition probability estimates, we can use the actual data to observe matrix B and attempt to deduce the probabilities that would explain such results occurring. But what do we do with these estimates? We cannot then use these estimates to predict the proportions finishing in each absorbing state because these predictions would be bound to correspond to what was observed in the experiment, since the probabilities were estimated from this information. Either we must use these estimated transition probabilities to predict the outcome of a different set of experiments or devise predictive tests for the original experiments that are not bound to succeed. Kemeny and Snell,* in a development of Cohen's work, chose to do the latter and, with their estimated transition probabili-

* J. G. Kemeny and J. L. Snell, *Mathematical Models in the Social Sciences*, Ginn & Co., Boston, 1962.

ties and the help of some mathematics again a little too sophisticated to be dealt with here, predicted the number of subjects that one would expect to have made a specific number of switches from one state to another. The number of such switches is observable directly and the procedure is legitimate since this information was not used to estimate the probabilities. Suffice it to say that they found that their absorbing Markov chain model was in reasonable agreement with Cohen's observations.

Exercise

As an exercise in arithmetic here is Kemeny and Snell's estimated transition probability matrix for Cohen's experiment.

		1	2	3	4
Permanent non-conformist	1	1	0	0	0
Permanent conformist	2	0	1	0	0
Temporary non-conformist	3	.06	0	.63	.31
Temporary conformist	4	0	.05	.46	.49

$$= \begin{bmatrix} I & 0 \\ R & Q \end{bmatrix}$$

The reader is recommended to compute the matrix $N = (I - Q)^{-1}$, the matrix $B = NR$ and the vector $t = Ne$ and give interpretations to their elements. If your arithmetic is correct you may well find yourself shocked by the susceptibility of the guinea-pigs, who were in fact students, to group pressure. (You should find that, on average, it took about 18 repeats of the experiment before a guinea-pig made up his or her mind. In addition, about 34 per cent of those that started as non-conformist bowed to group pressure in the end, and about 40 per cent of those originally conforming finished as conformists despite the evidence of their own eyes.)

A Review of the Problems Encountered in Markov Models

We saw in chapter seven that the original Markov chain model of industrial mobility by Blumen, Kogan and McCarthy was poor at forecasting the number of people staying in an industry. The consistent underestimation of this number led to them developing their mover-stayer model. This underprediction of elements in the main diagonal is indeed common to many studies that use Markov processes to analyse social actions and this perhaps points to a general weakness in the method. One of the fields in which workers have often noted this *deficient diagonal* is that of market research.* To estimate the eventual market share of a particular brand of goods, market researchers examine the way in which consumers change brands from one purchase to the next. Transition probabilities are estimated from these observations, assumed to remain constant in the future, and a Markov process is then used to predict the future sales of the various brands. These predictions tend to underestimate the number of individuals loyal to the same brand.

Coleman† gives an example of this form the United States from some observations on a sequence of three purchases of something called 'pancake mix' by a number of people whom chauvinistically Coleman refers to as housewives. There were three brands of this apparently popular food. The transition probabilities estimated from the first two in the sequence of purchases were

$$\begin{array}{c} \\ \text{Brand X} \\ \text{Brand Y} \\ \text{Brand Z} \end{array} \begin{array}{ccc} X & Y & Z \\ \left[\begin{array}{ccc} .72 & .17 & .11 \\ .16 & .66 & .18 \\ .09 & .16 & .74 \end{array}\right] \end{array} = P.$$

That is of those buying brand X at the first observation 72 per cent bought it again next time they bought pancake mix, 17 per cent bought Y and 11 per cent bought Z.

Now we know that if these probabilities remain constant P^2 will tell us the proportion of people, divided into categories according to their first purchase, buying X, Y and Z for the third purchase. Matrix multiplication yields

$$P^2 = \left[\begin{array}{ccc} .55 & .25 & .20 \\ .24 & .49 & .27 \\ .16 & .24 & .60 \end{array}\right],$$

and we can compare this matrix with the observed proportions of

---

*For a survey of the use of Markov chains in analysing what goods people buy see W. F. Massey, D. B. Montgomery and D. G. Morrison, *Stochastic Models of Buying Behavior*, MIT Press, Cambridge, Mass., 1970.

† J. S. Coleman, *The Mathematics of Collective Action*, Heinemann, London, 1973.

individuals buying the various brands on the third purchase

$$
\begin{array}{c}
& \textit{3rd purchase} \\
& \begin{array}{ccc} \text{X} & \text{Y} & \text{Z} \end{array} \\
\textit{1st purchase} \begin{array}{c} \text{X} \\ \text{Y} \\ \text{Z} \end{array} &
\left[\begin{array}{ccc}
.67 & .20 & .13 \\
.21 & .58 & .21 \\
.10 & .16 & .74
\end{array} \right].
\end{array}
$$

We can see that all the elements on the diagonal of P^2 are much less than those on the diagonal of the observed matrix, and all the off-diagonal elements are overestimated. Thus we have a deficient diagonal.

We have discussed two methods that could be used to amend the model and perhaps give better results. The first was that of the mover–stayer model. In general this method assumes that there are two distinct groups of individuals – one with significantly higher probabilities of changing brands than the other. In the industrial mobility model we took the extreme assumption that the probability of the group of stayers moving between industries was zero. Intuitively, we can see that this method has a tendency to help remedy the problem of the deficient diagonal. After the first step the people left in an industry or still buying the same particular brand of pancake mix will contain a higher proportion than previously of the group with a low probability of moving or changing pancake mix. Hence we would expect such a model to produce a higher estimate of people staying in the same industry or displaying brand loyalty in future time periods. As one might imagine, researchers with rather more mathematical sophistication than ourselves have developed the model to allow for more than two groups of the subjects having different transition probabilities. This leads to difficulties not only in the mathematical formulation of the models but also in estimating the size of such groups and their respective transition probabilities. We have to be careful that we do not use all the data to estimate these probabilities and leave none against which to test the predictive worth of the model.

The second method of attacking the problem is to consider the process as an absorbing rather than a regular chain. We have seen how this works. Effectively since all individuals have a chance of being absorbed (in the pancake example this means eventually showing complete brand loyalty to one particular mix) the proportion of people remaining in one state with no chance of moving will increase. Thus if we could estimate the transition probabilities to absorbing states we might remedy the problem of the deficient diagonal. We have also seen that this method creates other difficult if not insoluble problems in that the absorbing states are often states of mind and not directly observable. The idea that movers may eventually become stayers is appealing but it is difficult to identify when this transformation takes place. A deeper analysis of this problem requires the flexing of mathematical muscles slightly larger than those we are using.

These two modifications still have much in common with the basic Markov model. The probability of going from one state to another is simply dependent on the state in which we start. History prior to this is irrelevant. This may well be an accurate portrayal of some processes but will not be an adequate description of others. The probability of purchasing brand X after having previously purchased brand Y may well depend upon whether one has tried brand Z before or not. Similarly the determinants of mobility from one industry to another may to some extent depend on the whole previous pattern and experience of the worker concerned. To construct models allowing for this means setting up what are called higher-order Markov chains. Chains of first order have transition probabilities merely depending on the state the process is in presently; the probabilities in a second-order chain depend on the present state and the state the process was in one step before the present. We shall not go into details but can note that this method has had some success in analysing our market-research problem of examining how consumers switch between brands of goods.*

For different reasons all of these developments of the basic model result in the transition probabilities of moving from one observable state to another changing with time. We now turn to one example of a field of study where we may suppose that not only will probabilities change as a result of an individual's experience but also because the individual's environment changes.

The Spread of News

We discussed a model of the spread of rumour in chapter 6. The rumour was of a special kind in that it was either passed on in the form X is true or X is false. We concentrated on the outcome of the process in the sense of learning the proportion of people hearing that X was true and the proportion hearing that X was false. Most information is not of this

---

* For instance you can find the use of a higher-order chain to examine the purchasing of various brands of coffee in R. G. Frank, 'Brand Choice as a Probability Process', *Journal of Business*, Vol. 35, pp. 43–56, 1962.

kind. While messages may be distorted as they pass from individual to individual, distortion does not have to take the form of reversal. Now we concentrate on the description of the spread of the news rather than its content or accuracy. The first obvious question to ask is what determines the number of people learning the news. In our rumour model we assumed that each person passes on the rumour to just one other person who has previously heard nothing. Presumably this would go on until everybody in the population had heard one or other version of the rumour. The chain could, of course, be broken by somebody not relaying the news but we have nothing in the model to tell us when to expect such a break in the chain. To analyse the diffusion of information we must replace this assumption by something telling us more about the nature of gossip.

It seems reasonable to suppose that when gossips spread a particular piece of news they do so with more eagerness at first than later. This is because the news begins to lack topicality and becomes stale. A successful gossip does not tell news to people who already know it. Meeting people who know your new stops you telling it to more other people. We shall try to use this simple idea to build a model to explain some observed data on the spread of information.

In the 1950s the United States Air Force sponsored a series of experiments labelled 'Project Revere'. The basic objective behind this project was to gauge the effectiveness of dropping information from the air as a way of diffusing news through a population. One of the experiments started by telling forty-two out of 210 women in a village a slogan about some brand of coffee. They were asked to tell other women the slogan and were told that there would be a free pound of coffee for every woman that knew the slogan when the researchers returned. On calling back a couple of days later the interviewers were able to classify the women in the village according to whether they had received the information at all, heard it from one of the 'source women' or heard it second-hand, third-hand etc. Labelling those who heard first-hand as 1, second-hand as 2 and so on, and those who remained ignorant as I, the results could be tabulated as follows.

	1	2	3	4	5	I	TOTAL
Number of women	69	53	14	2	4	26	168

Nobody had heard the slogan at more than fifth-hand from source and twenty-six women remained in complete ignorance. The researchers believed that they had given sufficient time for the spreading of the news to have stopped; in other words that the news was completely stale before all members of the community had heard it. The experimenters were interested in what we shall call the generation (1, 2, 3, 4, 5) of the hearer, as well as the number remaining ignorant because the accuracy of the news is likely to diminish the more people the message has passed through.

We shall try to explain the distribution in the table above by means of our assumption about the nature of gossip. Firstly, we suppose that every woman is likely to meet all the other women with equal probability and that every woman meets another woman with the same regularity. Given that we know nothing about the social life of this village, this is the obvious assumption to make. If in fact the twenty-six who were not told the slogans were social outcasts or recluses then we would expect our model to predict badly the distribution of hearers. Secondly, we assume that if people know the news they tell it to anybody they meet, until they meet somebody who also knows the news. Immediately, then, they regard the news as having become stale and never mention it to anybody else – nobody in the village wants to be a purveyor of old news. Thus at any time we have a number of people spreading the news (gossips), a number of ex-gossips effectively stifling the spread of news (stiflers), and others totally ignorant of the news. The probability of an individual moving from the state of ignorance to that of being a gossip, and from being a gossip to that of a stifler obviously depends on the relative number of individuals in these three states. Thus the transition probabilities between such states do not remain constant through time. However, knowing the relative numbers in each state at the beginning of the process and hence the transition probabilities at the beginning, we should be able to trace the way these probabilities change and thus examine the outcome of the process.

We define G_0, G_1, G_2, G_3 and so on as being states of active gossiping – the subscript 0 meaning one heard the slogan directly from the researchers, 1 meaning one heard it from one of the forty-two women told originally, 2 meaning one heard it second-hand and so on. Similarly S_0, S_1, S_2 and so on are states of being a stifler of news – the subscript 0 meaning one had been one of the forty-two original gossips, 1 meaning one had been a first-generation gossip and so on.

These S states are, of course, absorbing states. Finally we define the state I as being in ignorance of the news.

We start with .2 of the population (42 out of 210) knowing the news and take the length of a step in the process to be the length of time between a woman of the village meeting any other woman. The probability, in the first step, of a gossip meeting and imparting the message to an ignorant is .8, and of meeting another gossip and thus becoming a stifler is .2. Since in the first step nobody can become a higher-generation gossip than first we can draw the transition probability matrix thus:

$$
\begin{array}{c}
 \\
From
\end{array}
\begin{array}{c}
 \\
S_0 \\
G_0 \\
G_1 \\
I
\end{array}
\overset{\textit{To}}{
\begin{array}{cccc}
S_0 & G_0 & G_1 & I \\
\end{array}}
\left[
\begin{array}{cccc}
1 & 0 & 0 & 0 \\
.2 & .8 & 0 & 0 \\
0 & 0 & 1 & 0 \\
0 & 0 & .2 & .8
\end{array}
\right] = P_1.
$$

(There is nobody in G_1 at the start of the first step so it does not matter what probabilities we put in the G_1 row – rather than leave it blank we have put zeros in all the columns except G_1 in which we have entered 1.)

The matrix is just a convenient way of summarizing what happens when people first meet after the news has been imparted. Alternatively we could draw a tree diagram.

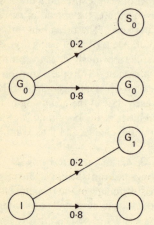

Now, as we have done before in several examples, we can find the proportion of people in each state by premultiplying this transition probability matrix by the starting vector of the proportions in each state.

This starting vector is

$$
\begin{array}{cccc}
S_0 & G_0 & G_1 & I \\
\end{array}
\left[
\begin{array}{cccc}
0 & .2 & 0 & .8
\end{array}
\right] = f_1,
$$

and so at the start of the second step our new starting vector is

$$f_1 P_1 = \begin{bmatrix} S_0 & G_0 & G_1 & I \\ .04 & .16 & .16 & .64 \end{bmatrix}.$$

Knowing these proportions we can calculate the transition probability matrix for the second step. For instance an ignorant will have a .16 chance of becoming a first-generation gossip, a .16 chance of becoming a second-generation gossip and a .68 chance (.64 + .04 since neither stiflers nor other ignorants mention the news) of remaining ignorant. So we have

$$\begin{array}{c} \\ S_0 \\ S_1 \\ G_0 \\ G_1 \\ G_2 \\ I \end{array} \begin{bmatrix} S_0 & S_1 & G_0 & G_1 & G_2 & I \\ 1 & 0 & 0 & 0 & 0 & 0 \\ 0 & 1 & 0 & 0 & 0 & 0 \\ .36 & 0 & .64 & 0 & 0 & 0 \\ 0 & .36 & 0 & .64 & 0 & 0 \\ 0 & 0 & 0 & 0 & 1 & 0 \\ 0 & 0 & 0 & .16 & .16 & .68 \end{bmatrix} = P_2.$$

Premultiplying P_2 by the starting vector for this second step

$$\begin{bmatrix} S_0 & S_1 & G_0 & G_1 & G_2 & I \\ .04 & 0 & .16 & .16 & 0 & .64 \end{bmatrix} = f_2,$$

we get the new expected proportion of women in each state

$$\begin{bmatrix} S_0 & S_1 & G_0 & G_1 & G_2 & I \\ .098 & .058 & .102 & .204 & .102 & .435 \end{bmatrix} = f_2 P_2.$$

We can repeat this process over and over again. This is equivalent to putting more and more branches on our tree diagram. As you can see the tree is going to look more confusing after every meeting. (As an exercise the reader should calculate the probabilities associated with the branches of the tree for the third meeting.)

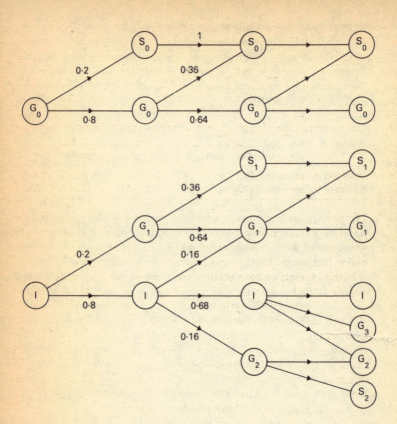

By repeating the calculations we started above we can work out P_3, P_4 and so on. After seven 'meetings' my pocket calculator came up with the following vector of proportions in each state.

$$\begin{bmatrix} S_0 & S_1 & S_2 & S_3 & S_4 & S_5 & S_6 \\ .200 & .321 & .235 & .091 & .020 & .009 & .001 \end{bmatrix}$$

$$\begin{bmatrix} & & & & & & G_0 & G_1 & G_2 & G_3 & G_4 & G_5 & G_6 & G_7 & I \\ & & & & & & 0 & 0 & .001 & .001 & .001 & .001 & 0 & 0 & .125 \end{bmatrix}$$

The process of news spreading is obviously coming to an end. To all intents and purposes there is a negligible number of gossips left and we are left with a substantial number of ignorant people. From this vector we can calculate how many of the 168 women in the village, not told the slogan originally, we should expect to remain ignorant, be first-, second-, third-, fourth- and fifth-generation hearers and compare these expected frequencies to those actually observed in the Project Revere experiment. (Since there are no gossips left we get this information from the values of S_1, S_2, S_3, S_4, S_5 and I.)

| | Generation of hearer | | | | | | |
	1st	2nd	3rd	4th	5th	Ignorant	Total
Observed in experiment	69	53	14	2	4	26	168
Predicted by our model	67.4	49.3	19.1	4.2	1.9	26.1	168

The predictions look very close to the numbers actually observed. A statistical test comparing these two distributions (known as the χ^2 test*) would tell us they are sufficiently alike for us not to want to reject the notion that our model was a true portrayal of the actual process.

In this example we have obtained estimates of transition probabilities not from data but from the assumptions of our model. The two assumptions that anybody is as likely to meet a particular person as everybody else, and that people stop relaying news as soon as they meet someone who already knows it, determined these probabilities. It may be a little surprising that two such extreme assumptions gave such good results and, of course, it may just be coincidence. However, we can be very optimistic that models with this kind of approach may be of considerable use in looking at social processes like the spread of news,† fashions and the growth and decline in purchases of new consumer goods.

---

* Calculation would tell us that $\chi^2 = 1.68$. We must amalgamate the hearers of the fourth and fifth generation because the expected numbers of these are so small. The critical value from χ^2 distribution tables is 9.49, at the 5 per cent level of significance, and because 1.68 is less than 9.49 this tells us we cannot reject the model as postulated.

Readers who have not heard of this test but would like to know more about it can consult any statistics text book such as Peter Sprent, *Statistics in Action*, Penguin, Harmondsworth, 1977 (chapter 3).

† Readers with very large mathematical armouries might consult chapter 8 of D. J. Bartholomew, *Stochastic Models of Social Processes*, Wiley, New York, 1967, where models of this type are set out in a very formal manner.

There is a close resemblance between this kind of model and the models used very successfully by medical statisticians to examine the spread of epidemic diseases. Replace the word news by measles and classify people as carriers, former sufferers now immune, and potential sufferers and you will see there is a very close analogy.

Exercise

Suppose we were quite wrong in supposing that news was stifled in the village. Instead let us suppose that if people knew the news they always transmitted it, but there was basically only time for four 'meetings' before the researchers came back to collect their results. Show that this model would predict the following table.

Generation of hearer				Ignorant
1	2	3	4	
84.8	59.2	16.6	1.7	5.9

Compare these results with those observed in the experiment.

10
The Seven Ages of Man and Population Problems

Life itself can readily be seen as an absorbing Markov chain. Sadly not everybody gets through all of Shakespeare's seven ages,* but all people once born embark upon the process of moving from one age to the next or to the absorbing state of death. This is a rather special and simple chain, in that unless at any time we die we move through the states (or ages) in strict chronological order.†

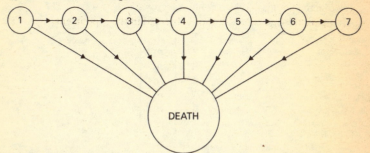

Let us construct a transition matrix that gives our chances of survival through the seven ages.

		Age Now							
		1	2	3	4	5	6	7	
	Infant, mewling and puking	1	0	0	0	0	0	0	0	
	Whining schoolboy	2	s_1	0	0	0	0	0	0	
Age	Lover, sighing like a furnace	3	0	s_2	0	0	0	0	0	= S
Next	Soldier, full of strange oaths	4	0	0	s_3	0	0	0	0	
	Justice, in fair round belly	5	0	0	0	s_4	0	0	0	
	Slipper'd pantaloon	6	0	0	0	0	s_5	0	0	
	Second childishness	7	0	0	0	0	0	s_6	0	

Survival Matrix

---

* See *As You Like It*, Act II, Scene vii.

† Our example of recidivism in prisons happens to be a chain of this kind. Ex-convicts could not be 'three years free' before they had been 'two years free', but there were two absorbing states in that example.

'Age now' is given by the columns and 'age next' is the rows. In all our previous examples and exercises we have gone from rows as 'now' to columns as 'next'. I am not being deliberately perverse in changing at this time, but merely following the convention of demographers who use matrices of this type. You will notice that we have not included the absorbing state of death in this survival matrix. All that can happen to a person in state i is to go next to state $i + 1$ or die. This means that the only non-zero entries in the transition matrix are the elements immediately below the main diagonal. Thus s_1 represents the probability of surviving from age 1 to 2; s_2 represents the probability of surviving from age 2 to age 3 and so on.

Now let us suppose that we start with a particular population in a country and that we have broken it down into the seven ages. We can describe the population by a column vector.

$$N_0 = \begin{array}{c} 1 \\ 2 \\ 3 \\ 4 \\ 5 \\ 6 \\ 7 \end{array} \begin{bmatrix} n_1 \\ n_2 \\ n_3 \\ n_4 \\ n_5 \\ n_6 \\ n_7 \end{bmatrix}$$

So at time 0 there are n_1 people in age 1 etc. If we want to find out how many of this existing population we can expect to survive into the next stage we merely postmultiply the survival matrix S by N_0.

$$SN_0 = \begin{array}{c} 1 \\ 2 \\ 3 \\ 4 \\ 5 \\ 6 \\ 7 \end{array} \begin{bmatrix} 0 \\ s_1\, n_1 \\ s_2\, n_2 \\ s_3\, n_3 \\ s_4\, n_4 \\ s_5\, n_5 \\ s_6\, n_6 \end{bmatrix}$$

(Obviously, if a proportion s_1 of those in age 1 can be expected to survive until age 2, then of the existing n_1 people in age 1 we can expect $s_1 n_1$ to survive to age 2.)

Whether SN_0 represents our expected future population depends on whether or not there are new entries into the population through birth or immigration, or people leaving through emigration. Keeping things simple, let us suppose that the society we are considering is closed – nobody leaves or enters – and that we can expect b_0 people to be born and hence enter age 1 while the current population is moving up an age or dying. Let us denote the vector

$$
\begin{array}{c}
1 \\
2 \\
3 \\
4 \\
5 \\
6 \\
7
\end{array}
\begin{bmatrix}
b_0 \\
0 \\
0 \\
0 \\
0 \\
0 \\
0
\end{bmatrix}
$$

as b.

Now if we add b to SN_0 we are adding new entrants to the society to those who are already there and have survived.* Thus, our new population is

$$
N_1 = b + SN_0 =
\begin{bmatrix}
b_0 \\
s_1\, n_1 \\
s_2\, n_2 \\
s_3\, n_3 \\
s_4\, n_4 \\
s_5\, n_5 \\
s_6\, n_6
\end{bmatrix}.
$$

Suppose that, as we move from this new stage to the next, exactly the same number of births are expected to take place. Repeating the same operation we have just performed we have

$$
\begin{aligned}
N_2 &= b + SN_1 \\
&= b + S\,(b + SN_0) \\
&= b + Sb + S^2 N_0.
\end{aligned}
$$

* Migration would not greatly complicate matters. The elements in b would be the *net* new entry into each age class.

And if b is expected to be constant into the foreseeable future we could similarly write

$$N_3 = b + Sb + S^2b + S^3N_0,$$

and

$$N_t = b + Sb + S^2b + \ldots S^{t-1}b + S^tN_0$$
$$= (I + S + S^2 + \ldots S^{t-1})b + S^tN_0.$$

We have seen before what happens to certain matrices when they are raised to successively higher and higher powers – the matrix tends towards a matrix with zeros everywhere. In the case of a survival matrix such as ours, the result is perhaps a little more dramatic. If there are, for instance, seven age classes then S^7, or indeed any higher power of S, is actually a matrix with zeros everywhere. It is fairly obvious that this must be so. In a society, like the one we are considering, where the number of births is *independent* of the current population, the population at time $0(N_0)$ can only influence the size of the future population while people from this population survive. Since, if there are seven ages, there are no survivors from the initial population in N_7 then

$$S^7N_0 = \begin{bmatrix} 0 \\ 0 \\ . \\ . \\ . \\ 0 \end{bmatrix} \text{ and } S^7 = \begin{bmatrix} 0 \end{bmatrix}.$$

This means that for t at least as large as the number of age classes;

so
$$N_t = (I + S^2 + \ldots S^{t-1})b$$
$$SN_t = (S + S^2 + S^3 + \ldots S^t)b.$$

Subtracting we have

$$N_t - SN_t = b - S^tb = b \text{ (since } S^t = [0])$$
$$(I - S)N_t = b$$
$$N_t = (I - S)^{-1}b.$$

$(I - S)^{-1}$ is, of course, the fundamental matrix* of an absorbing Markov chain and we could use it as we have done before.

$(I - S)^{-1}b$ tells us how many people we could expect to be in each age category if the whole population is to be stationary. This is the same as the number of people that we can expect to survive to each age class from some given number of new births.

To compute $(I - S)^{-1}$ is easy no matter how many age classes we have. For instance, suppose there are four age classes so

$$S = \begin{bmatrix} 0 & 0 & 0 & 0 \\ s_1 & 0 & 0 & 0 \\ 0 & s_2 & 0 & 0 \\ 0 & 0 & s_3 & 0 \end{bmatrix}.$$

We now know that

$$(I - S)^{-1} = I + S + S^2 + S^3$$

(S^4, S^5 are matrices with zeroes everywhere).

So

$$(I - S)^{-1} = \begin{bmatrix} 1 & 0 & 0 & 0 \\ 0 & 1 & 0 & 0 \\ 0 & 0 & 1 & 0 \\ 0 & 0 & 0 & 1 \end{bmatrix} + \begin{bmatrix} 0 & 0 & 0 & 0 \\ s_1 & 0 & 0 & 0 \\ 0 & s_2 & 0 & 0 \\ 0 & 0 & s_3 & 0 \end{bmatrix} + \begin{bmatrix} 0 & 0 & 0 & 0 \\ 0 & 0 & 0 & 0 \\ s_1 s_2 & 0 & 0 & 0 \\ 0 & s_2 s_3 & 0 & 0 \end{bmatrix}$$

$$+ \begin{bmatrix} 0 & 0 & 0 & 0 \\ 0 & 0 & 0 & 0 \\ 0 & 0 & 0 & 0 \\ s_1 s_2 s_3 & 0 & 0 & 0 \end{bmatrix} = \begin{bmatrix} 1 & 0 & 0 & 0 \\ s_1 & 1 & 0 & 0 \\ s_1 s_2 & s_2 & 1 & 0 \\ s_1 s_2 s_3 & s_2 s_3 & s_3 & 1 \end{bmatrix}.$$

---

* Rather it is the transpose of what we previously called the fundamental matrix (see p. 125) because we have changed rows and columns around.

(*Exercise*: Use the elementary row operation method of finding an inverse to invert $(I - S)$. Your method will show you how easy it is to invert any matrix that has elements that are all zero on one side of the main diagonal.)

We can give an explanation of the pattern of $(I - S)^{-1}$ by reminding ourselves of one of the results from our discussion of the theory of absorbing Markov chains. We showed that for starting in a particular state the expected time before absorption was the sum of the elements in the row in the fundamental matrix that corresponded to that state. Remembering that we have transposed rows and columns this means that the sum of the elements in column 1, for instance, of $(I - S)^{-1}$ gives the life expectancy of a person in age class 1, and the sum of the elements in column 2 gives the life expectancy of someone in age class 2 now and so on.

For example, the sum of the elements in column 1 is

$$1 + s_1 + s_1 s_2 + s_1 s_2 s_3 :$$

s_1 is the probability of survival to age 2 from age 1; $s_1 s_2$ is the probability of survival to age 3 from age 1; $s_1 s_2 s_3$ is the probability of survival to age 4 from age 1.

Adding these gives the expected further age a person will reach. In fact it gives an overestimate of life expectancy in that the above would only be strictly true if all deaths took place at the end of an age class. If deaths take place roughly evenly within an age class we would get a better estimate of life expectation by subtracting half the length of an age from this sum.

Let us look at what we have been doing again and consider some possible extensions by considering an actual population. We shall look at China – the largest country in the world and one with a very active population policy.

The People's Republic of China*

China's census in 1982 revealed that the country contained just under one quarter of the world's population. (Anybody who has attempted to walk down the Nanjing Road in Shanghai or visited the Great Wall just north of Beijing will readily believe that one quarter of the human race chose

---

* Nobody who learns anything about, let alone visits, China can fail to be fascinated by it. A good background to modern China and its population problems and policies is David Bonavia, *The Chinese*, Penguin, Harmondsworth, 1982 (revised edition).

the same day as themselves.) From the revolution in 1949 when the population was roughly 550 million it grew to over 1000 million in 1982. For much of this period the average female gave birth to five or six children; infant mortality rates have dropped dramatically as a result of public health work and rural medical care in the hands of what are known as barefoot doctors; and people of all ages have benefited from a general rise in health care, programmes of epidemic disease control, more food and better living conditions.

From the early 1970s the Chinese leaders have regarded the high growth rate of the population as a serious problem and the seriousness with which the problem is taken can be seen by the recent advent of the radical policy of the one-child family. Before analysing this policy using matrices, let us look at the present Chinese population with the help of the concepts we developed in the last section.

By looking at age-specific deaths in 1978, Chinese demographers have calculated the probability of survival from one age class to the next. To keep things relatively simple I have used rather wide age classes (ten years) and have averaged the survival rates of men and women.

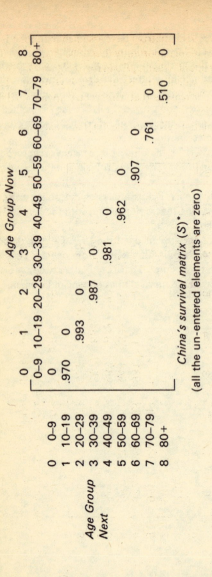

China's survival matrix (S)*
(all the un-entered elements are zero)

*The survival rates have been derived from census tables given in Tian Xueyuen, 'On changes in the age composition of the population and policy options for population planning', *Social Sciences in China*, Vol. V, No. 3, 1984.

To compile this survival matrix I have assumed that nobody lives beyond the age of 90, and more importantly that to be in age class 0 a person has to be a surviving infant – that is .970 in row 2 column 1 is the survival rate of a person who will live to be at least 1 year old. (I am ignoring infant mortality for reasons that will become apparent when we look at population policies.)

Routine calculation gives us the fundamental matrix $(I-S)^{-1}$ for China.

	0	1	2	3	4	5	6	7	8
0	1								
1	.970	1							
2	.963	.993	1						
3	.951	.980	.987	1					
4	.933	.961	.968	.981	1				
5	.897	.925	.931	.944	.962	1			
6	.814	.839	.845	.856	.873	.907	1		
7	.619	.638	.643	.651	.664	.690	.761	1	
8	.316	.325	.328	.332	.339	.352	.388	.510	1
Column Sums	7.46	6.66	5.70	4.76	3.84	2.95	2.15	1.51	1

The fundamental matrix $(I-S)^{-1}$ for China (elements un-entered are all zero)

Since the age classes are ten years long we can get an estimate of life expectancy in years by subtracting .5 from the column sums and multiplying by 10. Thus somebody aged 0 (but provided they are going to live to at least the age of 1 year old) can expect to live for 69.6 years, and somebody aged 10 can expect to live for another 61.6 years and so on.

The first column shows the proportion of any particular surviving infant group that can be expected to survive to further age groups. Multiplying this column by 100 million say will give us $(I - S)^{-1}b$, where

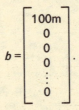

We have constructed what is known to demographers as a life table, showing the numbers from some given group that can be expected to survive to the various future age groups and the life expectancy of the different age groups.

			Number expected to survive to age group in millions	Further expectation of life, from age at beginning of age groups, in years
	0–9	0	100	69.6
	10–19	1	97	61.6
	20–29	2	96.3	52.0
	30–39	3	95.1	42.6
Age groups	40–49	4	93.3	33.4
	50–59	5	89.7	24.5
	60–69	6	81.4	16.5
	70–79	7	61.9	10.1
	80+	8	31.6	5.0

Life Table

Exercise

You might like to compare the life chances of surviving infants in modern China to those in the United Kingdom today and some time ago. The diagram below indicates approximate survival rates for male children reaching the age of 5 into higher age groups. The figures relate to 1982 (the top arrow) and 1902 (the bottom arrow) and are derived from statistics issued by the UK Office of Population Censuses and Surveys and published in the *Annual Abstract of Statistics* 1985 edition.

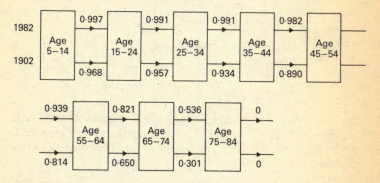

Construct life tables for the UK male for 1982 and 1902 and compare them with that of modern China.

Fertility and Leslie Matrices

China has a very active and definite population policy. Its long-term aim is to stabilize the population at about 900 million people by the middle of the next century, with the interim aim of keeping the population below 1200 million at the end of this century. If the mortality rates, or survival rates that we have been using, stay roughly the same then the crucial determinant of the future population will be the births in any year. If China succeeds in stabilizing its population we already know what the structure of such a population must look like. There will be the same number of births every year and these will exactly match the number of deaths. The age structure will look like our column vector $(I - S)^{-1}b$ for a fixed number of births – or equivalently we can get the relative proportion of the numbers that must be in each age class by reading down the life table.

This gives us a picture of the age structure of the population China is eventually aiming for.

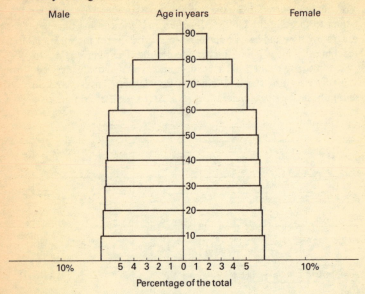

(We have assumed, for simplicity, that equal numbers of male and female children are born, and that men and women have the same survival rates.)

We can look at the age structure of China at the moment from figures taken from the 1982 census.

Age class	Age in years	Population in millions
0	0–9	205
1	10–19	258
2	20–29	169
3	30–39	127
4	40–49	99
5	50–59	74
6	60–69	48
7	70–79	23
8	80–89	5

China's Current Population

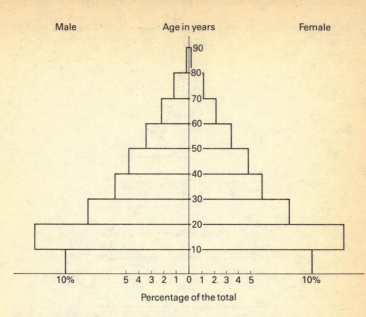

Male   Age in years   Female

Percentage of the total

Age structure (in 10-year classes) of China's population in 1982.

If we draw a picture of the current population we can see its shape is not very like that shape that would give a stationary population. In particular it slopes too quickly from age groups 1 upwards (reflecting a growing population in the past) and has a funny outward sloping form at the bottom of the pyramid (reflecting the slowdown in fertility rates that has taken place). Chinese demographers are particularly worried about the large number of people (258 million) in the 10–19 age group. The women in this group are just about to enter the important child-bearing years and this would cause a rapid expansion in population.

We shall work with the figures above, but having rather wide age classes can hide important features of a population. For instance if we chose to work with age classes of just one year long the detailed picture of the Chinese population looks a little different.*

* This diagram is taken from the 'Age distribution of China's population', *Beijing Review*, Vol. 27, No. 3, January 1984.

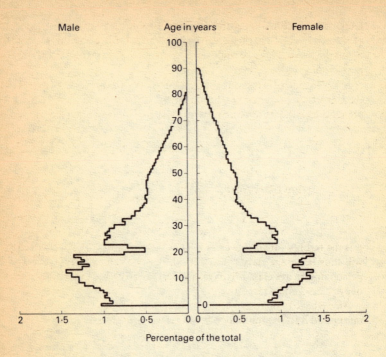

| Male | Age in years | Female |

Age structure (in one-year classes) of China's population in 1982.

Here we can clearly see a 'waistline' at the very early 20s age group that corresponds to the very high infant mortality rates that took place in the famines following the massive rural communization programme of the 'Great Leap Forward' of 1958–60. Also we can see clearly that while from 1972 to 1982 the number of women of child-bearing age was increasing, the number of children born must have been decreasing – the campaign to lower fertility rates that started in 1972 has had some success. However, we shall, for simplicity, continue to work with the more aggregated data to show, qualitatively if not totally accurately quantitatively, what will happen to the Chinese population under different assumptions about future fertility rates.

Whatever birth policy is adopted, if the survival rates we have listed above continue, then much of the population over the next seventy years is determined already. We can trace the survival of those already living to their deaths. The rest of future populations are not yet living and we must find a way of estimating births. Of prime significance will be the number of women of child-bearing age and their fertility. If we had information about these two things we could use a *Leslie matrix** to project the present population into the future.

A Leslie matrix is just our survival matrix S with the fertility rates of the age classes inserted in the first row. Thus a Leslie matrix for a population with just three age classes looks just like this:

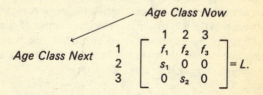

f_1 is the fertility rate of age class 1. That is the number of offspring, who will thus be in age class 1 next period, that we can expect the average person now in age class 1 to have. Similarly f_2 and f_3 are the fertility rates of age class 2 and 3 respectively.

All we have to do to project an existing population vector (N) forward one period is to postmultiply L by N. To see that this is so suppose

$$L = \begin{array}{c} 1 \\ 2 \\ 3 \end{array} \begin{bmatrix} .5 & .6 & 0 \\ .9 & 0 & 0 \\ 0 & .9 & 0 \end{bmatrix},$$

so that the fertility rates of age classes 1, 2, 3 are .5, .6 and 0 respectively.

Suppose there are at the moment 100 people in each age class

$$N_0 = \begin{bmatrix} 100 \\ 100 \\ 100 \end{bmatrix}.$$

---

* The matrix is named after P. H. Leslie whose influential article ('On the use of matrices in certain population mathematics', *Biometrika*, Vol. 33, pp. 183–212, 1945) was largely responsible for the present popularity of such matrices in demographic studies. An introduction to their use in demography can be found in chapter 2 of James Lighthill, *Newer Uses of Mathematics*, Penguin, Harmondsworth, 1978. A comprehensive treatment of the mathematics of populations can be found in Nathan Keyfitz, *Applied Mathematical Demography*, Wiley, New York, 1977.

The population after one period will be

$$N_1 = LN_0 = \begin{bmatrix} .5 & .6 & 0 \\ .9 & 0 & 0 \\ 0 & .9 & 0 \end{bmatrix} \begin{bmatrix} 100 \\ 100 \\ 100 \end{bmatrix} = \begin{bmatrix} 110 \\ 90 \\ 90 \end{bmatrix}.$$

There will be 90 people in both age class 2 and 3. This process is just the same for these age categories as postmultiplying the simple survival matrix by N_0. But as distinct from postmultiplying the survival matrix we now have a new entry in the first row of N_1. This, the number of new births, is got by adding up the number of new births from people of all age categories; and in each category the number of births is simply the number of people multiplied by their fertility rate. That is

$$\text{births} = .5 \times 100 + .6 \times 100 + 0 \times 100 = 110$$
$$= f_1 n_2 + f_2 n_2 + f_3 n_3.$$

Similarly

$$N_2 = LN_1 = L^2 N_0,$$

and, in general,

$$N_t = L^t N_0.$$

So let us return armed with the idea of a Leslie matrix to China.

To get a Leslie matrix for China we have to estimate the fertility rates of Chinese women in the various age classes. We shall look at three alternative futures by considering different estimates for these fertility rates.

It has been mentioned already that fertility rates in China have been falling since the early 1970s, when the growing population began to be recognized as a serious problem. The old view of Mao that 'every stomach was born with a pair of hands' was modified by the realization that a stomach did not come equipped with an acre of land or a tractor. In 1978 the national government began to promote the idea of the one-child family. At first the aims of the policy were fairly moderate – it was hoped that about a quarter of the urban families and rather less of the rural families would restrict themselves to one child. The policy rapidly escalated however. Rewards were given to couples pledging that they would have only one child. At first there were no penalties attached to having a second child (the two-child family had been promoted earlier in the 1970s) but there were economic penalties attached to having a third or more. By 1981 most provincial and local governments in both urban and rural regions had developed systems to penalize those couples having a second child.* The reward system still continues but the penalties for having a second child have become harsher and harsher.

In view of the nature of the campaign it is obviously rather difficult for us to predict future fertility rates. We certainly cannot simply use past ones, but we can look at what will happen for varying degrees of success of the campaign.

(i) Current Fertility Rates

Suppose the campaign is no more successful than the level it had reached in 1981. The 1982 sample census gives age-specific birth rates for 1981† and we can suppose they will carry on into the future. These figures tell us that we could expect (approximately) a woman in age class 1 to have produced an average of .9 of a child by ten years' time, a woman in age class 2 to have produced 1.37 children and a woman in age class 3 to have produced .27 of a child. The low fertility rates of other age groups can be ignored. These figures give us a Leslie matrix on the assumption that such rates will continue.

---

*Accounts of the one-child family campaign can be found in David Bonavia's book mentioned earlier or in Judith Banister, 'Population policy and trends in China, 1978–83', *China Quarterly*, No. 100, December 1984.

† See *Beijing Review*, Vol. 27, No. 12, March 1984.

| | | | Age class now | | | | | | | |
Age class next		0	1	2	3	4	5	6	7	8
0–9	0		.45	.69	.13					
10–19	1	.97								
20–29	2		.993							
30–39	3			.987						
40–49	4				.981					
50–59	5					.962				
60–69	6						.907			
70–79	7							.761		
80+	8								.510	

*Leslie matrix based on 1981 fertility rates
(all un-entered elements are zero)*

We have made one or two dramatic assumptions here that normally demographers would not make. We have divided the fertility rates by 2 assuming that there are exactly the same number of females as males in each age category, and we are assuming that in future there will be an equal number of male and female children born. Demographers normally stress the importance of female survival rates in determining population but we are just illustrating principles in a simple way at the cost of some accuracy.

Adding up the fertility rates of the age classes gives us an overall fertility rate of 2.54 children per couple, which suggests that at least by 1981 the one-child family campaign had not been a complete success. In fact, of the children born in 1981 about 47 per cent were first-born, 25 per cent second children and the rest were third-born or more. These aggregates hide relative successes and failures. For instance, in the large urban centres of Shanghai and Beijing over 85 per cent of the children born in 1981 were first-born, but this figure was as low as 25 per cent in some remote rural areas. The Communist Party has more control in urban areas and among people in the more educated strata of society.

With a fertility rate of about 2.5 per couple we could expect the population to grow and this is the outcome we get from projecting the present population forward. To get 1992's population we postmultiply L by our population vector (N_0) for 1982 to get

$$N_1 = LN_0,$$

and we get N_2 (2002) by calculating

$$N_2 = L^2N_0$$

and so on.

Here are the actual results we get from the matrix multiplications:

Age		N_0	N_1	N_2	N_3	N_4	N_5	N_6	N_7	N_8
		1982	1992	2002	2012	2022	2032	2042	2052	2062
0–10	0	205	249	288	278	316	343	359	400	424
10–20	1	258	199	242	279	270	307	333	348	388
20–30	2	169	256	197	240	277	268	305	331	345
30–40	3	127	167	253	195	237	274	264	301	327
40–50	4	99	125	164	248	191	232	269	259	295
50–60	5	74	95	120	157	239	184	224	258	249
60–70	6	48	67	86	109	143	216	167	203	234
70–80	7	23	37	51	66	83	109	164	127	154
80+	8	5	12	19	26	33	42	55	84	65
TOTAL		1008	1207	1420	1598	1789	1975	2140	2311	2481

China's future population in millions based on 1981 fertility rates.

It is these figures that so frighten the national government and Chinese demographers. China has already one quarter of the world's population and only 7 per cent of the world's arable land. There is already no space or privacy in the urban areas. The future indicated in these projections is a bleak, horrific one. Hence the escalation of the campaign for the one-child family. There is nothing planners can do about the existing population and in the table above I have drawn a bold line to indicate that below it we have the almost inevitable – the passage of the current population from one age category to the next. Family planning policy can influence only the figures above the bold line.

(ii) The Two-child Family

We have mentioned that China's long-term aim is to stabilize the population in the long run at about 900 million and to keep it below 1200 million at the end of this century. With an overall fertility rate of 2.5 these aims could not be achieved but we might ask about the implications of a two-child family. If every couple had two children, given that some people do not survive to child-bearing age, then this would mean that in the end the population must decline – people are not quite replacing themselves. Would this limitation not be enough to ease China's population problem? Certainly a two-child family policy would be more popular with individual couples than a one-child family.

To see what a two-child family policy implies for fertility rates, I extracted from the 1981 birth statistics the fertility rate of age class 1 for first- and second-born children only. Then I assumed that those only having one child when in this age class would have another when they are in age class two. I also assumed that women who had no children when in age class 1 would have their two children when in age class 2. There is a negligible number of first- or second-born children born to women in age class 3 and above.

This gave a new first row for the Leslie matrix.

Age class now

	0	1	2	3	4	5	6	7	8
FIRST ROW	0	.41	.59	0	0	0	0	0	0

First row of Leslie matrix for the two-child family

Using this new Leslie matrix to project the population forward gives us the table below:

Age	1982	1992	2002	2012	2022	2032	2042	2052	2062
0–9	205	205	233	198	209	211	196	203	198
10–19	258	199	199	226	192	203	205	190	197
20–29	169	256	197	198	224	191	202	203	189
30–39	127	167	253	195	195	221	188	199	200
40–49	99	125	164	248	191	192	217	184	195
50–59	74	95	120	157	239	184	184	209	177
60–69	48	67	86	109	143	216	167	167	189
70–79	23	37	51	66	83	109	164	127	127
80+	5	12	19	26	33	42	55	84	65
TOTAL	1008	1163	1322	1423	1509	1569	1578	1566	1537

China's future population in millions with a two-child family.

(Readers should check that they understand how to use Leslie matrices by checking these figures for some of the future years).

We said that under such a policy population will eventually decline but we can see that such a decline does not start until 2042. The population grows rapidly for the next forty years or so despite the less than replacement fertility rate. This is because the existing structure of the population is of vital importance in this period. The large numbers of people who are at present less than 20 years old produce children in this period. These forecasts of population are far too high for the liking of the Chinese planners.

(iii) The One-child Family

We shall now try to find out what would happen if the one-child family campaign were completely successful. If all couples just had one child and this carried on indefinitely, then eventually the population would decline very rapidly indeed. The society would basically be replacing two people by only one. Such a society would also be radically different from any we have ever known. Words like brother, sister, aunt, uncle and cousin would be redundant. Nobody would have any such relations. But this is not China's policy. The one-child family is seen as temporary and will last for one generation only. How exactly it will be relaxed in the future is not quite clear but we can assume a particular form of relaxation. It has been stated as part of the campaign that couples who are 'only children' may have two children – this is one of the exceptions to the one-child rule. While there are at present not many such couples there will be in the future. Thus in projecting forward the one-child policy, I have assumed that any female being born in the next twenty years will be an only child but eventually she will have two children. This means that fertility rates will change as we project into the future and we shall need different Leslie matrices in projecting from one year to another.

Using the birth statistics to find at which age women have their first-born child we get an estimate of fertility rates for the one-child family.

$$\begin{array}{ccccccccc} 0 & 1 & 2 & 3 & 4 & 5 & 6 & 7 & 8 \\ \begin{bmatrix} 0 & .28 & .22 & 0 & 0 & 0 & 0 & 0 & 0 \end{bmatrix} \end{array}$$

First row of Leslie matrix for the one-child family

We use the Leslie matrix made up of this row and the survival matrix to project the population from 1982 to 1992 and from 1992 to 2002.

Then, however, we have 'only children' in the child-bearing age class 1. These people may have two children so the first row of the Leslie matrix for the projection from 2002 to 2012 is (using our two-child family fertility rates)

$$[0 \quad .41 \quad .22 \quad 0 \quad 0 \quad 0 \quad 0 \quad 0 \quad 0]$$

and from 2012 to 2022 onwards we are back to the two-child family first row

$$[0 \quad .41 \quad .59 \quad 0 \quad 0 \quad 0 \quad 0 \quad 0 \quad 0].$$

Performing the calculations we get the following table:

Age	1982	1992	2002	2012	2022	2032	2042	2052	2062
0–9	205	109	112	87	107	98	92	100	93
10–19	258	199	106	109	84	103	95	89	97
20–29	169	256	197	105	108	84	103	95	88
30–39	127	167	253	195	104	107	83	101	93
40–49	99	125	164	248	191	102	104	81	99
50–59	74	95	120	157	239	184	98	101	78
60–69	48	67	86	109	143	216	167	89	91
70–79	23	37	51	66	83	109	164	127	68
80+	5	12	19	26	33	42	55	84	65
TOTAL	1008	1067	1108	1102	1092	1045	961	867	772

China's future population in millions under the one-child family.

We can notice several things here. Even with this very low fertility rate of replacing two adults by one child we find that the population increases for the rest of this century. This is because of the large numbers of people, as we have already noticed, who enter the child-bearing age at this time. As the already existing population gets older the total population starts to decline and to do so quite rapidly. Indeed the effect of the one-child family for just one generation is to halve the population in the middle of the next century compared with what it would be with a two-child family policy. The decline in population that we can see in the table would of course eventually slow down. Once the existing population have all died the population would begin to decline very gently as the overall fertility rate is only just below the replacement rate.

We can also see that the figures meet the aim of less than 1200 million people in the year 2000 quite comfortably. The Chinese national government does not expect to be as successful as these projections. In rural areas and in particular in areas where many of the national minorities live, it is expected that the campaign will not totally be successful. Indeed some minorities in China have been specifically excluded from the one-child rule. What we can see is that if the programme is reasonably effective there is no reason why China may not have a reasonably stable and balanced population of less than 1000 million towards the end of the next century. We can also see that unless the present generation of young Chinese is willing to restrict its child-bearing, China's population problems will increase.

Exercises

1. Repeat the projections with the assumption that China pursues its one-child family policy but allows 'only children' to have as many children as they wish. Assume this means that there is a return to 1981 fertility rates for only 'only children' and their offspring.
2. Compare the population structure that is projected for the year 2062 under the three different assumptions with the population structure that China needs for a stationary population.

11
Playing Games in Theory

There are many examples of conflict between individuals, groups, classes and nations. Individuals compete for jobs; political parties attempt to win elections; trades unions want higher wages for their members, while shareholders and managers would like wage cuts; wars are only too common. The understanding of how such important conflicts are resolved is obviously a major but difficult occupation of economists, political scientists and sociologists, and it is perhaps not surprising that new ideas on how to examine these conflicts are often greeted with much the same enthusiasm as would be caused by the discovery of the philosopher's stone. It is not the fault of the *Theory of Games* nor its originators, von Neumann and Morgenstern* that it was greeted in this fashion, that it has not fulfilled all the hopes of its devotees, nor that some of the applications of the theory have been simply silly. The initial insight of von Neumann and Morgenstern* that there is a close parallel between some social conflicts and many ordinary parlour games is a fruitful notion.

This does not mean we can learn much about society from studying a game like snakes and ladders where the players' moves are determined by the throw of dice. Many games, however, are games of strategy in the sense that the outcome is determined by the strategies of play of *all* the players. In chess, draughts or backgammon, for instance, in deciding a move a player has to take into account the possible and likely moves of the opponent. This is so even in very simple games such as matching pennies, in which the two players take a coin of the same value and place them simultaneously on a table choosing whether a head or tail is showing. If two heads or two tails are showing one of the players takes the money, and if the coins are not matched the other player is the winner. The theory of games describes the strategy a player of such games should adopt that will give him or her the best chance of winning. Thus, this theory describes what a rational player who wants to win should do, and not what players of such games actually do.

* J. von Neumann and O. Morgenstern, *Theory of Games and Economic Behavior*, Princeton University Press, New Jersey, 1944.

The game of matching pennies can be pictured as a matrix. Suppose Rachel (R for row) and Charles (C for column) play the game for tenpence a time with Rachel trying to match the coins and Charles winning if the coins are unmatched. The situation for Rachel can be represented by the following matrix.

$$
\begin{array}{c}
\textit{CHARLES} \\
\begin{array}{cc}
\text{Heads} & \text{Tails}
\end{array}
\end{array}
$$

$$
\textit{RACHEL}\;
\begin{array}{c}
\text{Heads} \\
\text{Tails}
\end{array}
\left[
\begin{array}{cc}
+10 & -10 \\
-10 & +10
\end{array}
\right]
$$

Rachel's pay-off matrix

Rachel's possible strategies of heads and tails are the rows and Charles's strategies are the columns. If Rachel plays heads and so does Charles, she wins tenpence so we write $+10$ in the 'heads' row and 'heads' column. However, if she plays heads and Charles plays tails she loses tenpence and so -10 is written in the 'heads' row and 'tails' column. Such a matrix is known as a *pay-off* matrix and, of course, one can construct another such matrix from Charles's point of view.

$$
\begin{array}{c}
\textit{CHARLES} \\
\begin{array}{cc}
\text{Heads} & \text{Tails}
\end{array}
\end{array}
$$

$$
\textit{RACHEL}\;
\begin{array}{c}
\text{Heads} \\
\text{Tails}
\end{array}
\left[
\begin{array}{cc}
-10 & +10 \\
+10 & -10
\end{array}
\right]
$$

Charles's pay-off matrix

In this case Charles's pay-off matrix is simply the negative of Rachel's. What Rachel wins, Charles loses. Adding the two matrices together would give a matrix in which all components were zero. A game with this property is known as a *zero-sum* game.

Suppose we alter the game slightly and make the winner pay a penny of the winnings in tax. The pay-off matrices for this amended game are

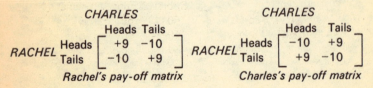

Rachel's pay-off matrix *Charles's pay-off matrix*

If we add these two we get another matrix

$$\begin{bmatrix} -1 & -1 \\ -1 & -1 \end{bmatrix}.$$

This matrix, which has all components equal, shows that the difference between the winner's winnings and the loser's losings is always the same (the amount of the tax) whatever strategies are adopted. This is an example of a *constant-sum* game. If we have a constant-sum game, then, since Charles's pay-off matrix can be derived from a knowledge of Rachel's matrix and the amount of the constant sum, it is usual in the interests of economy to picture the game as a matrix simply from the row player's point of view. As we shall see, the theory of games can tell us a great deal about how rational players should approach constant-sum games, but many conflicts in society are not of this extreme kind and for such cases the theory provides us with much less definite answers.

Dominant Strategies

We shall move from the parlour to the world of economics to demonstrate how to solve a constant-sum game. Imagine that Rachel and Charles are the heads of the only two television broadcasting companies and both have just one broadcasting channel. Economists would describe them as duopolists. They compete for the audience and to make sure they play a constant-sum game, we shall assume that the same number of people always watch television no matter what is broadcast. Plans are made in advance for a night's viewing and the programmes of the two channels are published simultaneously and cannot be changed. Rachel and Charles can choose to show sport, comedy or drama. The number of viewers watching Rachel's channel depends not only on the programme she shows but also on the programme Charles shows. The matrix below gives the pay-off to Rachel of the various possible combinations of programmes.

		CHARLES		
		Sport	Comedy	Drama
	Sport	50	55	65
RACHEL	Comedy	40	50	60
	Drama	30	40	50

Rachel's pay-off matrix

The numbers are the percentage of viewers watching Rachel's station and hence Charles's pay-off matrix would be that obtained by subtracting Rachel's matrix from a matrix that had all components equal to 100. What is good for Rachel is bad for Charles.

In this particular case a glance at the pay-off matrix tells us that for the viewing public sport seems to be more popular than comedy, which is, in turn, more popular than drama. Rachel, indeed, would be silly ever to adopt the strategy of showing comedy or drama. Regardless of what Charles does, showing sport will give her a bigger audience. The numbers in the comedy and drama rows are all less than the corresponding number in the sport row. The sport row is said to *dominate* both the comedy and drama rows. From Charles's point of view we can say much the same. The elements in the sports column are smaller than the corresponding elements in both the drama and comedy columns, and remembering that the smaller the pay-off for Rachel is the larger it is for Charles, we say that the sports column dominates the other two. It is rational for both Charles and Rachel to show nothing but sport. The solution to this game is that there will be undiluted sport on both channels every night and 50 per cent of viewers will watch each channel. This fictional game does illustrate a common result of duopoly. There would be a better chance of avoiding wasteful duplication if there was one controller in charge of both channels. Paradoxically, or at least contrary to saloon-bar wisdom, competition can lead to monotony.

Exercises

1. R and C have two tenpence coins each. They both hold either one or two in a clenched fist and open their fists together. If they are both holding the same number of coins, then R takes the coin or coins C is holding. If they are holding a different number of coins then C takes the coins R is holding.
    (a) What is R's pay-off matrix?
    (b) What is C's pay-off matrix?
2. The game in exercise 1 is slightly altered. Now a player can choose to hold 0, 1 or 2 coins. What are the pay-off matrices for this amended game?
3. The following matrices are the pay-off matrices for R in a variety of constant-sum games. For each of the games find whether R has a dominant strategy.

176

(a)

$$\begin{array}{c} \\ \text{\textit{R's strategy}} \end{array} \begin{array}{c} \\ \text{I} \\ \text{II} \\ \text{III} \end{array} \overset{\displaystyle \begin{array}{ccc} \text{\textit{C's strategy}} \\ \text{I} \quad \text{II} \quad \text{III} \end{array}}{\left[\begin{array}{ccc} 3 & 4 & 6 \\ 2 & 3 & 6 \\ 1 & 2 & 3 \end{array}\right]}$$

(b)

$$\begin{array}{c} \text{I} \\ \text{II} \\ \text{III} \end{array} \overset{\displaystyle \begin{array}{ccc} \text{I} \quad \text{II} \quad \text{III} \end{array}}{\left[\begin{array}{ccc} -2 & -1 & 0 \\ -1 & 0 & 1 \\ 0 & 1 & 2 \end{array}\right]}$$

(c)

$$\begin{array}{c} \text{I} \\ \text{II} \\ \text{III} \end{array} \overset{\displaystyle \begin{array}{ccc} \text{I} \quad \text{II} \quad \text{III} \end{array}}{\left[\begin{array}{ccc} -1 & -2 & 5 \\ 0 & 5 & 6 \\ 0 & 4 & 3 \end{array}\right]}$$

(d)

$$\begin{array}{c} \text{I} \\ \text{II} \\ \text{III} \end{array} \overset{\displaystyle \begin{array}{ccc} \text{I} \quad \text{II} \quad \text{III} \end{array}}{\left[\begin{array}{ccc} 2 & 1 & -2 \\ 1 & 1 & 0 \\ 3 & -2 & -3 \end{array}\right]}$$

Find C's dominant strategy (if it exists) for the above games.

In which games do both R and C have dominant strategies?

4. Are there any dominant strategies in the games of exercises 1 and 2?

Saddle-points and Pure Strategies

Obviously not all two-person games have a dominant strategy for each player. Suppose that Rachel's pay-off matrix was

$$\begin{array}{c} \\ \text{\textit{RACHEL}} \end{array} \begin{array}{c} \\ \text{Sport} \\ \text{Comedy} \\ \text{Drama} \end{array} \overset{\displaystyle \begin{array}{ccc} \text{\textit{CHARLES}} \\ \text{Sport} \quad \text{Comedy} \quad \text{Drama} \end{array}}{\left[\begin{array}{ccc} 65 & 40 & 20 \\ 55 & 50 & 60 \\ 30 & 45 & 70 \end{array}\right]}$$

Rachel's pay-off matrix

In this case we can see that the preferences of the viewers depend very much not only on the type of programme but also on which channel is showing it. In this matrix no row dominates any other and nor are any of the columns dominated. To find a rational strategy for Rachel we start by asking what is the worst that can happen to her when she chooses any particular programme. Thus if she shows sport the worst that can happen is that Charles shows drama and then she gets 20 per cent of the market. Similarly if she shows comedy the worst that can happen is to get 50 per cent of the market, and by showing drama her worst possible result is 30 per cent of the market. If she is security-conscious Rachel may well choose to show comedy on the grounds that the worst possible outcome in this case – that Charles also shows comedy and she gets 50 per cent of the market – is better than the worst possible outcome when showing the other programmes. Mathematically, this principle amounts to Rachel first finding the smallest (minimum) number in each row, then finding the largest (maximum) of these numbers and playing the strategy containing this number.

Suppose that Charles adopts the same approach and looks for the worst that can happen to him when playing the various strategies and then picks the best of these worst outcomes. Because the pay-off matrix is pictured from Rachel's point of view this amounts to finding the maximum element in every column and then finding the minimum of these maxima. The worst outcome for Charles if he shows sport is that Rachel gets 65 per cent of the audience, if he shows comedy the worst outcome is that Rachel has 50 per cent, and if he shows drama Rachel cannot get more than 70 per cent. The best of these worst outcomes for Charles is when he shows comedy and Rachel shows comedy and they both have 50 per cent of the audience.

In this case, if both Rachel and Charles adopt the strategies that this line of thinking indicates, their security-consciousness is justified. The worst that can happen to both Rachel and Charles if they broadcast comedy is that the other does likewise. When this happens, Rachel's search for the maximum of the minimum elements in the rows (often uglily called the *maximin*) yields the same element of the matrix as Charles's search for the minimum of the maximum elements in the columns (the *minimax*).

This coincidence of the maximin being the same as the minimax gives us the major reason for regarding the showing of comedy on both channels as the solution to this game. If Charles is showing comedy then any change Rachel makes from the strategy of also showing comedy will result in her being worse off. Similarly, given that Rachel always shows comedy, a change in strategy by Charles from also showing comedy will worsen his situation. There is no incentive for either to change strategy from always showing comedy, and hence we can regard this outcome of interminable comedy as an equilibrium. We only get this simple solution, that both players play one definite strategy (which we call a *pure strategy* solution), because the maximin for Rachel is equal to the minimax for Charles. In such circumstances we say that the element of the pay-off matrix at which this equality occurs is a *saddle-point*. As we shall now go on to see, if the matrix does not have a saddle-point then the game will not have a solution in terms of pure strategies.

Exercises

1. The following matrices represent R's pay-off matrix for various constant-sum games.

   Find, for each of the games, the maximin for R and the minimax for C. Which of the games have a saddle-point and hence have a pure strategy solution?

(a) $\begin{bmatrix} -1 & 1 \\ -2 & 3 \end{bmatrix}$ (b) $\begin{bmatrix} 3 & 1 \\ -4 & 2 \end{bmatrix}$ (c) $\begin{bmatrix} 3 & 1 \\ -4 & 0 \end{bmatrix}$

(d) $\begin{bmatrix} -1 & -1 & 2 \\ 1 & 0 & 0 \\ 0 & -1 & -2 \end{bmatrix}$ (e) $\begin{bmatrix} 4 & -1 & -3 \\ 2 & 1 & 3 \\ -2 & 0 & 5 \end{bmatrix}$

(f) $\begin{bmatrix} 1 & 2 & 3 \\ 3 & 3 & 4 \\ 2 & 5 & 4 \end{bmatrix}$ (g) $\begin{bmatrix} 3 & 2 & 1 & -1 & 0 \\ 1 & 0 & -2 & -2 & 3 \end{bmatrix}$

2. Show that the 'coin game' in exercise (1) above (p. 176) does not have a saddle-point but that the amended game of exercise (2) does.

Mixed Strategies

We suppose, at this stage, that once again the viewing preferences of the community alter and Rachel is faced by a new pay-off matrix:

		CHARLES		
		Sport	Comedy	Drama
	Sport	30	20	60
RACHEL	Comedy	60	50	40
	Drama	70	40	30

First, we look to see if we can get a solution to this game in terms of

179

dominant strategies. None of Rachel's pure strategies dominates any other, but whatever she does Charles will always do better showing comedy than he will showing sport. The comedy column dominates the sport column and hence Charles will never show sport. We can remove this redundant column from the game, as shown:

$$
\begin{array}{cc}
 & \textit{CHARLES} \\
 & \begin{array}{cc} \text{Comedy} & \text{Drama} \end{array} \\
\textit{RACHEL} \begin{array}{c} \text{Sport} \\ \text{Comedy} \\ \text{Drama} \end{array} & \left[\begin{array}{cc} 20 & 60 \\ 50 & 40 \\ 40 & 30 \end{array} \right].
\end{array}
$$

Acting on the assumption that Charles is rational, Rachel realizes he will never show sport and thus now finds that her drama strategy is dominated by comedy. The drama row is irrelevant and can be removed from the matrix, which leaves us with

$$
\begin{array}{cc}
 & \textit{CHARLES} \\
 & \begin{array}{cc} \text{Comedy} & \text{Drama} \end{array} \\
\textit{RACHEL} \begin{array}{c} \text{Sport} \\ \text{Comedy} \end{array} & \left[\begin{array}{cc} 20 & 60 \\ 50 & 40 \end{array} \right].
\end{array}
$$

We have succeeded in simplifying the game but can go no further by removing dominated strategies, and so must move to the second line of attack and look for a saddle-point. For Rachel, the worst that can happen if she shows sport is that Charles shows comedy and she gets 20 per cent of the market. When she shows comedy the worst outcome is that Charles shows drama and she gets 40 per cent. The best of her worst (her maximin) is this 40 per cent. For Charles, the worst of his best (his minimax) is when they both show comedy and both get 50 per cent of the audience. The maximin of the rows of this matrix does not correspond to the minimax of the columns. The matrix does not have a saddle-point.

If both players act with security in mind they will both play comedy but it is not an equilibrium in the sense it was in our last example. With Rachel showing comedy, Charles can improve his position by switching from comedy to drama. But if he does show drama, Rachel can gain by switching from comedy to sport. We are going round in circles and unlike our previous example there is no obvious solution to the game.

Intuitively we might guess that the players in this game will keep their opponent guessing by sometimes switching between strategies in successive plays of the game. Without being predictable, and hence avoiding Charles doing her down, Rachel will sometimes show a sports programme and sometimes a comedy programme. Likewise Charles will show a mixture of programmes. Our problem is to find out what the mixtures should be. In settling this problem we come across another. Suppose that Rachel decided her best strategy was to show four times as many comedy programmes as sports programmes. If she did this by showing a sports programme every fifth day then her actions would be just as predictable as if she showed a single kind of programme all the time. Charles could respond by showing drama every fifth day and comedy otherwise, and Rachel would do worse than by showing comedy all the time. To ensure unpredictability Rachel would have to show sport one fifth of the time but without there being a guessable pattern as to when it would be shown. A simple way of doing this would be for Rachel to put four red counters representing comedy and one blue counter representing sport in a bag, and decide on which programme to show every day by selecting a counter at random – say by closing her eyes and picking one from the bag. To find out how many counters of each colour she should put in the bag, that is to find her best mix of strategies, we need to examine the pay-off to Rachel when she assigns different probabilities to selecting the two strategies. This can be easily represented diagrammatically.

First we start by drawing a line A B of unit length. Rachel can choose to assign any probability (p_1) between zero and one to showing sport, and then the probability of her showing comedy (p_2) will be $1-p_1$. We shall describe Rachel's strategy by the probability vector p.

$$p = \begin{bmatrix} p_1 & p_2 \end{bmatrix}$$

If we measure p_1 from the left-hand end (A) of the unit line and p_2 from B then all possible probability vectors are represented by some point on the line.

A •⎯⎯⎯⎯⎯⎯⎯⎯⎯⎯⎯⎯⎯⎯⎯⎯⎯⎯⎯⎯⎯⎯• B

$p = [0,1]$ $p = [⅓, ⅔]$ $p = [⅔, ⅓]$ $p = [1,0]$

Now we measure Rachel's pay-off for all these possible probability vectors by a vertical distance above the line A B.

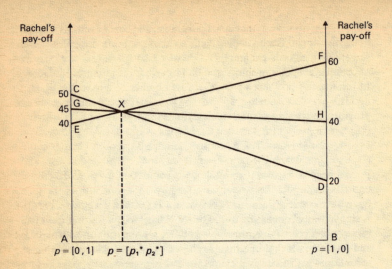

Rachel's pay-off (left axis): 50 C, 45 G, 40 E, X, A
$p = [0,1]$ $p = [p_1{}^* \; p_2{}^*]$

Rachel's pay-off (right axis): F 60, H 40, D 20, B
$p = [1,0]$

If Charles shows comedy all the time and so does Rachel her pay-off is 50 every time the game is played, but if she always shows sport her pay-off is 20. Thus for Charles playing comedy we have points C and D on the diagram. If Rachel shows sport a fraction p_1 of the time and comedy a fraction p_2 of the time, her average pay-off if Charles shows comedy will be

$$20p_1 + 50p_2,$$

which could be written as

$$p \begin{bmatrix} 20 \\ 50 \end{bmatrix}.$$

Or, since

$$p_2 = 1 - p_1,$$

Rachel's pay-off

$$= 20p_1 + 50 - 50p_1$$
$$= 50 - 30p_1.$$

For every .1 increase in p_1, Rachel's pay-off goes down by 3. Thus as we

182

increase p_1 from zero (that is, move along the line from A to B), Rachel's pay-off, when Charles shows comedy, declines evenly and can be represented by the straight line CD.

Similarly if Charles shows drama, Rachel's pay-off can be represented by the line EF showing a pay-off of 40 if she always shows comedy and 60 if she always shows sport. If Charles does adopt a pure strategy we can write the possible pay-offs to Rachel as

$$\begin{matrix} & \text{CHARLES} \\ & \text{Comedy} \quad\quad \text{Drama} \end{matrix}$$

$$\begin{bmatrix} p_1 & p_2 \end{bmatrix} \begin{bmatrix} 20 & 60 \\ 50 & 40 \end{bmatrix} = \begin{bmatrix} 20p_1 + 50p_2 & 60p_1 + 40p_2 \end{bmatrix}.$$

However, there is no reason to believe that Charles will adopt a pure strategy. Suppose that by tossing a coin Charles ensured that there were equal probabilities of him showing comedy and drama. Rachel's expected pay-off would simply be the average of the expected pay-offs that she would get with Charles playing the two pure strategies. This could be represented by the line GH on our diagram. For any probability vector p, Rachel's pay-off is given by the point half way between the line CD and EF. Similarly if Charles assigned different probabilities to showing comedy and drama (say $[q_1, q_2]$), the pay-off to Rachel would be represented by a line starting on the left-hand side of the diagram between C and E, going through the point X, and finishing somewhere between D and F.

Returning to algebra we can say that the expected pay-off to Rachel if Charles plays a mixed strategy is

q_1 (pay-off to Rachel if Charles plays comedy)

$+ q_2$ (pay-off to Rachel if Charles plays drama),

which is from above

$$(20p_1 + 50p_2)q_1 + (60p_1 + 40p_2)q_2$$

or, in matrix form,

$$\begin{bmatrix} p_1 & p_2 \end{bmatrix} \begin{bmatrix} 20 & 60 \\ 50 & 40 \end{bmatrix} \begin{bmatrix} q_1 \\ q_2 \end{bmatrix}.$$

Writing G as the pay-off matrix for the game we can say that the expected

183

pay-off to the row player is

$$pGq'$$

where p is a row vector of probabilities that the row player assigns to her strategies, and q' the column vector of probabilities the column player assigns to his strategies. The object of the row player is to choose p so as to maximize her expected pay-off (pGq') given that the column player can choose any q', and the column player tries to minimize it given that the row player can choose any p. These are none other than our old friends maximin and minimax. For all p, Rachel sees what happens when Charles picks the q that does worst damage. She picks the p that means with the appropriate q' Charles can do her least harm.

Our diagram is illustrating this problem for Rachel in this simple two by two game. Whenever one has a diagram with a few lines on it that intersect at one point then it is never a surprise to learn that this point is of special interest. In this diagram the point X, at which let us suppose Rachel's probability vector is $[p_1^* \ p_2^*]$ is of great significance. If Rachel shows sport with any probability less than p_1^*, then the worst that can happen to her is that Charles shows comedy and her pay-off for each probability vector is given by the points on the line EX. If she shows sport with a probability of greater than p_1^* then her worst outcome is always that Charles shows drama and her expected pay-off is given by the line XD.

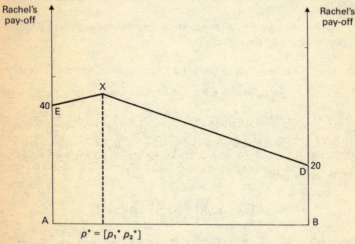

Rachel's worst possible outcomes

We can immediately see that the best of these worst outcomes occurs at the point X. Her expected pay-off at this point gives her the greatest possible share of the audience that she can guarantee to expect. Playing a different strategy from $[p_1{}^* \; p_2{}^*]$ could lead – and given a sensible opponent will lead – to a worse outcome for her.

It is fairly trivial to work out this best strategy for Rachel. At X the expected pay-off to Rachel is the same whatever Charles does. We know that if Charles plays comedy Rachel's pay-off is

$$20p_1 + 50p_2,$$

and if he plays drama, it is

$$60p_1 + 40p_2.$$

Since these must be equal at X,

$$20p_1{}^* + 50p_2{}^* = 60p_1{}^* + 40p_2{}^*$$

which yields

$$4p_1{}^* - p_2{}^* = 0,$$

and since, by definition,

$$p_2{}^* = 1 - p_1{}^*$$

then

$$p_1{}^* = \tfrac{1}{5}.$$

Thus Rachel's strategy should be to make sure she has a one in five chance of showing sport and a four in five chance of showing comedy. If she adopts this strategy, then the average percentage of viewers that she can expect to watch her programme each night, regardless of what Charles does, is

$$20p_1{}^* + 50p_2{}^* = 20(\tfrac{1}{5}) + 50(\tfrac{4}{5}) = 44.$$

This is called the *value* of the game. It represents the average audience she can expect if she adopts this mixed strategy over a long period of time.

In matrix terms we have shown that there is a vector p^* such that

$$p^*Gq' = 44,$$

regardless of what q Charles chooses, and if Rachel chooses a vector p that is not equal to p^*, Charles can always choose a vector q such that

$$pGq' \leqslant 44.$$

In our diagrammatic discussion Charles has played a rather secondary role. Rachel sees him as reacting to any strategy she plays by doing the best he can given her strategy. We could equally well have reversed these roles. This is done by representing Charles's possible probability vectors q as points on a line of unit length. Remembering that q_1 is the probability that he will show comedy and q_2 the probability that he will show drama we can draw a new diagram.

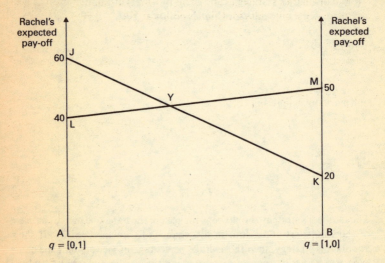

Rachel's expected pay-off for Charles's different strategies can be measured as before. If Rachel always shows sport then Charles showing drama gives Rachel a pay-off of 60 and we are at point J, while if he shows comedy her pay-off is 20 and we are at K. The line JK, then, gives Rachel's expected pay-off when showing sport for all of Charles's possible strategies. Similarly L M gives Rachel's expected pay-off when she shows comedy.

The value of the pay-off along J K is

$$20q_1 + 60q_2$$

and along L M is

$$50q_1 + 40q_2.$$

Using the same argument as before, if Rachel adopts a mixed strategy, we could represent the consequences by a line starting from somewhere between J and L, going through Y, and ending between K and M.

Looking at this diagram through Charles's eyes we see that the worst that can happen to him when he plays the different strategies is given by the kinked line J Y M; for along it Rachel's pay-off is the largest possible for all of Charles's strategies and so his pay-off is at a minimum. The best of these worst outcomes for Charles occurs at Y.

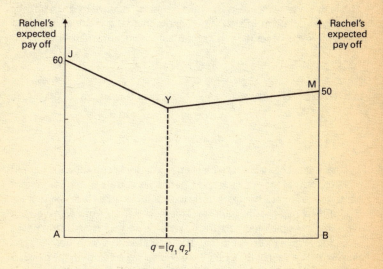

Charles's worst possible outcome

Letting q^* be Charles's probability vector corresponding to the point Y we can write

$$20q_1{}^* + 60q_2{}^* = 50q_1{}^* + 40q_2{}^*,$$

because the pay-off to him is the same at this point regardless of whether Rachel plays sport or comedy. Remembering that

$$q_2{}^* = 1 - q_1{}^*,$$

we can solve the equation to yield

$$q^* = \begin{bmatrix} q_1{}^* & q_2{}^* \end{bmatrix} = \begin{bmatrix} \frac{2}{5} & \frac{3}{5} \end{bmatrix}.$$

Charles should show comedy with a probability of $\frac{2}{5}$ and drama with a probability of $\frac{3}{5}$. If he does this, then Rachel's expected pay-off is

$$20\left(\tfrac{2}{5}\right) + 60\left(\tfrac{3}{5}\right) = 44,$$

which, by no coincidence, is the same result we obtained by analysing the game from her point of view. For Charles there is a vector q^* such that whatever Rachel does the value of the game is no more than 44;

$$pGq'^* = 44,$$

and if Charles chooses q' not equal to q'^* then Rachel can choose p such that

$$pGq' > 44.$$

Thus Rachel has a strategy that can guarantee her an expected pay-off of 44 per cent of the audience and Charles has a strategy that can restrict her to this amount. By exploring mixed strategies we have found that the best of the worst possible outcomes for Rachel is the same as the best of the worst possible outcomes for Charles. We have, using our previous terminology, a saddle-point, but this time it occurs with both players playing mixed strategies. Again it is a convincing solution to the game. If either player deviates from the calculated best mixed strategy, the other player can benefit by altering their strategy. There is no incentive to move from these optimal strategies.

Our game started with a three by three matrix. Conveniently, because

188

certain strategies were dominated it reduced to a two by two. However, using more powerful tools, it can be shown that there are solutions to all two-person constant-sum games no matter how large, in terms of dominant strategies, or saddle-points with pure strategies, or saddle-points with mixed strategies. Solving for the optimal strategies in $m \times n$ matrix games (where m and n are bigger than two) is a little more difficult than for two by two games. In theory they can be solved using computational methods devised to solve linear programmes.* In practice, even with the help of computers, the saddle-points of some very complicated games such as chess have yet to be discovered.

Before turning to the use of constant-sum games in analysing social conflict, it is wise to recap the theory we have just covered by working quickly through another example.

Another Worked Example

Let us consider a version of a game known as two-finger Morra. There are two players (R and C). Each player holds up either one or two fingers. If they hold up the same number of fingers R gets the sum (in pence) of the digits, and if they hold up a different number C gets the sum.

Without much difficulty we can write down R's pay-off matrix

$$
\begin{array}{c}
 \quad\quad\quad\quad C \\
 \quad \text{1 finger} \quad \text{2 fingers} \\
R \begin{array}{c} \text{1 finger} \\ \text{2 fingers} \end{array}
\left[\begin{array}{cc} 2 & -3 \\ -3 & 4 \end{array} \right] = G
\end{array}
$$

R's pay-off matrix

Neither R nor C has a dominant strategy, and the maximin for R (–3) is not equal to the minimax for C (2). This means that the game is not soluble in terms of pure strategies.

Suppose, then, that R adopts the mixed strategy of

$$
\left[\begin{array}{cc} p_1 & p_2 \end{array} \right] = p;
$$

* See for instance K. Sasaki, *Introduction to Finite Mathematics and Linear Programming*, Wadsworth, California, 1970.

R's expected pay-off for C's two possible strategies are given by the row vector

$$\begin{array}{cc} & \mathbf{C} \\ & \begin{array}{cc} \text{1 finger} & \text{2 fingers} \end{array} \\ pG = \begin{bmatrix} p_1 & p_2 \end{bmatrix} \begin{bmatrix} 2 & -3 \\ -3 & 4 \end{bmatrix} = \begin{bmatrix} 2p_1 - 3p_2 & -3p_1 + 4p_2 \end{bmatrix}. \end{array}$$

Now we know that the essence of the solution of the game for R is to guarantee herself the best expected pay-off possible regardless of what C does. This means that if p is optimal the expected pay-off to R is the same whether C holds up one finger or two.

Hence, the optimal mixed strategy ($p^* = [p_1{}^* \ p_2{}^*]$) for R is such that

$$2p_1{}^* - 3p_2{}^* = -3p_1{}^* + 4p_2{}^*$$

$$5p_1{}^* = 7p_2{}^*$$

and since

$$p_2{}^* = 1 - p_1{}^*$$

$$p_2{}^* = \tfrac{7}{12}.$$

So

$$p^* = \begin{bmatrix} \tfrac{7}{12} & \tfrac{5}{12} \end{bmatrix}.$$

Player R should play the one-finger strategy with probability $\tfrac{7}{12}$. If R did adopt this strategy then her expected pay-off is

$$2p_1 - 3p_2 = \tfrac{14}{12} - \tfrac{15}{12} = \tfrac{1}{12}$$

whatever C does. So the best R can guarantee to do is to expect to make on average a small loss from every play of the game.

We must also look at the game from C's point of view. Suppose C plays the mixed strategy

$$q' = \begin{bmatrix} q_1 \\ q_2 \end{bmatrix},$$

then the amount that C can expect to lose for R's two strategies are given by the column vector

$$Gq' = \begin{bmatrix} 2 & -3 \\ -3 & 4 \end{bmatrix} \begin{bmatrix} q_1 \\ q_2 \end{bmatrix} = \begin{matrix} R & \text{1 finger} \\ & \text{2 fingers} \end{matrix} \begin{bmatrix} 2q_1 - 3q_2 \\ -3q_1 + 4q_2 \end{bmatrix}.$$

(This vector gives the amount C expects to lose rather than win because G is R's pay-off matrix and not C's.)

Now once again we use the idea that the best strategy for C is the one that minimizes the level of guaranteed losses. That is, the expected loss (and hence pay-off) to C is the same whatever R does. So the optimal strategy

$$q'^* = \begin{bmatrix} q_1^* \\ q_2^* \end{bmatrix}$$

is such that

$$2q_1^* - 3q_2^* = -3q_1^* + 4q_2^*$$

and since

$$q_2^* = 1 - q_1^*$$

$$q_1^* = \tfrac{7}{12}.$$

In this game, the optimal strategy for C, that of playing the one-finger strategy with probability $\tfrac{7}{12}$, happens to be the same as that for R. Regardless of this happenstance, the expected loss to C when C plays his optimal strategy is the same as the expected pay-off to R when she plays her optimal strategy.

$$\text{C's expected loss} = \begin{matrix} R & \text{1 finger} \\ & \text{2 fingers} \end{matrix} \begin{bmatrix} 2q_1^* - 3q_2^* \\ -3q_1^* + 4q_2^* \end{bmatrix}$$

$$= \begin{bmatrix} -\tfrac{1}{12} / -\tfrac{1}{12} \end{bmatrix}.$$

That is, C will on average win $\tfrac{1}{12}$ of a penny a game regardless of what R does, if C plays his optimal strategy. To sum up then for this game the optimal strategies are:

$$p^* = \begin{bmatrix} \frac{7}{12} & \frac{5}{12} \end{bmatrix}; \quad q'^* = \begin{bmatrix} \frac{7}{12} \\ \frac{5}{12} \end{bmatrix}$$

and the value of the game to R is $-\frac{1}{12}$.

Exercises

1. Show for the game

$$\begin{array}{c} & & \text{C} \\ & & 1 \quad\ \ 2 \\ R \begin{array}{c} 1 \\ 2 \end{array} & \begin{bmatrix} 0 & 1 \\ 3 & -4 \end{bmatrix} \end{array}$$

that the optimal strategy for R is $p = \begin{bmatrix} \frac{7}{8} & \frac{1}{8} \end{bmatrix}$, and for C is $q' = \begin{bmatrix} \frac{5}{8} \\ \frac{3}{8} \end{bmatrix}$ and that the value of the game to R is $\frac{3}{8}$.

2. Consider R's pay-off matrix

$$\begin{array}{c} & & \text{C} \\ & & 1 \quad\ 2 \quad\ 3 \\ R \begin{array}{c} 1 \\ 2 \\ 3 \end{array} & \begin{bmatrix} 0 & -1 & 3 \\ 3 & 2 & 1 \\ 4 & 1 & 0 \end{bmatrix} \end{array}.$$

By looking for dominated strategies show that this game can be reduced to a 2×2 matrix.

Hence show that it is optimal for R to play strategy 1 with probability $\frac{1}{5}$ and strategy 2 with probability $\frac{4}{5}$, while C should play strategy 2 with probability $\frac{2}{5}$ and strategy 3 with probability $\frac{3}{5}$.

3. Consider the game for which R's pay-off matrix is

$$\begin{array}{c} & & \text{C} \\ & & 1 \quad\ \ 2 \quad\ \ 3 \\ R \begin{array}{c} 1 \\ 2 \\ 3 \end{array} & \begin{bmatrix} 2 & 1 & 0 \\ 1 & -2 & -1 \\ -3 & 3 & -2 \end{bmatrix} \end{array}.$$

Find a row that is dominated. Remove it. Now a column in the remaining matrix is dominated – remove it. Carry on in this way to find the solution of this game.

4. R's pay-off matrix is

$$
\begin{array}{c}
& \quad C \\
& \quad 1 \quad\; 2 \quad 3 \\
R\;\begin{array}{c} 1 \\ 2 \end{array} & \left[\begin{array}{rrr} 5 & -10 & 5 \\ -10 & 5 & 5 \end{array}\right].
\end{array}
$$

Find the optimal strategies for R and C and the value of the game.

5. 'Scissors, paper, stone' is a well-known game. Two players acting simultaneously either hold out two fingers (scissors), a flat hand (paper) or a fist (stone). The rules are 'scissors cuts paper', 'paper covers stone' and 'stone blunts scissors'. If you win in this way you get one point, and if both players do the same thing neither gets a point.

Check that the pay-off matrix for the game is

$$
\begin{array}{c}
& C \\
& \text{Scissors} \;\; \text{Paper} \;\; \text{Stone} \\
R\;\begin{array}{c} \text{Scissors} \\ \text{Paper} \\ \text{Stone} \end{array} & \left[\begin{array}{rrr} 0 & 1 & -1 \\ -1 & 0 & 1 \\ 1 & -1 & 0 \end{array}\right].
\end{array}
$$

Check that no strategy is dominated and that the game is not soluble by pure strategies.

What are the optimal strategies for R and C?

(Even though we have not dealt with the mechanics of solving 3 × 3 mixed strategy games you should be able to work it out easily in this case.)

12
Magic, Fishing and Farming –
Some Applications of Constant-sum
Games Theory

At the beginning of the last chapter it was emphasized that the theory of constant-sum games gave a prescription for how rational people should play such games, and not necessarily a description of how people actually do play them. Psychologists have undertaken laboratory experiments, usually with supposedly intelligent students, to discuss whether or not people repeatedly playing a game find the optimal strategy.* It is fair to summarize the results of the studies by saying that in small games most students found the optimal strategy if the solution of the game required the playing of a pure strategy, but that the students did not discover what we have called the solution to the game if a mixed strategy was required. Indeed they do not seem to develop independently the notions of a strategy based on using a random device to assign different probabilities to playing different moves. Of course these were laboratory experiments and it may be wrong to suggest that these results will carry over into 'real world' games, but they do indicate that it should be no surprise if there are many conflicts in which the actors do not behave as the theory prescribes.

Another problem in applying the theory is that most social conflicts are not constant-sum games. In our fictional example we assumed that either the same number of people in total watched television regardless of what was broadcast, or that Rachel and Charles were only concerned with their share of the audience and not its absolute size. If the number of viewers varied according to the combination of programmes shown and if the television companies were concerned with the absolute size of the audience then we would no longer have a constant-sum game. A change of programme can result in the loss or gain of viewers to both channels rather

* Examples of such studies are: Bernard Liebermann, 'Human behaviour in a strictly determined 3 × 3 matrix game', *Behavioural Sciences*, Vol. V, 1960, pp. 317–22, and Bernard Liebermann and David Malcolm, 'The behaviour of responsive individuals playing a two-person game requiring the use of mixed strategies', *Psychoanalytic Science*, Vol. II, 1965, pp. 373–4.

than just the transfer of viewers between channels. Although the study of duopoly is an obvious choice for the use of game theory, the problem never seems to be perfectly describable as a constant-sum game. An early application was the study of two firms competing by advertising.* One can expect that the amount of soap powder that people use is roughly fixed, but that advertising may cause people to change brands. Thus one might picture Proctor and Gamble and Unilever as being engaged in a constant-sum game where the constant-sum is the total fixed amount of soap powder people buy. Or at least one might if advertising were costless. It is of no great benefit for Unilever to secure the whole market if the advertising strategy required is so costly as to remove profitability. Presumably the firms are interested in profits rather than mere shares in the market, and there is not some constant total of profit to be earned.

For these reasons it is not surprising that examples of the use of the theory to describe social phenomena are rare and also sometimes a little inadequate. The conditions necessary for such applications – two rational players or teams, and a constant-sum outcome – are also rare, but some of the examples are nevertheless interesting, instructive and worth describing.

Magical Practices

Faced with the need to make a decision many groups of people resort to mumbo-jumbo or magical practices. The Azande, of the Sudan, use a poison oracle. Fowl are given poison of some kind and decisions are taken according to whether the birds live or die. The ancient Chinese burned tortoise shells and decisions were determined by the shape of the resulting cracks. Many societies including the Assyrians, Etruscans, Greeks and Romans have practised haruspicy, the reading of the entrails of sacrificed beasts. The state of the liver of the beast seems to have been a very popular basis for decision-making. Some people still read tea leaves before taking a new job or setting out on a journey.

Omar Khayyam Moore, an American anthropologist, has suggested that these apparently absurd magical practices may be rational and efficient.† We have seen that the solution to a game may involve playing

---

* See for instance A. Charnes and W. W. Cooper, 'A constrained game formulation of advertising strategies', *Econometrica*, 1954.

† 'Divination – a new perspective', *American Anthropologist*, Vol. 59, 1957, pp. 61–74.

a mixed strategy with a certain probability being attached to the play of all the pure strategies. To adopt such a strategy requires a random device, such as pulling different coloured counters out of a bag or tossing coins which will ensure such probabilities and yet avoid a predictable pattern of behaviour. It is possible that these odd rites may be random devices that have proved successful in the achievement of the goals of the society concerned. Certainly many modern games of chance are thought to have developed from such magical rites. Several Greek and Roman oracles used cleromancy – the throwing of dice or little bones and interpretation of the dots that turned up, or the alignment of the bones.

Moore illustrated his thesis with an account of the Naskapi Indians from Labrador who use scapulimancy to determine where to go hunting. If they want to hunt caribou and have no information about where the beasts are, they take the shoulder blade of a previously killed caribou and, after a lot of ritual, hold it for a time over hot coals. Burnt spots and cracks appear. There is an elaborate but fixed method of interpreting these signs, and this interpretation tells the Naskapi in which direction to go to hunt.

The hunt can be presented as a game between the Naskapi and the caribou. Suppose there are four hunting grounds around the Indian camp – call them north, south, east and west – and that if the hunters come across the caribou herd they always manage to kill one beast. The pay-off matrix for the Naskapi can be easily constructed.

		CARIBOU			
		Feed north	Feed south	Feed east	Feed west
	Hunt north	1	0	0	0
NASKAPI	Hunt south	0	1	0	0
	Hunt east	0	0	1	0
	Hunt west	0	0	0	1

It is a zero-sum game in that if the Naskapi kill a caribou the herd loses a caribou. Looking at the pay-off matrix we can see that there are no dominated strategies and nor is there a saddle-point. The solution to the game must be in terms of mixed strategies. Although we have not discussed the techniques necessary to solve matrix games that are larger than two by two, we can see that since this game is completely symmetrical there can be no advantage in assigning a higher probability to hunting at one point of the compass than another.* The optimal probability vector for both the Naskapi and the caribou must be $[\frac{1}{4} \ \frac{1}{4} \ \frac{1}{4} \ \frac{1}{4}]$.

Although Moore does not present an actual pay-off matrix for the game, he interprets the shoulder-blade augury as a device for getting the randomness required to adopt a mixed strategy. Without such a device there may be a pattern to the hunting expeditions which the caribou could consciously or unconsciously learn and hence supposedly avoid the hunters.

Put in this way, Moore's case is less than convincing but not entirely unappealing. The argument breaks the prime assumption of game theory that there is a conflict between two rational players. However, while caribou may not be famous for their rationality, it may be that unlike humans they naturally act in some kind of random fashion and do not require auguries or roulette wheels to achieve this randomness. One might attempt to argue that an evolutionary process could lead to the development of a randomly wandering herd. But whether Moore's thesis is convincing or not it does have the merit of pointing out that what may appear to be irrational – acting on the basis of tossing coins or throwing dice, for instance – may, in certain circumstances, be very sensible behaviour. The Greek generals who sacrificed a succession of animals, examining each liver in turn for good signs, and not entering a battle until omens were good, could at least guarantee that the enemy did not know when the attack was coming.

In our sophisticated society it is easy for us to ensure that our behaviour is random if we so wish it; we even have special tables of random numbers. Yet it is a very difficult concept to grasp that sometimes it may be best to behave randomly. The students in Liebermann's experiments with simple games failed to develop the idea of a mixed strategy. It is not surprising that societies may have given random devices some religious significance in order to justify the use of some successful practice. At the same time Moore's case is rather weakened if these practices are such that the interpretation of the signs is not fixed or definite. It is easy to read hands and tea leaves in a variety of ways. The palmist or the witch doctor may be tempted to twist the signs to tell people what they want or expect to hear. Even tossing a coin to make a decision is open to this possibility. Bob Dylan illustrates this beautifully in a song entitled 'Bob Dylan's 115th Dream'. Having escaped from jail, Dylan is deciding whether to return to

---

* The game of matching pennies that was mentioned earlier is also of this type. Readers can check that the optimal mixed strategy for both players in that game is to assign equal probabilities to showing heads or tails.

jail to help his friends or leave them stranded and escape on a ship. He writes

> 'I decided to flip a coin
> Like either heads or tails
> Would let me know if I should go
> Back to ship or back to jail
> So I hocked my sailor suit
> And I got a coin to flip
> It came up tails
> It rhymed with sails
> So I made it back to the ship'*

Fishing in Jamaica

Perhaps the most famous example of the application of constant-sum game theory in social science is William Davenport's analysis of a Jamaican fishing village.† As we shall see, Davenport explained the behaviour of fishermen to a remarkable degree of accuracy using, or rather abusing, game theory to portray the supposed conflict between man and nature. A description of the work not only alerts one to the dangers of applying blindly mathematical techniques to descriptions of society, but also illustrates some further technicalities of solving games.

There were twenty-six fishing crews in the village, all with a captain and a boat. The captains had a choice about where to set their fishing pots. They could set them far out at sea where the bigger and better fish were to be found, or they could set them near the shore, inside some sandbanks, where the fish were inferior but the catch was less susceptible to the condition of the current. These fishermen were playing a game against the sea which could send a current to destroy the catch and equipment of those placing pots out at sea, or remain tranquil and thus reduce the value of the poorer-quality fish caught inside the sandbanks because of the glut of fish on the market.

Somehow Davenport calculated a pay-off matrix for the fishermen. He listed three possible strategies every boat could adopt. They could set all their pots inside the banks, all outside, or some pots inside and some outside.

*Bob Dylan's Writings and Drawings, Granada, London, 1974, p. 279.
† W. Davenport, 'Jamaican fishing: a game-theory analysis', Yale University Publications in Anthropology, Vol. 59, pp. 3–11, 1960.

		SEA	
		Current	No current
	Inside	17.3	11.5
FISHERMEN	In-out	5.2	17.0
	Outside	−4.4	20.6

Catch in pounds

The pay-offs for a month's fishing by a crew are measured in pounds and the implicit assumption is that the sea, for some reason, wants to minimize the return to fishing; so we have a zero-sum game.

There is no strategy in this game which dominates another strategy nor does the matrix have a saddle-point; the maximin of the rows (11.5) does not equal the minimax of the columns (17.3). Thus we have to look for the solution of the game in terms of mixed strategies. This game is three-by-two but there is a theorem that tells us that its solution will be the same as that of a two-by-two game obtained by omitting one of the

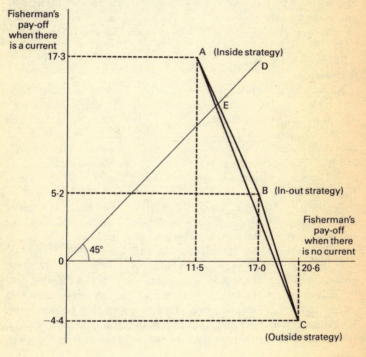

rows. The problem is to determine which of the rows should be omitted. In the figure above, the pay-offs for the various strategies are represented by the points A, B and C.

For instance, the point A represents the fisherman's strategy of placing all pots near the shore. The distance of A along the horizontal axis gives the pay-off to the fishermen if the sea remains calm and its distance along the vertical axis gives the pay-off when the sea runs a current. Similarly the co-ordinates of B(5.2,17.0) give the returns to the fishermen when an in-out strategy is used. The co-ordinates of the mid-point of A B will give the expected returns to the fishermen, for the sea's two possible strategies, if they adopt the inside strategy half the time and the in-out strategy the other half. We can give a similar interpretation to every point on A B, B C and A C. We can also give an interpretation of points within the triangle A B C. For instance if we joined B to the mid-point of A C and consider the point half-way along this line, it would represent the pay-off to using the in-out strategy half the time and the inside and outside strategies for one quarter of the time each. Thus we have that the vertices of the triangle give us the consequences of the use of pure strategies, points on the sides give the consequences of a mix of two strategies, and points in the interior of the triangle give the results of using a mix of all three. The triangle A B C gives the pay-offs for all feasible mixed or pure strategies played by the fishermen.

Now, as far as the fishermen are concerned, a point on this diagram is preferable to another if it lies to the north-east of it. This is because such a point would have a higher pay-off regardless of what the sea does. The only feasible strategies that do not have other strategies definitely better than them in this way are those represented by the points on the lines A B and B C. Thus we can definitely say that the fishermen will use a mix of at most two strategies and will not use a mix of purely inside and purely outside strategies.

We can go further than this. In the game we solved before in terms of mixed strategies, we noted that the expected pay-off for a player at the solution point was the same regardless of what the other player did. It was this fact that we used to solve the game. If we draw a line (O D) at 45° from the origin then every point on it has equal pay-offs for the fishermen regardless of whether the sea sends a current or not. This common pay-off is greatest for the feasible strategies of the fishermen where O D intersects A B at E. This point gives us the game's solution. Intuitively this is obvious. If the fishermen play a strategy somewhere between A and E the sea can ensure they receive a lower pay-off than at E by remaining calm; if the fishermen choose to be on EB or BC the sea can again guarantee them a lower pay-off than at E by sending a current.

An accurate drawing of the figure would tell us nearly all we want to know. The value of the game can be read off from the co-ordinates of E; the ratio of the lengths of AE to AB would give the probability the fishermen should assign to playing the in-out strategy and the ratio EB to AB the probability of playing the inside strategy. Not entirely trusting our draughtsmanship, we shall solve the game algebraically.

Knowing that the fishermen will never use the purely outside strategy we can remove it from the game matrix:

$$
\begin{array}{cc}
 & SEA \\
\end{array}
$$

$$
\textit{FISHERMEN} \quad
\begin{array}{c}
\text{Inside} \\
\text{In-out}
\end{array}
\begin{bmatrix}
17.3 & 11.5 \\
5.2 & 17.0
\end{bmatrix} = G.
$$

$$
\begin{array}{cc}
\text{Current} & \text{No current}
\end{array}
$$

If the fishermen's probability vector for playing the inside and in-out strategy is $p\,(=[p_1\,p_2])$ then their expected pay-offs for the two strategies of the sea are given by the row vector

$$
pG = \begin{bmatrix} p_1 & p_2 \end{bmatrix}
\begin{bmatrix}
17.3 & 11.5 \\
5.2 & 17.0
\end{bmatrix}
$$

$$
\begin{array}{cc}
& SEA \\
\text{Current} & \text{No current}
\end{array}
$$

$$
= \begin{bmatrix} 17.3p_1 + 5.2p_2 & 11.5p_1 + 17.0p_2 \end{bmatrix}.
$$

Remembering that the solution of this game requires that these two pay-offs be equal, and that by definition $p_2 = 1 - p_1$, we can calculate the probability $(p_1{}^*)$ that optimally the fishermen should assign to playing the inside strategy:

$$
17.3p_1^* + 5.2\,(1 - p_1^*) = 11.5p_1^* + 17.0\,(1 - p_1^*).
$$

With trivial manipulation this yields to two places of decimals

$$
p_1^* = 0.67
$$

and

$$
p_2^* = 0.33.
$$

The fishermen's best strategy is to fish inside and in-out in the ratio of 67 to 33. Or, since there are 26 canoes the fishermen should use them in such a way that .67 × 26 of them fish inside and .33 × 26 fish inside and outside. Thus the theory of games tells the fishermen to use 17.4 canoes for solely inside fishing, 8.6 canoes for in-out fishing and none for solely outside fishing. Davenport observed that in fact 18 canoes fished entirely inside the sandbanks, 8 fished both inside and outside, and none fished solely outside. These observations correspond remarkably well to the strategy prescribed by the theory of games.

It is left as an exercise for the reader to show that the strategy prescribed by the theory of games for the sea is to run a current about 31 per cent of the time and remain calm for the other 69 per cent. Davenport's observations were that the sea actually ran a current about 25 per cent of the time, which, while not as close to the prescribed strategy as were the fishermen, is not that far away from it.

Not only are these results surprising in their accuracy, but even more surprising is the fact that Davenport conceptualized the problem in terms of game theory. This conceptualization requires a view that either nature is, or the fishermen behave as if it is, a malevolent rational force attempting to minimize the market value of the catch. Further, it supposes that the fishermen act in a co-operative fashion as a team trying to defeat nature. Davenport presents no evidence to suggest that there is such co-operation; indeed there appears to be considerable rivalry between the crews. They do not share the income from fishing; they keep the positions in which they set their pots a closely guarded secret because the price an individual crew gets for its catch depends on the success or otherwise of the other crews. Particular crews consistently adopt either the inside or the in-out strategy. No individual crew seems to pursue the optimal strategy for itself, this not even being an option for many because outside fishing requires a superior boat.

Further, the pay-off matrix itself is open to doubt. Davenport's estimates for the return to solely outside fishing are simply estimates. No crew adopted this strategy and it is difficult to understand Davenport's logic in arriving at his figures. The other entries in the matrix are observed figures but these would alter by the laws of supply and demand if the proportion of crews adopting the different strategies changed. The price of the better-quality fish caught outside the banks compared to the fish caught inside depends on the relative supplies of the two kinds of fish. This depends not only on whether the sea is calm or rough, but also on how many crews adopt each strategy. One must conclude that the correspondence of the solution of the game to the observations is mere coincidence.

This is a case where a most inappropriate theory seemingly provides a successful explanation of events. It has been chosen as an example not merely as a warning to anthropologists to keep their feet out of economics, nor just to teach a salutary lesson about the dangers of a little learning. There is a dearth of satisfactory examples of the use of constant-sum games to provide explanations of social phenomena. We must accept that perhaps the conditions required for the use of such games are seldom met with in practice.

Exercises

Using the techniques above show that R will never use strategy 3 for games with the following pay-off matrices. Find the optimal mix of strategies 1 and 2 for R and C.

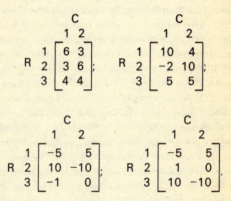

Farming in Ghana

We would not like to give the impression that anthropology has a monopoly of the misuse of game theory. All social sciences have examples of abuses of techniques derived from other disciplines. Geography is no easy exception to this rule. Peter Gould's grandly titled article 'Man against his environment: a game theoretic framework',* seems to be the

---

* In *Annals of the Association of American Geographers*, Vol. 53, 1963, pp. 290–97.

most cited example of a geographer's use of game theory. Having praised Davenport's work on the fishermen, Gould applies the same techniques to the farmers of Jantilla in Western Ghana. They can choose to plant various crops but the return to each depends on whether the growing season is wet or dry. Gould's pay-off matrix for the farmers is given below.*

		ENVIRONMENT	
		Wet years	Dry years
	Yams	82	11
FARMERS OF	Maize	61	49
JANTILLA	Cassava	12	38
	Millet	43	32
	Hill rice	30	71

The pay-offs are fictitious (although Jantilla apparently does exist) and Gould does not even tell us what units they are to be measured in – he hints vaguely that calorific or nutritional content might be what we want.

We can see straight away that the cassava and millet strategies are both dominated by maize and we can thus remove them from the game matrix. Thus we are left with a three-by-two game which does not have a saddle-point, and hence there is no solution in terms of pure strategies. If we use the techniques we have developed to solve such games, it can be shown (and this is left as a useful exercise for the reader) that the solution is for the farmers to grow maize with probability .77 and hill rice with probability .23. Likewise it can be shown that the environment should produce dry years .58 of the time and wet years .42 of the time. Gould concluded that farmers will or should put 77 per cent of their land down to maize and 23 per cent of their land to hill rice each year.

He goes on to suggest some questions that could be asked after such a study has been completed: 'Does the land-use pattern approach the ideal? If the land-use pattern does not approach the ideal, does this imply a conscious departure on the part of the people, or does their less-than-ideal use of the land reflect only the best estimate they can make with the knowledge available to them, rather than any degree of irrationality? ... If one were in an advisory position would this help to make decisions regarding the improvement of agricultural practices?'† While the last

* Gould, *op. cit.*, p. 291.
† Gould, *op. cit.*, p. 293.

question may be answered with a definite negative, the first two are meaningless. The solution to the game does not tell us what ideal land use is. The environment is not a rational opponent intent on minimizing the nutritional, calorific, money value, weight or any other attribute of the farmers' crops that we might display in a pay-off matrix. The use of game theory, with this assumption that nature does its worst, could lead to the advice that Britain divide its lands between coconuts and reindeer pasturage because of the possibility of the weather randomly altering between tropical and arctic conditions. Different crops are grown in different parts of the globe largely because of differences in climate. To find the ideal use of land in a place we need to know amongst other things the probability of different climatic conditions in that place, the farmers' attitudes towards the choice between high but risky pay-offs and low but safer pay-offs, the possibility of storing crops from year to year, and, not least, what it is that farmers are trying to maximize.

While this example serves as an exercise for readers to practise their new-found skills in solving games, it is also intended as a serious warning of the dangers of the misapplication of mathematical techniques to important social problems. Nor do I think I am using a straw man, not taken seriously by other geographers, to illustrate this point. A random walk through the geography sections of the local library produced some interesting views on game theory and Gould's work. The views were in general laudatory but also showed rather nicely how people can misread information or jumble it during the process of transmission.*

Michael Chisholm, in a well-known text commenting generally on game theory,† says that it is not much use in the study of conflict between humans. 'However if one of the "players" is conceived to be "nature" then a two-person game can be extremely useful.'** This, of course, is the opposite of the truth. In citing Gould's work as an example of its usefulness, Chisholm writes that 'Gould collected data'‡ whereas Gould explicitly states that his numbers are fictional. It is easy to forgive this misreading in that Gould does, for some unaccountable reason, draw a map illustrating the position of Jantilla in Ghana and this has the effect of adding spurious realism to his work. It is harder to understand the misreadings by some other commentators who believe that not only were

---

* See chapter 6.
† M. Chisholm, *Human Geography: Evolution or Revolution*, Penguin, Harmondsworth, 1975.
** *ibid.*, p. 141.
‡ *ibid.*, 142.

the data real but that Gould compared the game-theory solution to actual land-use. Thus, for instance, Morgan and Munton write that Gould had a 'close fit between reality and the predicted land-use pattern',[*] and even more amazingly David Rhind and Roy Hudson attribute reasons for this non-existent correspondence: 'Gould in fact found that actual land-use patterns in Jantilla in the Middle Belt of Ghana approximated to this optimal pattern, a correspondence reflecting learning and adaptation by the resident population.'[†]

A fictional study using inappropriate techniques has somehow been transformed into an example of a good theory successfully surviving a confrontation with fact. We turn from this blemish on the academic scene to some more fruitful avenues for the theory of games.

[*] W. B. Morgan and R. J. C. Munton, *Agricultural Geography*, Methuen, London, 1971.
[†] D. Rhind and R. Hudson, *Land Use*, Methuen, London, 1980.

13
Conflict or Co-operation

In the games considered so far the players' interests have been diametrically opposed. We turn now to games where the conflict is not of such an extreme form but in which it is possible for players sometimes to adopt strategies that are mutually advantageous. Many of these games do not have such definite solutions as constant-sum games but the analysis of them does help to see the structure of many conflicts and hence the difficulties that may arise in attempts at resolution.

We have seen that the solution of some games is that players should adopt the deliberately random behaviour of mixed strategies. I was thinking about this while I was on holiday in France and soon after was confronted with the random behaviour of British Customs officials. Standing nervously in the queue in the 'green channel' I realized that I was in a game where a mixed strategy may well be the solution yet it was certainly not a constant-sum game.

Smuggling

Customs officers have two strategies when faced with a traveller. They can search the person or let them into the country untouched. Travellers can choose to smuggle or not. No doubt officials do act on any information they have about particular travellers, and perhaps even gain information by looking for such things as perspiration in the palms of hands or roving nervous eyes. However, casual observation suggests that in addition they basically choose a random sample of people to search. Questions to be answered are whether this is a sensible policy and if so how large should this sample be. We start by constructing pay-off matrices for the Customs and the typical traveller.

$$
\begin{array}{c}
\textit{HM CUSTOMS} \\
\begin{array}{cc}
\text{Search} & \text{Not search}
\end{array} \\
\textit{TRAVELLER} \begin{array}{l} \text{Not smuggle} \\ \text{Smuggle} \end{array}
\left[
\begin{array}{cc}
T & S \\
W & B
\end{array}
\right]
\end{array}
$$

Traveller's pay-off matrix

Key: B = best outcome; S = second best: T = third best: W = worst.

For the traveller the best outcome is that he is not searched and manages to get some contraband into the country. Not smuggling and not being searched is preferable to being searched when not smuggling because of the effort of repacking bags and the wasted time that results from a search. The worst outcome for the traveller is, of course, to be caught with contraband.

Her Majesty's Customs have a different pay-off matrix.

$$HM\ CUSTOMS$$

		Search	Not search
TRAVELLER	Not smuggle	S	B
	Smuggle	T	W

H. M. Customs pay-off matrix

For the Customs the worst outcome is that the traveller smuggles but is not searched. The costs of this are the loss of duty and the social costs of lawlessness. Next worse is the traveller smuggling and being searched. This is worse than searching a non-smuggler because not only are there the labour costs of searching but also there are costs involved in prosecuting smugglers. The best outcome for the Customs is not searching a non-smuggler.

In a constant-sum game the better the outcome for one player the worse it is for the other. Clearly this is not a constant-sum game. It is usual with non-constant-sum games to put the two pay-off matrices together, the first element of each pair representing the pay-off to the row player and the second the pay-off to the column player.

$$HM\ CUSTOMS$$

		Search	Not search
TRAVELLER	Not smuggle	T,S	S,B
	Smuggle	W,T	B,W

Even without assigning numerical values to the various outcomes we can see that neither player has a dominant strategy, but the problems facing the player may be made clearer by replacing the symbols with fictitious numbers.

$$HM\ CUSTOMS$$

		Search	Not search
TRAVELLER	Not smuggle	−1, −2	0, 0
	Smuggle	−51, −5	10, −20

d that no pure strategies are dominant, let us see what happens if the players adopt the cautious tactic of a maximin approach. Clearly the traveller will not smuggle but the Customs will search. This is hardly an equilibrium for if the travellers never smuggle the Customs can benefit by altering their strategy to not searching. (Indeed this change of strategy would benefit the traveller as well as the Customs.) However, if the Customs do not search people the travellers may as well smuggle, but then the Customs would benefit by starting to search. We are just going round the matrix in a clockwise direction for ever and ever.

Looking at the matrix again it can be seen that although the Customs have no dominant strategy, their pay-off is greater, whether they search or not, when the traveller does not smuggle. They must look for a way of ensuring that the traveller plays the 'not smuggle' strategy. Similarly we can argue that the traveller should try to ensure that the Customs play the 'not search' strategy, but let us first concentrate on the game from the Customs' point of view.

Obviously the Customs could guarantee that no smuggling took place by announcing that they will always search travellers and carrying out this policy. However they can do better than this by searching a sufficient proportion of travellers to deter any smuggling. Suppose they adopt a policy of searching a proportion q and hence not searching a proportion $1-q$. Using the techniques developed for constant-sum games we can determine the minimum percentage of travellers that the Customs should search. With this random-search policy we have for the traveller that

the expected pay-off for not smuggling $= -1q + 0(1-q) = -q$

and

the expected pay-off for smuggling $= -51q + 10(1-q) = 10 - 61q$.

For small values of q the expected pay-off for smuggling is greater than not smuggling and vice versa for large values of q. The minimum value of q that will deter smuggling (q^*) is that value for which the two expected pay-offs are equal.

Then

$$-q^* = 10 - 61q^*$$
$$q^* = \tfrac{1}{6}.$$

Provided the Customs search at least one in six travellers should stop smuggling. In such circumstances we have that

$$\text{the expected pay-off for the traveller} = -\tfrac{1}{6}$$

and

$$\text{the expected pay-off for the Customs} = -2 \times \tfrac{1}{6} + 0 \times \tfrac{5}{6} = -\tfrac{1}{3}.$$

In one sense this is a solution to the game. If the Customs search more or less than one in six travellers the travellers will act so as to lower the expected pay-off to the Customs. In another sense it is an unsatisfactory solution. For both players the outcome is worse than if they agreed respectively to not smuggle and not search. The random-search solution gives a negative pay-off to both players while this better alternative would yield both sides a zero pay-off. If the Customs could trust the travellers not to smuggle then everybody would be happier. In this example one suspects that this nice co-operative outcome is unlikely to be achieved. Strikes by Customs officials tend to lead to large plastic bags full of dutiable items such as alcohol and tobacco being carried off ferry boats. Given that trust is likely to be misplaced the random search or conflict solution is a much more likely outcome than the more efficient one of co-operation.

We have deliberately looked at the game from the Customs point of view, having noted that equally the traveller could try to ensure the Customs never searched. Going through the exercise again from the point of view of the traveller the reader can calculate that if the travellers declare and carry out a policy of smuggling not more than twice out of seventeen occasions then it will pay the Customs not to search at all. We have omitted this possibility on the grounds that HM Customs would not condone such lawlessness – even though they would benefit from it – and, without the random search of the Customs, there is no way of checking that the travellers are sticking to their declared policy. Without searching it is impossible for the Customs to know what proportion of travellers are smuggling. However, we can see that with two different players and a different social context the solution of a game of this type may well be rather elusive.

We have, of course, simplified the problem of smuggling to a considerable extent. Every traveller will not have the same pay-off matrix. People value the inconvenience of being searched differently; they also, no doubt, place different values on the costs of being sent to gaol; smuggling is not homogeneous in that one can smuggle different amounts of goods and the returns to and penalties for smuggling different goods are not the same. There is no reason, however, to suppose that allowing for such complications will fundamentally alter the game. Random search will still be the rational method of trying to deter big-time smugglers even if it is difficult to calculate the appropriate proportion of travellers to be searched. As far as small-scale smugglers are concerned, where the costs of search and prosecution may approach or be greater than the costs of letting goods into the country duty-free, the Customs may offer a gesture of trust. They can encourage co-operation by allowing limited smuggling and calling it a duty-free allowance.

This game gives us some basis for supposing that the actual behaviour of Her Majesty's Customs has a rational basis. It is interesting to note that there is little complaint about allowing the Customs legally to pursue this strategy. In a similar fashion it would no doubt be rational for the police to breathalyse a random sample of people driving cars away from public houses. This is not allowed and it is generally thought that such a policy would involve a considerable incursion into the liberties and rights of the individual. Unless one supposes that the police would be more likely to abuse such a strategy than do Customs officers this seems to be rather inconsistent. In this case it may be the public's lack of trust in the police that allows the carnage caused by drunken drivers to continue.

Prisoner's Dilemma

In the smuggling game it turned out that the likely outcome was a situation in which both players could improve their pay-offs, if they could trust each other and co-operate. Many non-constant-sum games have this problem of conflict or co-operation but it is perhaps most starkly illustrated in a very famous game known as *prisoner's dilemma*. The original formulation of the game goes roughly as follows. Two prisoners have been arrested on suspicion of committing a serious crime. In fact they are guilty but there is not enough evidence to convict them of it. They are kept in separate cells and questioned by police. If they both confess to the crime they will receive fairly long gaol sentences. If neither confesses they will be 'fitted up' on some minor charge and receive a short gaol sentence. If one confesses and turns Queen's evidence while the other doesn't the confessor will go scot-free and receive a reward from the police, while the one who does not confess will receive an even larger gaol sentence than if

211

he had admitted his guilt. This information can be collected in a pay-off matrix representing a game between the two prisoners, using the same symbols as in the previous section and where again the first entry of a pair gives the pay-off to the row player and the second entry the column player's pay-off.

		PRISONER C	
		Not confess	Confess
PRISONER R	Not confess	S, S	W, B
	Confess	B, W	T, T

Key: B = best outcome; S = second best; T = third best; W = worst.

The configuration of Bs, Ss, Ts and Ws is noticeably different from the smuggling game and this unsurprisingly leads to different results. For those who like arithmetic rather than algebra we can put in some numerical values for these pay-offs to reflect the outcomes of the story.

		PRISONER C	
		Not confess	Confess
PRISONER R	Not confess	−1, −1	−5, +1
	Confess	+1, −5	−3, −3

In this game the solution at first sight appears to be simple. The game is symmetrical and whether we choose to examine the algebraic or numerical matrix it is apparent that for both prisoners the strategy of confessing dominates the strategy of not confessing. So if they are rational they both confess, end up with fairly long gaol sentences and leave the police delighted. The prisoners have plenty of time to reflect that they both ended up with their next to worst outcome when a bit of trust and co-operation in the form of not confessing would have left them both with their second best outcome. It is this dilemma – that individual interest dictates confession regardless of what the other prisoner does, while it is in their collective interest that neither confesses – that has caused this fascinating game to be extensively studied. Such a dilemma cannot occur in constant-sum games. With diametrically opposed players there can never be a possibility of a change in strategy producing mutual benefit.

Before looking at examples of conflicts of interest that may be represented by the prisoner's dilemma game let us extend the rather contrived story of the prisoners a little further. An obvious way to remove the dilemma is to alter the rules of the game or alter the pay-offs for the various strategies. This may seem a cheating method of removing the dilemma but in many conflicts the actors or interested outsiders do often play a role in formulating the rules or determining amendments to existing rules. The ability or otherwise to amend the rules may well determine whether a co-operative or an inefficient conflict solution is reached. In the case of the prisoners an important part of the story was that they were kept in separate cells. This prevents them agreeing not to confess and observing that the agreement is carried out. Co-operation is more likely where there is negotiation between the players and where there can be effective policing of agreements. Alternatively another outside body may alter the pay-offs. In the story the pay-offs are presumably determined by the police and the judiciary. However, it is rumoured that in the underworld there are severe penalties for squealing. The reward given to a man for turning Queen's evidence may be small in comparison to the costs incurred when he is caught by other members of the criminal fraternity. If this reduces the pay-off to confessing, when the other prisoner does not, to something worse than the pay-off when neither confesses then the dilemma may be removed. Let us suppose that in our numerical matrix this pay-off is lowered to -2. There is now a new pay-off matrix.

$$
\begin{array}{cc}
 & \textit{PRISONER C} \\
 & \begin{array}{cc} \text{Not confess} & \text{Confess} \end{array} \\
\textit{PRISONER R} \quad \begin{array}{c} \text{Not confess} \\ \text{Confess} \end{array} & \begin{bmatrix} -1,\ -1 & -5,\ -2 \\ -2,\ -5 & -3,\ -3 \end{bmatrix} \\[2em]
= & \begin{bmatrix} \text{B, B} & \text{W, S} \\ \text{S, W} & \text{T, T} \end{bmatrix}
\end{array}
$$

Now neither prisoner has a dominant strategy. If both adopted the maximin approach that we associated with rationality in constant-sum games then both would confess and again we would have the unco-operative solution. However in a non-constant-sum game there is nothing rational about the maximin approach. Unless a player is very spiteful he will be trying to secure the best outcome for himself rather than the worst for his opponent. On this assumption both prisoners in this new game will not confess on the assumption that the other will behave rationally and act in the same manner. The imposition of sanctions for departing from the co-operative solution has led to a better outcome for everybody than if the sanctions were not there. We turn to some important examples where our analysis of prisoner's dilemma games may be illuminating.

213

The Arms Race

The Cold War or arms race with its horrendous waste is the most popular example of a social conflict to be depicted as a prisoner's dilemma game.* The convincing story starts by assuming that the United States and the Soviet Union are considering whether or not to increase their '*defences*' by building an anti-anti-anti-missile system (or whatever number of antis the game is in at the moment). Suppose that both governments rate having the system when the other does not as being worth, say, 150 units per year, and rate not having the system when the other does as being worth -150 units. Suppose the cost of building and servicing such a system is 100 units per year (the cakes and ale people would have had instead). If both countries build the system neither sees any benefit or loss to the present status quo apart from the loss of these alternative goods. We can put this information into a pay-off matrix.

		US	
		Not build system	Build system
USSR	Not build system	0, 0	$-150, +50$
	Build system	$+50, -150$	$-100, -100$

Writing B for the best outcome and so on, we can see that this game is exactly of the same form as the original prisoner's dilemma story.

		US	
		Not build system	Build system
USSR	Not build system	S, S	W, B
	Build system	B, W	T, T

The strategy 'build system' is dominant for both players. Without co-operation, and following their dominant strategies, they will both develop the new defence system and both be worse off than if neither had done so.

As one would expect, this same unfortunate outcome appears to be likely if one considers disarmament instead of new armament. The US and USSR have the capacity to destroy each other several times. A reduction of armaments of equal amounts would leave them in the same

* See, for instance, Thomas C. Schelling, *The Strategy of Conflict*, Harvard University Press, Cambridge, Mass., 1960; and Michael Nicholson, *Conflict Analysis*, The English University Press, London, 1970.

214

strategic position and release resources for other uses. Suppose having built the new system of the previous game they both consider dismantling it. We have a new pay-off matrix.

		US	
		Reduce arms	Retain present level
USSR	Reduce arms	100, 100	−50, 150
	retain present level	150, −50	0, 0

Not surprisingly, since the pay-offs in this matrix are obtained by adding 100 units to the corresponding pay-offs in the previous matrix, we have another prisoner's dilemma game with no incentive for either side to disarm unilaterally but both benefitting if they both disarm. We could extend all this to show that there will be a tendency for defence expenditure always to be increased if the supposed strategic benefits from the increase, that would occur if the other side did not make a corresponding increase, are greater than the costs of this extra defence. With both sides acting in the same manner these strategic benefits never do accrue and the outcome is mere waste.

Is there any route to co-operation in this depressing tale? Sadly, unlike in our fictitious extension of the original prisoner's game, there is no Mafia to alter the pay-offs to ensure co-operation. The United Nations can encourage it but not enforce it. There is a slight hope in that, unlike the prisoners, the US and USSR have no need to take decisions sitting independently in separate cells. They can meet round a table and attempt to negotiate for mutual co-operation but the history of disarmament talks is not one of success. Without a thorough inspection by both sides of the other's armaments it is possible to cheat on any negotiated agreement. Thus without such an inspection we would have another prisoner's dilemma game with the strategies 'cheat' and 'not cheat' replacing 'retain present level' and 'reduce arms'. To cheat would be the dominant strategy for both sides. Arms talks tend to founder on the policing of agreements. Any policing naturally gives one's enemies information and it is difficult to persuade negotiators that these two piles of intelligence would balance out. Nor is it easy for two enemies to agree upon what agency would be a neutral referee. We are left with a very bleak outlook and the paradox that it appears to be rational for the US and USSR to continue amassing weapons of war. Perhaps we should question this view of rationality.

OPEC, Trade Unions, Public Parks and Lamp-posts

The Organization of Petroleum Exporting Countries was set up to promote the collective interest of its members. In 1974 it succeeded in quadrupling the price of oil and hence increased massively the revenues received by the oil-producing nations. Before that occasion the price of oil had been falling in real terms and since 1974 there has been a similar erosion in the price. The problem OPEC faces is quite simple. In order to raise the price of oil on the world market, less oil must be produced. Members of the cartel must be prepared to sell less if they want to get a higher price.

Let us suppose, for simplicity, that there are five nations all producing 100 units of oil and receiving a price of one million pounds per unit. Let us also suppose that if the quantity produced goes down by 1 per cent the price they will receive will, by market forces, go up by 2 per cent. Thus we get the following table.

Total Production	Price Per Unit in £ million
500	1
490	1.04
480	1.08
470	1.12
460	1.16
450	1.20

Seeing the benefits that can accrue from restricting oil production, the members of OPEC make an agreement to cut output by 10 per cent. The problem that faces each nation is whether or not to honour this agreement. The change in revenue for each nation will depend on how many others break or keep their word. These changes in revenue can be represented in a pay-off matrix for member A.

Number of other nations keeping agreement

		0	1	2	3	4
Member A	Leave production unchanged	0	4	8	12	16
	Cut output by 10%	−6.4	−2.8	0.8	4.4	8

Pay-off as change in revenue in £ million

These figures are easily calculated. For instance if member A reduces its output by ten units and so do two other members the price of oil rises to 1.12 million pounds per unit and hence A's revenue is $90 \times 1.12 = 100.8$ which is an increase in revenue of .8 million pounds.

Leaving production unchanged as a strategy is better for member A regardless of what other nations do. It is a dominant strategy. This, of course, is true for all the members. Thus we have a five-person prisoner's dilemma game in which collective interest demands that everybody cuts production but self-interest and rationality dictate that nobody should. The cartel will collapse unless OPEC can enforce production quotas. Again one is in the situation where, without trust, there has to be agreed policing arrangements before co-operation can be achieved. It is perhaps surprising that with the economic and political differences of the members of OPEC that such a degree of co-operation was achieved in 1974. Of course, while the model presented does indicate the difficulties of getting a cartel to work it is not a perfect representation of OPEC. The members are certainly not all equal and the recognition of the importance of Saudi Arabia might make considerable differences to the analysis.*

The above analysis could apply to the producers of many goods. In agriculture if there is a general and widespread bad harvest the consequent increase in price of crops may well result in an increase in income for farmers. From this it follows that if all farmers agree to grow less no doubt they could all benefit. At the same time it would pay any individual farmer to produce more. In this prisoner's dilemma game with very many players one certainly, and luckily for non-farmers, does not expect the co-operative outcome to be realized. On the other hand, if the number of players are few and the agreement readily policed, cartel agreements can last for long periods of time. It is only recently that Sealink and Townsend Thoresen abandoned their agreement on fares on cross-Channel ferries.

Prisoner's dilemma games with many players do portray many social situations. Consider a factory with a work-force of 100 people. The more people that join a trade union the better are the chances of the union securing a pay rise. Suppose that the union will press for a ten pound per week pay rise and that the workers believe that every additional member of the union gives the union a 1 per cent better chance of being successful

* For instance Ali D. Johany, in *The Myth of the OPEC Cartel* (John Wiley, Chichester, 1980), argues that OPEC has never been an effective cartel and that the rise in oil prices in 1974 came about not by co-operation between oil producers but in consequence of the change in control of oil resources from the petroleum companies to the governments of the oil-producing nations.

in the claim. The cost of joining the union is fifty pence per week. The expected gain or loss from joining or not joining the union for any worker depends then on the number of other workers joining.

Number of other workers joining union

		0	1	2	...	50	...	99
Worker A	Don't join union	0	.10	.20	...	5.00	...	9.90
	Join union	−.40	−.30	−.20	...	4.60	...	9.50

Expected pay-off to worker A in pounds per week

If fifty other workers join but worker A does not the union has a 50 per cent chance of getting the pay rise so the expected pay-off is five pounds. If in addition worker A also joins his pay-off is the expected £5.10 wage increase minus the 50 pence union dues. Because all workers benefit from union activity regardless of whether they are members, the pay-off from not joining is always greater than the pay-off from joining regardless of how many others join. We are back in the prisoner's dilemma with it being rational for nobody to join the union. That unions do exist suggests that there may be other considerations that stop people acting in this supposedly rational and self-interested manner. Basically to get people to join the union, other than by appealing to their immorality in free-riding on the backs of the union members, one must provide benefits that do not accrue to non-joiners. Thus an important part of most unions' activities is providing protection against the unfair dismissal of a member. This alters the pay-off matrix and removes the dilemma. Similarly if a union can get a closed shop in a factory then not joining the union results in the loss of employment at that factory. Rather than being seen as a severe restriction on individual liberties, the closed shop may be better seen as a way of promoting co-operation, avoiding conflict and furthering the collective interests of workers.

From the union example we can see that prisoner's dilemma games are going to be common when one cannot exclude people from the benefits or use of a good or service. In economics these goods are called collective goods or public goods.* Once goods such as public parks, street lighting, defence, police services and clean air have been provided it is difficult to exclude citizens from the benefit of them. If the provision of such goods were left to individuals then there would be very little of any of them. The dilemma in these cases is resolved by government action. The government raises taxes, preferably those that are difficult to evade, and with these

* See for instance chapter 15 of D. K. H. Begg, S. Fischer and R. Dornbusch, *Economics*, McGraw-Hill, Maidenhead, 1984.

resources provides what it thinks is the *right* amount of these goods for the collective interest. Whether there is such a thing as the *right* amount and if so whether the government finds it is yet another question.

Pollution

Following the lines of argument of the previous examples it can readily be seen that the polluted state of the environment may be the non-co-operative outcome of a game. If it is cheaper to pollute than not to pollute then individual greed will result in the nasty outcome of all individuals polluting. Governments sometimes do recognize this problem and legislate to prevent or limit the pollution a firm or individual can produce. Intervention of this kind, altering the rules of the game, may be very successful but sometimes such legislation may be impossible to enforce or even enact. The sad state of the Great Lakes of North America illustrates such difficulties. These once beautiful and fruitful lakes are steadily dying from the waste of the United States and Canadian cities that are on their shores. That the lakes lie between two countries leads to a discouragement of any one country taking action to clean them up. This can be presented as a prisoner's dilemma.

Let us suppose that for both countries the costs of preventing their own pollution amount to 200 million dollars and that the benefits to both of totally pollution-free lakes are estimated at 300 million dollars, while if just one country carries on polluting the benefits are 150 million dollars to both. From these data we can work out the net benefits to each country of the consequences of controlling pollution or taking no action.

			CANADA			
			Control pollution		Take no action	
	Control	Costs	300,	100	Costs	300,	0
UNITED	pollution	Benefits	600,	200	Benefits	450,	150
STATES	Take no	Costs	0,	100	Costs	0,	0
	action	Benefits	200,	65	Benefits	0,	0

Costs and benefits in millions of dollars

The 'take no action' strategy is dominant for both countries but both could benefit by agreeing to take anti-pollution measures. The best, second-best, third-best and worst outcomes for both nations are positioned in the matrix in the same configuration as for our previous prisoner's dilemma games. Once again the superior outcome of co-operation may be difficult to achieve – laws and customs differ from country to country and neither may believe the other will do the job properly. We have already simplified the game by suggesting that there are only two players. This presupposes that within each country a co-operative outcome can be achieved by the individual polluters, the firms and the city authorities within each country. Without legislation within each country we have an *n*-person prisoner's dilemma game comparable to our previous example of cartels and unions. To ensure co-operation within a nation requires altering the pay-offs by laws regulating pollution or taxes on pollution or subsidies to encourage pollution prevention. The efficacy of such measures depends on amongst other things the likelihood of prosecution for breaking the law and the severity of punishment, and the magnitude of the taxes or subsidies. In addition to these internal difficulties, for a co-operative international solution both nations must believe that the other's method of control is adequate.

Perhaps luckily not all conflicts are of the prisoner's dilemma kind. Indeed Rapoport and Guyer* suggest that for a two-by-two matrix there are seventy-eight ways that the best, second-best, third-best and worst outcomes of the players can be arranged to produce significantly different games. While pollution may often be rightly seen as the unfortunate outcome of a prisoner's dilemma situation, it has been suggested that our particular example of the Great Lakes is a rather different game.† It is quite easy to get the flavour of this new game.

Our model assumed that the costs and benefits to the United States and Canada were equal. This is silly when one realizes that Canada has only about a quarter of the population and industry that borders the lake. Let us suppose, therefore, that the costs to Canada of preventing its pollution are only one third of that of the United States and that the benefits to Canada of clean lakes are similarly smaller. We can construct a table to picture the amounts we are assuming such costs and benefits to be.

		CANADA	
		Control pollution	Take no action
UNITED STATES	Control pollution	100, 100	−50, 150
	Take no action	150, −50	0, 0

* A. Rapoport and M. J. Guyer, 'A taxonomy of 2 × 2 games', *General Systems*, Vol. 11, 1966, pp. 203–14.

† Michael Sheehan and K. C. Kogiku, 'Game theory analyses applied to water-resource problems', *Socio-Economic Planning Sciences*, Vol. 15, No. 3, 1981, pp. 109–18.

In this table the first number of any pair gives the costs or benefits to the United States of a particular combination of strategies, and the second number is the costs or benefits to Canada. The countries are, of course, only interested in the net benefits accruing to them so we get our game matrix by subtracting the costs from the benefits in each section of the table.

		CANADA	
		Control pollution	Take no action
UNITED STATES	Control pollution	300, 100	150, 150
	Take no action	200, −35	0, 0
		Net benefits	

Using our code we can see that this game is not of the prisoner's dilemma type.

		CANADA	
		Control pollution	Take no action
UNITED STATES	Control pollution	B, S	T, B
	Take no action	S, W	W, T

However, like the prisoner's dilemma, both players do have a dominant strategy. It appears that whatever Canada does the United States should control pollution, while whatever the United States does Canada should take no action. Canada, not being a large polluter, can save its money and benefit from the expensive measures taken by its neighbour. Again, like the prisoner's dilemma, the outcome from both players choosing their dominant strategy is stable in the sense that neither player can improve his lot by unilaterally altering his strategy. Unlike prisoner's dilemma there is no other outcome that is better for both players, so at least in this case rationality apparently works in favour of one of the players. Canada secures her best outcome while the United States makes do with her third best.

Of course this is not the end of the story. We must remember that the countries can alter the rules of the game. Seeing Canada riding on her

221

back the United States might declare in advance that her strategy will be to take no action unless Canada controls her pollution. If Canada believes that the United States will actually follow this strategy and if necessary sacrifice the benefits from independently controlling pollution, then Canada may succumb to the threat and agree to take action. An equilibrium outcome that allows the possibility of a threat of this kind is called a *threat-vulnerable* equilibrium. However, the threat may not be effective. Canada may decide that the United States is bluffing and will eventually take action to benefit herself whatever Canada does. Whether a threat is taken seriously or not will depend upon many things including the amount the threatener has to lose by carrying out the threat, the show of determination and the past behaviour of the threatener in similar situations. In the political world threats and the attempts to convince opponents of their seriousness – brinkmanship – have led to many potentially explosive and explosive situations.*

There are other possible outcomes in this deceptively simple game. Once we recognize the possibility of threats it is automatic to consider the possibility of bribes. Suppose that the United States decides to pursue her dominant strategy of controlling pollution. If Canada also takes action the United States is 150 million dollars better off than if Canada does nothing while Canada is only 50 million dollars worse off. Thus any side-payment of between 50 and 150 million dollars from the United States to Canada to persuade Canada to act against pollution will leave both sides better off than if Canada does nothing. What is happening here is that while the sums of the pay-offs to both players for the various strategy combinations are unchanged, the players can agree to alter the distribution of these sums between themselves. (This is possible for money pay-offs but a little more difficult in the prisoner's game where it may be difficult to persuade the authorities to divide a gaol sentence.) Thus if the United States offers to pay Canada 100 million dollars to pursue anti-pollution measures we have a new pay-off matrix.

		CANADA	
		Control pollution	Take no action
UNITED STATES	Control pollution	200, 200	150, 150
	Take no action	100, 65	0, 0

* For a comprehensive discussion of the use of game theory for analysing such situations see S. J. Brams, *Game Theory and Politics*, Free Press, New York, 1975.

which in our code looks like

$$\begin{bmatrix} B, B & S, S \\ T, T & W, W \end{bmatrix}$$

Controlling pollution is now the dominant strategy for both countries and both are better off than with the equilibrium outcome of the original game.

So why are the Great Lakes still so polluted if international agreement between the two countries could lead to great benefits for both? It may be simply that the freedom-loving United States and Canada are unwilling to force their citizens to co-operate and hence the pollution is there as the outcome of an n-person prisoner's dilemma game. The right to pollute may be considered as inviolable as the right to carry firearms.

Co-operation within a nation, let alone international co-operation, may be impossible. However, in recent years the United States has intervened in dilemma games to force co-operation. There are stringent laws on the safety of cars, on the levels of poisons in the exhaust gases of cars and rigidly enforced speed limits on public highways. So one can be slightly optimistic about the future willingness of the United States to care for the environment.

However, we are still left with difficult international negotiations. The lack of action by the United States may be seen as an attempt to threaten Canada and force joint action. This threat with no response by Canada could carry on for years. Even if the threat fails and the United States starts to clean up the lakes we are left with Canada's pollution. While it may be in the United States' interest to pay Canada to pursue joint action it may be difficult politically. Even if one could sell the idea to United States citizens of paying Canada to clean up Canada's mess the actual value the side-payment would take would be a matter of difficult negotiation. With our fictitious numbers a payment of anything between 50 and 150 million dollars would be beneficial to both sides, but the United States would prefer to give 50 million while Canada would like 150 million dollars. Stubbornness at negotiation can lead to no settlement or a long period of time before there is a settlement. The environment meanwhile continues to deteriorate.

Several writers have used game theory to analyse the lack of co-operation between states in undertaking potentially mutually beneficial environmental projects. Perhaps even more dramatic than our example

223

of the Great Lakes is Rogers's examination* of the benefits to India and Bangladesh of work to even out the flow of the Ganges. In the wet season in Bangladesh the Ganges floods, lives are lost but rice is grown. In the dry season nothing grows. Upstream storage facilities, almost entirely in India, to control the flow of the river and to generate electricity would be of benefit to both countries. India, of course, would not consider doing the work required to benefit Bangladesh without payment. Bangladesh knows this work would also benefit India. We have much the same game as our pollution game for the Great Lakes. It is difficult to imagine agreement on a side-payment between these two not totally friendly neighbours. The Ganges continues to produce disasters and famines.

How Do People Actually Play Games?

So far our analysis of non-constant-sum games has been based upon the notion that players are *rational*. In the games we have discussed this *rationality* can lead to outcomes which are worse for the players than if they had behaved in a less *rational* manner. In this section we shall look at the results of various laboratory experiments that researchers have undertaken. We shall not discuss whether these experiments give us a guide to behaviour outside the laboratory but merely report some of the interesting findings. The dilemma of conflict or co-operation occurs in many of the possible seventy-eight two-by-two games but since it is particularly vivid in the prisoner's dilemma game and since this game has been the most popular game for experiments, we shall restrict our attention to it.

The pioneers of the experimental work are Rapoport and Chammah who conducted a large number of experiments using students of the University of Michigan as players.† The students were asked to play various prisoner's dilemma games about 300 times in succession. Because the size of the awards for co-operation or the penalties for conflict may well influence the outcome seven different games were used. Two of them are represented below.

---

* P. Rogers, 'A game-theory approach to the problem of international river basins', *Water Resources Research*, Vol. 5, 1969, pp. 749–60.

† A. Rapoport and A. M. Chammah, *Prisoner's Dilemma*, University of Michigan Press, Ann Arbor, 1965.

		PLAYER B	
		Strategy C	Strategy D
PLAYER A	Strategy C	+1, +1	−10, +10
	Strategy D	+10, −10	−9, −9

R and C's game II

		PLAYER B	
		Strategy C	Strategy D
PLAYER A	Strategy C	+1, +1	−50, +50
	Strategy D	+50, −50	−1, −1

R and C's game V

Although these are both prisoner's dilemma games the rewards and penalties are very different. In game II the penalty for conflict (strategy combination DD) is relatively very high while in game V the incentive to co-operate is small compared with the temptation to double-cross. These rewards and penalties were real to the players as their gains or losses were converted into money and added to or subtracted from their fee for taking part in the experiments.

These experiments are rather different from our previous examples of prisoner's dilemma games in that the same game is played between the same players many times in succession. However, it is still *rational* for the players to adopt the unco-operative strategy (strategy D) in all plays. This is easily seen. Suppose the game is to be played 300 times then even if the players have co-operated for 299 times it is apparent that on the 300th a *rational* player should choose D. On the last play there is no chance of retaliation – we have a one-play prisoner's dilemma. However, if both players believe the outcome of the 300th game to be DD then as far as strategic thinking is concerned the 299th game becomes the final game. Whatever has happened before this, it is rational to play D in this game since both players know that the other will not play C in the next game. Working backwards from 300 to 1 the *rational* player will always act in an unco-operative fashion. We can illustrate this numerically by using Rapoport and Chammah's game II and constructing a pay-off matrix for the players if the game is to be played twice and twice only.

It turns out that there are eight strategies for each player in such a game. In four of them the player ignores what the opponent does in the first play and in the other four the opponent's first play influences the player's second choice. It is useful to write a list of these strategies.

1. Play C in both plays regardless of the other player's first move.

2. Play C first and on the second play choose the same move as the opponent's first play.

3. Play C first, then the opposite of the opponent's first move.

4. Play C first and D second, regardless of the opponent's first move.

5. Play D first and C second, regardless of the opponent's first move.

6. Play D first and then the same move as the opponent's first.

7. Play D first and then the opposite of the opponent's first move.

8. Play D followed by D again, regardless of the opponent's first move.

There are no other possible strategies. Routine computation allows us to work out the total pay-offs from the two plays for the two players for all different strategy combinations.

	PLAYER 2							
	1. C,C	2. C,SAME	3. C,OPP	4. C,D	5. D,C	6. D,SAME	7. D,OPP	8. D,D
PLAYER 1 1. C,C	2,2	2,2	-9,11	-9,11	-9,11	-9,11	-20,20	-20,20
2. C,SAME	2,2	2,2	-9,11	-9,11	0,0	0,0	-19,1	-19,1
3. C,OPPOSITE	11,-9	11,-9	-8,-8	-8,-8	-9,11	-9,11	-20,20	-20,20
4. C,D	11,-9	11,-9	-8,-8	-8,-8	0,0	0,0	-19,1	-19,1
5. D,C	11,-9	0,0	11,-9	0,0	-8,-8	-19,1	-8,-8	-19,1
6. D,SAME	11,-9	0,0	11,-9	0,0	1,-19	-18,-18	1,-19	-18,-18
7. D,OPPOSITE	20,-20	1,-19	20,-20	1,-19	-8,-8	-19,1	-8,-8	-19,1
8. D,D	20,-20	1,-19	20,-20	1,-19	1,-19	-18,-18	1,-19	-18,-18

Pay-off matrix for two plays of Rapoport and Chammah's game II

227

The game is, of course, symmetric and a rational strategy for one player will be rational for the other. Looking at the game from either player's point of view we can see that strategy 8 (D,D) dominates strategies 7, 6 and 5 but not the first four strategies, and strategy 4 (C,D) dominates strategies 1, 2 and 3 but not the last four strategies. Thus a *rational* player should choose either strategy C,D or strategy D,D. This confirms our verbal argument that in repeated plays of the game the first thing we can be certain of is that *rationality* demands unco-operative behaviour in the last play. The two strategies CD and DD are the only strategies which definitely lead to choosing D in the final play.

We have now reduced this complicated game into a simple two-by-two game knowing that rational players will not adopt strategies 1, 2, 3, 5, 6 or 7. The reduced pay-off matrix, just involving strategies 4 and 8, can be extracted from the original matrix.

		PLAYER 2	
		4	8
		C, D	D, D
PLAYER 1	4. C, D	−8, −8	−19, 1
	8. D, D	1, −19	−18, −18

This reduced game is another prisoner's dilemma with the strategy D,D dominant for both players. It is *rational* for both players to adopt unco-operative behaviour in all plays of the game.

As one would suspect, the subjects of experiments with such games do not always choose this *rational* strategy. In fact for game II, illustrated above, the co-operative solution was achieved in no fewer then 77.4 per cent of the plays. For game V, in which the incentives to co-operate are smaller, the co-operative solution was only achieved 26.8 per cent of the time. Rapoport and Chammah found in general that co-operation did increase with the size of the reward and decrease with the size of the possible benefits from non-co-operation.

Other interesting results emerged from the experiments. Not only were the games played with the pay-off matrices displayed but they were also played without such a display but with the pay-offs being quickly announced after each game. The researchers originally guessed that this might increase co-operation. The argument was that by chance the players would stumble across the co-operative solution and since it gave nice results stick to it. It might encourage co-operation if players did not have the *rational* strategy of conflict before their eyes. In fact the reverse turned

228

out to be the case and there was markedly less co-operation when the matrix was not displayed. For instance in game II the co-operative outcome was only achieved 44.6 per cent of the time compared with 77.4 per cent when the matrix was displayed. Overall the absence of display led to a fall of about half in the number of co-operative outcomes achieved. Considering that the players could have easily constructed a pay-off matrix after a few plays this result is rather surprising. However, perhaps we can learn that co-operation is more likely if the benefits of it are firmly kept in front of our eyes.

For no apparent reason Rapoport and Chammah also compared the behaviour of men and women players. They found that men playing against men were almost twice as likely to be co-operative as women playing against women. Mixed pairs tended to be somewhat more co-operative on the first play of the game than single-sex pairs. Later studies seemed to confirm these findings and no doubt psychologists could produce explanations that would sound convincing to some people. More interesting, to me at least, is a study done by V. Shotko, D. Langmeyer and D. Lundgren* which yielded rather different results from all the previous experiments. They noted that as far as they could gather all previous experiments had been conducted using male experimenters – that is, the people giving instructions to and recording the strategies played by the subjects were men. Shotko *et al.* conducted a similar experiment to the many previous studies but sometimes used male and sometimes female experimenters. Broadly speaking when using male experimenters they confirmed the results of the earlier workers. However, in the presence of female experimenters the female pairs of subjects no longer showed such competitive behaviour and were roughly as co-operative as male pairs. Male subjects behaved in roughly the same way regardless of the experimenter's sex. In other words the different results for the two sexes in prisoner's dilemma experiments may well illustrate that the design of the experiment affects the sexes differently and nothing about whether women are in some way more rational or competitive than men.

Following from this we can see that it may be rather naive to suppose we can use the results of such experiments to predict the way that people will behave when faced with prisoner's dilemmas in the *real world*.

Thus we should probably treat these experiments as nothing more than experiments. In one study, games were played after giving some subjects

* V. Shotko, D. Langmeyer and D. Lundgren, 'Sex differences as artefact in the prisoner's dilemma game', *Journal of Conflict Resolution*, Vol. 18, 1974, pp. 207–13.

a tranquillizer (Librium) and others a placebo.* It was found that those given Librium showed more mutual co-operation than those given the placebos. While this shows that Librium does seem to affect human behaviour one would hardly wish to suggest that all the negotiators in disarmament talks should be continually drugged. Game theory gives us an insight into the structure of many problems in which there are incentives to co-operate but temptations to compete. It may not tell us much about how decisions are actually made in such situations.

* Allan H. Stix, 'The effect of a minor tranquillizer on strategic choice behaviour in the prisoner's dilemma', *Journal of Conflict Resolution*, Vol. 18, 1974, pp. 373–94.

Epilogue and Further Reading

'Give a small boy a hammer and he will discover that everything in sight needs pounding.'*

There are considerable incentives for misusing a skill that one has spent time in mastering. Thus there is a temptation, having conquered the theory of Markov chains or the theory of games, to see all social situations or processes as games or chains. We noticed, for instance, that some attempts to apply game theory have been of a contrived nature. These examples were deliberately selected to illustrate the danger of letting one's armoury of research techniques determine the way one approaches a problem. If we avoid this pitfall, and certainly I believe that most of the work that has been discussed in this book does avoid it, then mathematical techniques can be of considerable power in helping us to study and understand society. Putting our ideas into the language of mathematics clarifies these ideas, forces us to think in a logical fashion and brings order to our analysis of apparently messy and complicated social situations. But this formalization of a problem may itself bring dangers. The economy, social mobility, population movements, power relations and kinship are all complex processes or phenomena. We must not imagine we have captured all the complexities within a cosy cocoon of mathematics.

What this means is that we should probably never be satisfied with any particular model. Models can be improved by questioning the reasonableness of the assumptions on which they are based, and by confronting the models with data. We saw, for instance, in our discussion of industrial mobility how researchers, having first seen the process as a simple Markov chain, developed the model beyond this illuminating insight. Equally in our example of input-output analysis, where there is no doubt that matrix methods help us capture the important and fundamental notion of the interdependence of the different sectors of an economy, we tentatively questioned how the model might be improved. Economists have asked questions like: 'How far is the assumption of constant input-output

* A. Kaplan, *The Conduct of Social Inquiry. Methodology for Behavioral Sciences*, Chandler, San Francisco, p. 28, 1964.

coefficients justified? If it is not justified what would we do about it?' These are difficult questions but ones which must be answered. Any model is a simplification of reality and we want to make this simplification in the most sensible fashion. We want neither to simplify at the cost of losing important parts of reality nor to create a model which is a one-to-one map of reality. Doing the latter does not help us get from A to B, nor help us with anything for that matter.

Having taken heed of these warnings we can say that mathematics and, in particular as we have seen, matrix algebra can be of considerable help to social scientists of all kinds. Economists and psychologists have recognized for a long time the need to be numerate in order to practise their disciplines in a competent fashion. This numeracy involves a knowledge of various branches of mathematics. Some other social scientists have been a little slower at coming round to this point of view. The intention of this book has been to illustrate some possible uses of a single branch of mathematics in many disciplines. It is hoped that the reader will have been sufficiently convinced of this that he or she will wish to pursue the study of such possibilities.

Further reading

There are many suggestions for further reading in the text of the book. These are not all repeated here but a few that cover rather more material than the context of the reference suggests have been listed. The list is only a selection from a vast literature, but by following up the references given in these articles and books the reader should not have any great difficulty in pursuing particular interests. While I have put the reading into sections, much of it is of an interdisciplinary kind and the boundaries between the sections are not rigid.

(1) General Texts

J. W. Bishir and D. W. Drewes, *Mathematics in the Behavioral and Social Sciences*, Harcourt, Brace, New York, 1970.
    A general text that covers matrix algebra and Markov chains. The mathematics goes beyond that used in this book. It contains examples of applications from most of the social sciences.

J. G. Kemeny, J. L. Snell and G. L. Thompson, *Introduction to Finite Mathematics* (3rd edition), Prentice-Hall, New Jersey, 1974.
    This excellent standard text covers much of the mathematics used in this book and is replete with examples.

R. Bronson, *Matrix Methods,* Academic Press, London, 1970.

F. E. Hohn, *Elementary Matrix Algebra* (3rd edition), Macmillan, New York, 1973.

E. D. Nering, *Linear Algebra and Matrix Theory*, Wiley, New York, 1970.

These three books are examples of many mathematical texts which start at an elementary level but take the reader to higher levels of matrix algebra than we have reached.

H. Hamburger, *Games as Models of Social Phenomena*, Freeman, San Francisco, 1979.

A good introduction to the theory of games, with examples from economics, political science and psychology. Very little mathematical knowledge is presumed or required.

M. Shubik, *Game Theory in the Social Sciences*, MIT Press, Cambridge, Mass., 1982.

Unlike Hamburger's book this is mathematically very rigorous and only for the determined student. It indicates the frontiers that the practitioners of game theory have reached.

(2) Economics and business studies

Economists use matrices in much the same way that they use toothpaste – with familiarity and without thinking too much.

G. Mills, *Introduction to Linear Algebra for Social Scientists*, Allen and Unwin, London, 1969.

This is a clear exposition of matrix methods that are particularly useful to economists. It starts at an elementary level but supplements the theory we have developed.

A. C. Chiang, *Fundamental Methods of Mathematical Economics* (3rd edition), McGraw-Hill, Tokyo, 1984.

This covers more mathematics than just matrix algebra but it gives an intermediate-level account of the use of matrix methods in such things as input-output analysis and finding efficient production and output plans.

G. Heal, G. Hughes and R. Tarling, *Linear Algebra and Linear Economics*, London, Macmillan, 1974.

This book sets out well the concepts of linear algebra that are frequently encountered in economic and statistical theory. It also provides an introduction to their use in economic planning.

J. G. Kemeny, A. Scheifer, J. L. Snell and G. L. Thompson, *Finite Mathematics with Business Applications*, Prentice-Hall, New Jersey, 1962.

Although this book is rather old now there is still no better work to introduce students of business and finance to the uses of probability theory, Markov chains and the theory of games.

R. O'Connor and E. W. Henry, *Input-Output Analysis and Its Applications*, Griffin, London, 1975.

A clear account of input-output analysis, with examples of actual input-output matrices and their use in examining the consequences of national and regional economic policies.

R. Stone, *Aspects of Economic and Social Modelling*, Librairie Droz, Geneva, 1981.

Richard Stone was responsible for building the first input-output model for the United Kingdom. His work and the developments of it are summarized in the first half of this very readable book.

E. R. Weintraub, *Conflict and Co-operation in Economics*, Macmillan, London, 1975.

A straightforward guide to the use of game theory in economics. It discusses wages and bargaining, exchange, externalities, public goods and voting in a game-theory framework.

J. W. Friedman, *Oligopoly and the Theory of Games*, North Holland, Amsterdam, 1977.

Not always an easy book but a comprehensive guide to the analysis of competition in markets in which there are just a few large firms.

L. Friedman, 'Game theory models in the allocation of advertising expenditures', *Operations Research*, Vol. 6, 1958, pp. 699–700.

A. K. Klevorick and G. H. Kramer, 'Social choice on pollution management: the *Genossenschaften*', *Journal of Public Economics*, Vol. 2, 1973, pp. 102–46.

M. Laver, 'The great British wage game', *New Society*, 6 March 1980.

The above three articles are examples of the many individual studies on subjects such as advertising, pollution and inflation that have fruitfully used game theory.

I. Adelman, 'A stochastic analysis of the size distribution of firms', *Journal of the American Statistical Association*, Vol. 53, 1958, pp. 893–904.

A. R. Horowitz and I. Horowitz, 'Entropy, Markov processes and competition in the brewing industry', *Journal of Industrial Economics*, Vol. 16, 1968, pp. 196–216.

These two articles are examples of the power of Markov chains in analysing economic phenomena. The first explains the size distribution of firms within an industry. The second explains the demise of breweries in an absorbing Markov chain process.

J. K. Shank, '*Matrix Methods in Accounting*, Addison-Wesley, Reading, Mass., 1972.

Bookkeeping and accountancy which show the inflows and outflows of money are almost natural subjects for the use of matrix algebra.

S. Koshimura, *Capital Reproduction and Economic Crisis in Matrix Form*, Wako University Press, Tokyo, 1984

Much of Karl Marx's economic thought might have been better expressed if he had known matrix algebra. This book puts Marx's theory of capital and later developments of it into matrix form.

(3) Geography, Population Studies and Social Demography

R. W. Thomas and R. J. Huggett, *Modelling in Geography – a Mathematical Approach*, Harper and Row, London, 1980.

This text discusses the use of various matrix methods in geography. It includes the use of Leslie matrices in geographical population studies and how matrices help to solve transportation problems.

K. Chapman, *People, Pattern and Process*, Edward Arnold, London, 1979.
D. Unwin, *Introductory Spatial Analysis*, Methuen, London, 1981.

Both of these books contain clear discussions of how matrices can be used to analyse transport networks like the road system of the UK or the London Underground. The matrix used is called a connectivity matrix and it is very like, and used in the same way as, the dominance matrix we used in Chapter 5.

W. Isard, *Introduction to Regional Science*, Prentice-Hall, New Jersey, 1975.

Written by the leading regional scientist, this book includes accounts of regional input-output matrices and their uses, and of the usefulness of pay-off matrices in analysing regional problems.

P. Gould, 'Wheat on Kilimanjaro', *General Systems*, Vol. 10, 1965, pp. 157–66.

This is another attempt by Gould to apply game theory to crop growing. Gould argues that when wheat was first introduced as a crop near Kilimanjaro, farmers, in ignorance of the properties of the crop and the weather, regarded the weather as a vindictive cost-minimizing game player. This showed in the conservative locational strategies that the farmers adopted. Gould shows that after the initial years the farmers tended to alter their strategies to high pay-off, high-risk ones – suggesting they were maximizing their expected pay-off taking into account weather patterns and not regarding weather as a rational opponent. This is a very interesting application of matrix methods to an important problem, and if Gould is right there are important policy implications.

A. Rogers, *Matrix Analysis of Interregional Population Growth and Distribution*, University of California Press, Berkeley, 1968.

This book uses matrix methods to analyse population changes in regions with migration, different fertility rates and so on.

N. Keyfitz, *Introduction to the Mathematics of Population*, Addison-Wesley, Reading, Mass., 1968.
N. Keyfitz, *Applied Mathematical Demography*, Wiley, New York, 1977.

The first of these two books by Keyfitz is the standard work on mathematical demography. It includes a thorough account of Leslie matrices and other mathematics useful to demographers. The second book, as well as containing a section on matrices in demography which supplements this book, has a discussion of how similar methods may be used to analyse health and medical care, educational systems and delinquency. These are examples of social demography. People can be seen as moving from states of being sick to well, from primary school to secondary school, or from non-delinquent to delinquent.

R. Stone, *Aspects of Economic and Social Modelling*, Librairie Droz, Geneva, 1981.

The first half of this book was mentioned under 'Economics'. Richard Stone has led the way in using matrices in social demography and the second half of the book summarizes a great deal of his work. In particular he uses an adaptation of a Leslie matrix to analyse the educational system and future educational requirements.

R. Stone, *Demographic Accounting and Model Building*, OECD, Paris, 1971.

Demography is about human stocks and flows. This book shows how matrix methods like input-output matrices and Markov chain matrices can be used to describe and analyse the movements of populations through life, education, occupation and so on.

J. Meredith, 'A Markovian analysis of a geriatric ward', *Management Science*, Vol. 19, 1973, pp. 604–12.

An interesting example of the use of transition matrices to appraise the cost-effectiveness of providing a home outside hospital for elderly patients.

(4) Sociology, Social Psychology and Anthropology

R. Mapes, *Mathematics and Sociology*, Batsford, London, 1971.

This is a very simple introductory text specially written for sociologists. It includes simple accounts of matrix algebra, Markov chains and graph theory.

R. K. Leik and B. F. Meeker, *Mathematical Sociology*, Prentice-Hall, New Jersey, 1975.

T. J. Fararo, *Mathematical Sociology*, Wiley, New York, 1973.

Both of these intermediate-level texts use matrix methods to discuss kinship structure, social mobility, game theory in sociology and so on.

O. Bartos, *Simple Models of Group Behavior*, Columbia University Press, New York, 1967.

This book is particularly strong on Markov chains and game theory and their use in sociology and social psychology.

P. F. Lazarsfeld and N. W. Henry, *Readings in Mathematical Social Sciences*, MIT Press, Cambridge, Mass., 1966.

This well-known collection of readings contains many of the classic papers we have referred to, for example, White on kinship, Blumen *et al.* on occupational mobility and Kemeny and Snell on Asch's experiment.

J. S. Coleman, *The Mathematics of Collective Action*, Heinemann, London, 1973.

This book contains an excellent discussion of the deficient diagonal problem in

Markov-chain models and includes a matrix analysis of such things as committee decision making and who controls what in bureaucracies.

C. H. Coombs, R. M. Dawes and A. Tversky, *Mathematical Psychology*, Prentice-Hall, New Jersey, 1970.

This contains an analysis of the use of dominance matrices to analyse relationships, game theory, and Markov-chain models to analyse 'how we learn things'.

R. Boudon, *Mathematical Structures of Social Mobility*, Jossey-Bass, San Francisco, 1973.

It discusses and extends the matrix models of social mobility that we have discussed. This book is useful not only to students of social mobility but to anybody interested in the development of mathematical thinking in sociology.

P. Krishnan, 'A Markov-chain approximation of conjugal history'; and J. Stafford, 'Urban growth as an absorbing Markov process'. These are two articles included in *Mathematical Models of Sociology, Sociological Review*, Monograph 24, 1977.

In Krishnan's article conjugal history is seen as the process through the states of married, widowed, divorced, death. Stafford uses Canadian data to describe urban growth and decline and to predict the size of towns in Alberta in the future.

A. M. Colman, *Game Theory and Experimental Games*, Pergamon, Oxford, 1982.

A good survey of game theory and the vast number of experimental games that have been reported in recent years. The book is written by a psychologist but there are discussions, in addition to examples from psychology, of game theory in economics, politics (the strategy of voting), biology (the theory of evolution) and moral philosophy (ethical conduct).

C. A. Gregory, *Gifts and Commodities*, Academic Press, London, 1982.

This thought-provoking book is written by a political economist who attempts to marry economics and anthropology. It analyses the exchange of gifts and commodities in Papua New Guinea. The mathematical appendix shows the considerable clarity one gains by using a matrix approach to kinship relations.

I. R. Buchler and H. G. Nubini (eds), *Game Theory in the Behavioral Sciences*, University of Pittsburgh Press, Pittsburgh, 1969.

Despite its title this book is a collection of anthropological essays. It includes matrix games of African tribal politics, a matrix approach to marriage systems and a discussion of Davenport's matrix-game approach to the behaviour of Jamaican fishermen.

J. J. Honigmann (ed.), *Handbook of Social and Cultural Anthropology*, Rand McNally, Chicago, 1973.

Chapter 9 (by D. R. White) is a survey of the extensive work done in mathematical anthropology. It includes a Markov analysis of residence changes (between nuclear, extended etc. families) on the island of Andros and also an account of work on the use of Markov chains to analyse society in Ethiopia (sons must go through the same cycle or set of age groups as their fathers).

(5) Political Science and the Study of Conflict

Politics is obviously a field where the theory of games, by identifying the players and looking at the outcome of strategies, can be very illuminating.

The *Journal of Conflict Resolution* has many examples of the application of game theory to particular situations.

T. C. Schelling, *The Strategy of Conflict*, Harvard University Press, Cambridge, Mass., 1963.

This is a famous standard work. Schelling discusses many provocative simple games and analogies to international conflict situations.

S. J. Brams, *Game Theory and Politics*, Free Press, New York, 1975.

A clear exposition of the myriad applications of game theory to politics including competition between political parties.

S. J. Brams, *Paradoxes in Politics*, Free Press, New York, 1976.

Further examples of the theory of games in politics including vote trading and a discussion of the Cuban missile crisis.

S. J. Brams and M. D. Davis, 'A game-theory approach to jury selection', *Trial*, Vol. 12, 1976, pp. 47–9.

S. J. Brams and D. Muzzio, 'Game theory and the White House tapes case', *Trial*, Vol. 13, 1977, pp. 49–53.

These are two short articles illustrating the use of game theory in particular circumstances. The latter is an illuminating account of the Supreme Court's decision to end President Nixon's efforts to withhold evidence in the Watergate case.

M. Dresher, *Games of Strategy: Theory and Applications*, Prentice-Hall, New Jersey, 1961.

Still the best survey of the use of game theory in military situations. It answers questions like 'What target should you attack with what weapon?'